The Hour

Sporting Immortality the Hard Way

Michael Hutchinson

YELLOW JERSEY PRESS
LONDON

Published by Yellow Jersey Press 2007

13

First published in Great Britain in 2006 by
Yellow Jersey Press
Random House, 20 Vauxhall Bridge Road,
London SW1V 2SA

www.randomhouse.co.uk

Addresses for companies within The Random House Group Limited can
be found at: www.randomhouse.co.uk/offices.htm

The Random House Group Limited Reg. No. 954009

A CIP catalogue record for this book is available from the British Library

ISBN 9780224075206

Penguin Random House is committed to a sustainable future for
our business, our readers and our planet. This book is made from
Forest Stewardship Council® certified paper.

Printed and bound in Great Britain by Clays Ltd, St Ives plc

The Hour

Michael Hutchinson became a full-time cyclist in 2000 after becoming disillusioned with an academic career. Over the following six years he has won more than twenty national titles, and the gold medal in the Masters' Pursuit World Championships. He is now a writer and journalist (and cyclist) and lives in south London.

Here is a simple question. How far can you ride a bicycle in one hour? No assistance, no pace-makers. A rider alone on a track, with only the time elapsed and the distance covered to occupy his mind. The very purest of physical efforts. This is the World Hour Record, and it took over my life.

CHAPTER 1

FEBRUARY CAN BE COLD IN MANCHESTER. ON THIS particular day, it's very cold. I'm riding my bike on the track at Manchester Velodrome and, even though it's indoors, as I ride faster I can feel cold air sting against my face and tumble over my back. Today, I can feel everything. The hum of the tyres on the wooden track, the way the bike flexes ever so slightly, the hard smoothness of the bare metal handlebars. As I whisk past my coach, standing by the track, I can smell the milk in her coffee. I can absorb so much detail that these don't even rank as distractions.

Best of all, what makes what I'm doing now so glorious, is how I can feel my whole body as it moves with the bike. The way my legs spin lightly in a fluid motion that betrays none of the force they're generating. How I move my shoulders to make almost imperceptible corrections to my steering. Then I can feel my breathing. It's harsh and quick, but each breath is still deep. Breathing is where the rhythm of my riding starts. If I'm breathing right, then everything else just happens. Today, I'm breathing perfectly.

Near the track's inside edge there is a simple painted black line. This is the shortest, fastest route. Following it is not as easy as it looks. When I go this fast, the centrifugal forces in each curve push the bike up the steeply banked track. In the flatter straights it wants to drift down and off the track altogether. To ride the fast route I have to time the transitions from straight to curve and from curve to straight just right, and do it four times in every 18-second lap.

I'm in a trance-like state of almost-concentration. If I let myself think too clearly about any one of the many things that I must get right, I'll lose my grip on the rest. They're all hovering in front of me, but I mustn't let my eyes focus. I have to leave them all in soft focus, all perfectly balanced.

The track has brightly coloured advertising hoardings round its outside, left over from the last major event held here. I remember thinking, when I arrived today, that they looked out of place in the big, empty building on a quiet Tuesday morning. But now I can see them whirl past in my peripheral vision, the colours merging into an ecstatic audience.

Like I said, today is a good day. It's all happening easily. I'm balanced and relaxed, yet right on the limit of what I can do physically. My heartrate is only a few beats off its maximum, but I can still wiggle my toes. It feels very powerful to be this close to the edge, and yet so in control. Bikes have certainly been ridden faster than this, but just now I doubt if one has been ridden better.

Days like this are not as frequent as I'd like. They're not as frequent as they used to be either, or maybe I've just grown harder to please. I've never found any other way of so fully engaging mind and body, of functioning so completely. The rewards of racing a bike have more to do with feeling like this than they have to do with winning. Winning just means going faster than everyone else, and it's winning that pays the bills. This is more profound.

Some years ago I shared a house with a truly gifted pianist. He knew what a day like this was like. 'Sometimes,' he said, 'I can forget about my hands and fingers, and I just get pulled into the music. I hear it the way it was always meant to be. That it's me who is playing it isn't important any more. It's an effortless rapture. I feel like it's my purpose.'

I can remember what he said so accurately, partly because I have a soft spot for pretentious crap, but mainly because at the time I had him pinned to a wall by the throat. This was the better to reinforce the suggestion that perhaps, after four fortissimo hours, he might like to give it a rest with the bloody piano. Otherwise, I explained, I and the rest of the household would dismantle it into pieces small enough to pass through his alimentary canal. We would, we assured him, give a whole new meaning to the expression 'a musical passage'.

That's the problem with this kind of thing. It's all about you. Even if they understand it, no one else can really feel it. You come off the track feeling like a divine combination of Mozart and Roger Bannister and discover that, instead of marvelling at your skill, the two cleaners in the track centre are sniggering at the way your ears go pink when you're riding fast.

For the riders, cycling is about the feeling. For everyone else, it's the sheer grandeur of it all. There is no other sport that demands so much from its athletes, or weaves so much of their effort into drama for the fans. At one extreme, epic contests like the Tour de France pit up to 200 riders against each other in an intricate network of individual and team rivalries. For added value, this is played out across three weeks, over some of the most beautiful countryside and mountain-scenery in Europe.

At the other end of the scale, you get over-muscled sprinters rough-housing their way round a small track at over 40mph with all the pushing and shoving of a school-lunch queue. It's not uncommon to see the kind of pile-up on which motor racing has depended for its popularity for years. Except that real men don't wear protective clothing – they wear Lycra and shave their legs so that it's easier to put on bandages afterwards.

All of this, and featuring some of the greatest athletes in any sport. Everyone knows about Lance Armstrong's journey from almost a dead man to seven-times Tour de France winner. Understandably, the story distracts attention from the man. What not enough people appreciate is just what a phenomenal athlete he was, taken on any terms you like, cancer or not. The same goes, at least in most English-speaking countries, for almost all the great champions.

In continental Europe, on the other hand, you can tell by the nicknames the fans gave the riders that there is a deep understanding and respect. No one was christened 'the Eagle of Toledo' or the 'Angel of the Mountains' (Federico Bahamontes and Charly Gaul respectively) for any reason other than admiration. Other names tell you about the attitude that their owners brought to their racing. Bernard Hinault won the Tour de France five times, and is called (almost universally) 'the Badger'. It gives me visions of Dickie Davies, but apparently it's because badgers are quick to take offence, and vicious when cornered. This was Hinault to a T. And it would have been for exactly those reasons that I'd have given him a more flattering name: 'the Golden Lion of France', 'Sir', anything less likely to provoke him.

Other riders' names are more dignified, but no less telling. Jacques Anquetil was one of the all-time greats, dominating the cycling world during the late 1950s and '60s. He was never known as anything other than 'Maître Jacques' – Master Jacques. He was notorious for preparing for races by staying up half the night drinking, and he won several events while suffering from the kind of hangover that would have kept the rest of us in bed for the day. Somehow he managed to do this without it denting a rather cold public image, and his dominance meant that he was never especially popular. Cycling fans always cheer for the underdog – in Master Jacques's era, the most popular rider was Raymond 'Pou-Pou' Poulidor, whose lot it was to come second in most of the races that Anquetil won. Master Jacques versus Pou-Pou. There was only ever going to be one winner there.

The best nicknames are reserved for the best riders. Eddy Merckx was the greatest cyclist of all time, as well as the only properly famous Belgian that history has to offer. Merckx didn't just win a phenomenal number of races through the 1960s and '70s, he did it in crushing style. With an insatiable appetite for competition and for victory, he was simply 'the Cannibal'.

Merckx's only serious rival for the all-time top spot was the Italian star of the 1940s and '50s, Fausto Coppi. He had the best name of all, '*Campionissimo*', Champion of Champions, though I've always liked the literal mistranslation, Most-Champion. You really can't argue with that. (He was also occasionally, and less reverentially, known as 'the Heron', because on a bike that was just what he looked like. Go and look on the Internet – really, it's worth seeing.)

In Britain, of course, most of these names mean little or nothing to non-cyclists. Cycling has never really been a big part of the landscape. There have been a few false dawns. Tom Simpson won the BBC Sports Personality of the Year award in 1965 following his World Championship win. Chris Boardman caused a brief flurry of interest in the mid-1990s, and every Olympics brings medals from the GB track-cycling squad. But none of this really generates any sustained interest. It gets picked up when the Tour and the Olympics are on, or when someone fails a dope test, and that's about it.

This puzzles me. British sports fans have a grasp of the epic like few others. Ellen MacArthur, for example, gives good epic, as does Paula Radcliffe. It's not just their physical achievement, but the whole story that goes along with it: the soap-opera narrative of underdog to favourite, to thwarted or old athlete, to underdog again, to winner, to BBC TV presenter.

Cycling, especially the major stage races, has this with knobs on. You don't just have the extraordinary demonstrations of ability and skill; they come packaged in a grand-scale story with big players, bit players, surprises, disasters, celebrations and tragedies. As a fans' sport, it is perfect. Yet it just doesn't seem to catch alight. Some stories, like Armstrong's, do make an impression. But I can't quite shake off the suspicion that had he been in a different sport – marathon running, say, or boxing – it would have been even bigger.

It's not even as if cycling's low profile is simply down to a lack of British big hitters – tennis is not exactly awash with talented Brits, but it attracts huge (if sporadic) audiences. The very American flavour of golf doesn't put people off. Sports fans can be parochial, but not usually so parochial as to ignore the kind of freewheeling physical opera offered by bike riders every day of the season.

I can't claim much in the way of the high ground here. Unlike most of the small number of riders from the British Isles who manage to make a living at cycling, I didn't grow up with much interest in it. I knew what the Tour de France was, yes, but that was it. I didn't even make the connection between that and the occasional time-trial race that I saw on the road that ran in front of my parents' house – though I rapidly made the connection between stopping work in the garden to lean on my child-sized rake and watch the riders go by and my father scolding me for laziness. It was my misfortune that my parents had a large garden, and only one son.

My early cycling history did not bode well. My first bike was an orange imitation of the Raleigh Chopper. Because I was older than normal for a rookie cyclist, and a bit on the large side anyway, I needed a bike so big that the little training wheels didn't reach the ground until it was an alarmingly long way off vertical. A sharp turn would result in a flop from one side to the other that could be vicious enough to throw me out of the saddle. As I got up, the bike would sit there at a rakish angle and laugh at me. It was like a nasty older brother.

The thing is that if, as I did, you grow up in an isolated house in rural Northern Ireland, you have to get the hang of riding a bike or you'll be an unpaid garden labourer for ever. By the time I was in my teens I was racking up a lot of miles. But it was never riding for its own sake – it was just about independence. There are not many bike racers for whom the main attraction of a bike at the age of sixteen was the ability to ride to a quiet forest clearing on a sunny afternoon to lie in the grass and read Tolstoy. It was for me.

Tolstoy and Elizabeth Martin, if I'm being totally honest. Liz was my first girlfriend, and if you wanted to pretend you were having some sort of grown-up relationship, you needed a bike. It was the only thing that made it possible to get to nowhere in particular, or at any rate somewhere that wasn't politely drinking tea in either of our parents' front rooms, or requiring that we catch the bus to Belfast.

The only problem was that it was impossible to escape the sophisticated espionage network of parents' friends. 'Saw you and some girlie cutting across a field out past Dunadry last week,' I'd be told with a lecherous wink – which was entirely unjustified since we'd gone there to do nothing much more libidinous than sit by the river holding hands and discussing bloody Tolstoy. We might as well have been being tracked by means of models on a map-table in a dimly lit room.

Cycling was transport – freedom. I didn't think there was anything more to it than that. As soon as I'd learned to drive, and scraped enough money together to buy a clapped-out Volkswagen Golf, I stopped cycling altogether. The bike that I'd ridden through my teenage years ended up ferrying my father to the village to buy his newspaper every morning, until a few years ago the frame rusted through and it was thrown into a skip.

What I certainly never guessed was that I had a considerable latent talent for riding a bike. It was well buried. It took a long time, several coincidences and a later, more grown-up girlfriend before I realised that I had the ability to ride fast. That I could sustain the quickest of paces, for mile after mile, and that I could learn to relish the blissful mental state that I often attained when I did so. And, along the way, I could win.

What I should have been doing instead of reading *War and Peace* and making daisy chains on riverbanks was training for the hour record. Of course, I'd never heard of it.

The record is awfully simple. One bike, one man, one hour. No help, no tactics, no brakes, no gears. No hiding place. It started in 1893, and the challenge has remained exactly the same ever since. It's the only endurance cycling record that matters. If you want to be a great champion, it has to be on your CV. Like nothing else it tests the purest element of riding ability – how fast you can go, alone.

In most sports, records come and go. They're just something that happens in the normal course of things. The hour record isn't like that: it's an event in its own right. There is no hour racing, or hour championship. An hour record *can't* just happen; it has to be specially organised, and it stands on its own. A man making an attempt on the hour is in as exposed a position as modern sport has to offer. If you make an attempt and fall short, you can't claim any fall-back consolation, like a race win or a medal.

If the hour goes wrong, the best you can hope for is that you fail with some dignity. Even this is not easy. When you attempt the record, you have to stand up and make some pretty big claims about your ability. Then you have to race against all the greatest champions the sport has ever had. Even in the worst-case scenario of most sports, you can count on the dead staying dead. In the hour record, there is the very real danger that a rider who has been deceased for thirty years is going to rise from the grave, dust himself off and kick you all over the velodrome.

And you can't kid yourself that failure is easily shrugged off. To this day, the great Italian Alfredo Binda is almost as well remembered for his failure to beat the hour in 1929 as for the rest of an astonishingly prolific career. A failed hour attempt will follow you all your days.

For its purity, for the courage required, for its constancy, the hour is at the top of the cycling tree. It's often described as coming second only to the Tour de France in its prestige. It's more complicated than that. The Tour is the greatest race on Earth, but it starts afresh every year. The hour record is the essence of cycle sport, continuous almost since the invention of the bicycle. It's not just a record: it's a race across the generations.

You can race Fausto Coppi – the *Campionissimo* died in 1960, eighteen years after he set his hour record in Milan. It took weeks for word of Coppi's record to spread across war-time Europe. In Britain, the news appeared in an issue of *Cycling* magazine full of advice on how to make black-out masks for cycle lamps, and details of the shocking number of deaths on the road caused by the black-out regulations. It was still the biggest story of the year, and *Cycling* made numerous apologies for not being able to offer more information.

You can race Jacques Anquetil. He broke the record twice, in 1956 (when he beat Coppi's mark) and 1967. Except that the 1967 record was never ratified, because Master Jacques refused to take the dope-control test afterwards. He felt that such a test was an indignity to which a rider of his stature should not be subjected. It was just about the first great doping scandal, and for a few days at least it was not at all clear who was going to win – the defiant Anquetil or the authorities. Ironically, the whole affair did great things for his public image in France, where in the weeks after the record attempt he was cheered as never before. Cyclists, cycling authorities and cycling fans have always had a rather confused attitude to doping.

Of course you can also race Eddy Merckx. Fittingly, he set what's probably the most significant record of them all, in the thin air of Mexico City in 1972. It was far from a perfect ride; with more careful preparation he could have done much better. But it was still so intimidating that almost no one was prepared to try to match it for more than a decade.

Merckx's record, one way and another, lasted for twenty-eight years. When it was finally broken, it was in Manchester, on the track where we began. And it was a British rider who did it. The bettering of Merckx's distance in 2000 marked the end of a strange period in the history of the record, distinguished by a battle for supremacy between technology and rider. It seems likely that it also marked the end of a brief, distinctly British-flavoured interlude.

For most of the twentieth century, despite the achievements of a handful of talented riders, no British cyclist had held the hour record. Tom Simpson had attempted and failed the amateur hour, and he made plans that he never realised for an attempt on the professional hour in the 1960s. Before that, in 1937, Harry Hill set an amateur record in Milan. (The report in *Cycling* notes that he refused to shave his legs as suggested by an Italian coach, because 'like any Englishman he was justly proud of his hairy legs'.) But all of that was about as close as the British had come. It was a record for the hardened continental professionals only, not for hairy-legged Brits.

In 1993, all that changed. For a few years the hour record was dominated by two British riders. Their names were Graeme Obree and Chris Boardman. It was because of them that I first heard about the record. And ultimately it was because of them that I ended up trying to break it myself.

CHAPTER 2

IN 1993, WHEN THE HOUR RECORD HIT THE headlines, I was a student in Durham. I didn't know much about cycling, but I'd heard of Chris Boardman. Boardman was a cabinet-maker from Merseyside who had catapulted himself to national fame the previous summer when he won gold at the Barcelona Olympics. It was Britain's first Olympic cycling medal since 1920, but that wasn't why I remembered him.

It was because of the 'superbike', a profoundly sexy black carbon-fibre bike with a smooth fluid shape and only one front fork blade. It had rapidly become more famous than its rider, and it made cycling look like an exciting, cutting-edge sport. Less with the flat caps and whippets, more like Formula 1. It was built by Lotus – yes, *that* Lotus – and apparently it was so good that your granny could ride it to Olympic glory.

Now Chris, this time without the Lotus, was planning an attempt on this hour-record thing. Normally this would have been good for a few days' worth of 'Sport in Brief' paragraphs in the papers.

What made it an international media event was

Graeme Obree. Obree was an almost unknown Scottish cyclist who popped up – in Norway of all places – the week before Boardman's attempt and broke the record. For months Boardman had been meticulously planning an attack on the nine-year-old record of the Italian star Francesco Moser. Now the *arriviste* Obree had snatched it from under his nose.

Obree could not have been less like Boardman if he had tried. Boardman, the Olympic champion, was the darling of the British cycling establishment. He had been destined for greatness from an early age; at sixteen he had been the youngest rider ever selected to represent Britain at a senior world championships. Boardman's sheer speed in a time-trial was phenomenal – most of the records he set in British time-trial events in the early 1990s look as inaccessible now as they did then. He was a new kind of rider: achingly scientific in his preparation (he trained in a laboratory), cold and methodical in his racing. He was not so much unruffled, as incapable of being ruffled. He was almost German.

Graeme Obree was a trainee receptionist, a bad trainee receptionist at that, and made his attempt on a bike he'd built himself out of washing-machine spare parts and a bit of steel he found lying on an Ayrshire road near his home. He'd been the only rider consistently able to mount any challenge to Boardman on the domestic scene, but he'd just as consistently come out of the encounters second best. He'd won the Scottish championships, which from the viewpoint of the London-based media was probably worse than winning nothing. His impact on the international scene had been exactly zero. He certainly hadn't won an Olympic gold medal.

The biggest contrast with Boardman was in personality. Obree was an eccentric, a maverick who trained according to his own instincts, rather than to a plan worked out by a man in a white coat. If he felt like training, he trained. If he didn't, he didn't. While Boardman used specially formulated sports drinks, Obree trained on a diet of marmalade sandwiches.

It was an almost perfect rivalry, and it was happening at the perfect time, when the newspapers were looking for things to fill the quiet summer issues. British papers had always been reluctant to give much coverage to cycling – not only was it a sport in which Britain had enjoyed rather limited success over recent years, but it was often difficult to explain the tactical intricacies of most forms of racing. By contrast, the hour record was blissfully easy to explain, and it was very clearly a big deal. The papers explained – without much in the way of hyperbole – that it had been held by everyone who mattered in the entire history of cycling. Now, not one, but two British riders were involved in it.

Everyone I knew divided into one camp or the other. It was like the days when the whole country supported Oxford or Cambridge in the boat race on the basis of whatever prejudice fell easily to hand. Probably a majority went for the bloke with the washing-machine bike. Me? I was a Boardman supporter. I liked the boffinish approach, I liked the high-tech bikes. I liked his apparently dispassionate way of doing the thing, and I liked to see hard work being rewarded. So I raised a smile the week following Obree's record, when my newspaper reported that Boardman, on another carbon-fibre wonder-bike, had taken it off him with a distance of 52.27km, 674m further than Obree.

Then, more or less immediately, I forgot all about it.

Since the last rainy summer before I left home, I'd done almost no cycling at all. I did own a bike, but by 1993 it had been chained up outside my college for so long that it had begun to merge with the railings. It had ivy growing on it. Obree's bike may have been unconventional, but it didn't feature much vegetation.

Buying the bike in the first place had been a misjudgement. Durham is not a place for cycling; it's built on an incised meander in the River Wear, and consists entirely of steep hills. Add to that the narrow cobbled streets, and any attempt to locomote by bike quickly turned into a bit of an adventure, especially if, like mine, your bike was light in the brakes department. (It was also broken in the lights department.) For the most part, all I did was wheel the bike uphill, then freewheel squeakily down the far side. I had to drag my feet along the ground so that I didn't attain the critical momentum that would prevent me from stopping without having to crash into something. I almost never actually pedalled – so whatever talent I had stayed hidden.

Anyway, athletic greatness was not what was on my mind. I liked my subject, and I wanted to be an academic. The majority of students avoided working. They absolutely avoided being caught working. I worked and I didn't care who found out. The result of this brazenness was, of course, that no one noticed; they just wondered where it was I got to every day between about 10 a.m. and 5 p.m. It gave me a pleasing air of mystery. Since few of my friends went to the library, and none of them went there regularly, no one ever worked it out.

I got through a lot of newspapers when I was at the library. Reading the case-law of the European Court of Human Rights was an activity that called for frequent breaks. Even so, it sent me to sleep on a regular basis – as it would anyone – usually face down on the newspaper. Often I spent the rest of the day with the news headlines printed backwards across bits of my face. Boardman's and Obree's records are still closely tied up in my mind with the reading room at the back of Palace Green Library, overlooking the river. Most of my friends learned about the records by reading about them from my forehead.

From Durham, I went to Cambridge University to do a Ph.D.; more dusty case-law, dusty libraries and even dustier librarians. Everyone in Cambridge had a bike except me, because mine was incapable of being separated from its railings when I left Durham. For all I know, it's still there. I was just about the only student in Cambridge who walked everywhere.

In Durham, as well as a degree, I had acquired a girlfriend, Louisa. ('Acquired' doesn't really do justice to weeks of carefully choreographed pursuit.) When I went to Cambridge, she went back home to London to try to get a job. Crucially, her father was a racing cyclist. He was also cunning enough to lay an inviting trap for his daughter's new boyfriend.

Thus it was that my cycling career started with a protective father's attempt to kill me. 'Fancy a ride round the park?' he asked, offering me his spare bike. It seemed like a kind offer on a sunny evening. But, as I was to find out in short order, busy London streets are no place to learn to ride a racing bike. The handling was sufficiently sharp that I'd almost fallen off spontaneously before I even reached the road.

Then I discovered that the brakes worked in a manner that suggested that someone had tied the bike to the house and I'd just run out of rope. The bike stopped dead, and I fell over before I had time to put out a foot to save myself. Louisa clung to a small tree with tears of laughter running down her face. Her father didn't even look round at the sound of me falling over. 'The brakes probably work better than you're used to,' he shouted without a hint of irony as he headed off down the road.

I picked myself up and chased after him, only momentarily delayed by my shoelaces getting reeled into the chain. I'd just about begun to feel not actively terrified when we got to the five-lanes-wide circus of Wandsworth roundabout, at rush-hour, in the days when it didn't have any traffic lights. 'Be careful,' said my tormentor, 'this is a bit of a pig.' He accelerated, blended himself into the blur of traffic, and vanished. It was like a conjuring trick. I stood with one foot on the ground, looking at the whirl of cars and lorries. I couldn't even get off and walk; I was stranded in the middle of the road. There was impatient honking behind me.

Nothing in life had prepared me for this. There'd been nothing like it in Durham, or Cambridge, or even Belfast, a city of which the troubles had flattened so much that there was no real need for extravagant traffic management. In Belfast, you could just drive where you wanted. I'd never even negotiated anything like this in a car. After a bit more honking, I decided that I'd just try riding into the maelstrom and hope that at least everyone else had the reaction times to save me. I wasn't going to be beaten by certain death. More honking, squealing tyres, swearing. And, no doubt to the disappointment of Louisa's father, out the far side in a charmed bubble of calm, planning to find a different route back even if it went via Birmingham.

But riding a racing bike appealed to me. It felt like flying. It was as though there was no mechanical linkage involved – I just thought 'faster', and I went faster. Magic! I started to borrow the bike when I was in London. I even learned to go round Wandsworth roundabout without having to depend on pure dumb luck for my survival.

I also discovered that I could ride a bike faster than almost all of the more serious-looking riders in the park, the ones with the Lycra, the shaved legs and the multicoloured kit. They waved to each other, but none of them waved to me, with my flapping tracksuit trousers and running vest. They felt, I'm sure, that I was rather lowering the tone. They liked me even less whenever I overtook them and they found they couldn't keep up.

This was where it began. Charging round the park, blasting past innocent riders who'd wanted nothing beyond a quiet evening's exercise. None of them ever said anything in reply to my cheery, and in retrospect immensely irritating, 'Hi there!' as I breezed by. For my part, I couldn't understand why they all went so damn slowly. It was a lot more fun when you rode fast. This was something I wanted to do. I didn't really care if I was any good at it or not; it just felt right. I whooped with pleasure as I flew downhill, and the other riders looked at me murderously.

I wasn't a cyclist, though. I was just an annoying little

shit on a bike. In an attempt to blend in better, I started reading copies of *Cycling Weekly*. I needed to learn the etiquette. At first, though, I just goggled at the incomprehensible adverts. What the hell was a 'Continental Tempo 22'? How could a bicycle chain, however superior, possibly cost £30? I'd bought bikes for less than that. Best of all were the classified ads, where in the midst of the techno-jargon ads ('Dave Lloyd 56cm c–t, 8sp Shim D/A Ultegra, Open CD, Rolls, ITM etc. Lovely £750') you would always find a lonely one that said, 'Gents' 12-speed racing cycle, very good condition, complete with saddle bag and puncture repair kit'.

The magazines also had the blow-by-blow account of Boardman and Obree. By this time, summer 1994, Obree had taken the record back off Boardman. Still the maverick, still riding a home-made bike. But the most remarkable thing about Obree, I learned, was not where the bikes came from, but their design.

The crucial factor for an hour record or time-trial race is aerodynamics. An essential part of that is getting your head and shoulders low over the front of the bike, with your torso more or less horizontal. Boardman, and everyone apart from Obree, used low-set handlebars, well below the level of the saddle. They placed their elbows on top of the bars, as close together as felt comfortable. Their forearms pointed horizontally forwards, and their hands held onto twin extensions that ran from near the handlebars' centre. It looks uncomfortable, but because your elbows support your body weight, it's a surprisingly relaxed position.

Obree used much higher, narrower handlebars, and rode with his hands on the bars and his shoulders resting on his hands. To accomplish this, his elbows were bent double and tucked into his sides. He looked a little like a weightlifter who had completed the clean, but not yet the jerk, tilted forwards 90 degrees and placed on a bicycle. Gainly? No. Comfortable-looking? No. But you didn't need a degree in fluid dynamics to see that he'd got it right and everyone else had got it wrong. He wasn't an eccentric at all. He was a genius. And to fly in the face of so much conventional wisdom!

It was clear that that was not a universal opinion. Rising from the pages of the magazines were complaints that the Obree position was dangerous; that it was impractical; that it would prevent older riders from competing because they couldn't bend their elbows due to arthritis; that everyone would have to buy a new bike (I don't suppose that one came from a bike-builder); and a hundred others.

They could be boiled down to one: that was just not how things were done.

Don't get me wrong, most appreciated his exploits. After all, he'd broken the hour record twice and then beaten Olympic champion Boardman to win the world track pursuit championships – a short 4km race (the equivalent of the 1500m in athletics) where you chase an adversary on the opposite side of the track and win by either catching him or recording the faster time. No one could ignore all this. But most of the admiration centred on what he'd achieved, rather than how he'd done it. For many cyclists, the comedy bike and the odd position that attracted such attention from the general public were a bit of an embarrassment, rather than an exhibition of brilliance.

It just looked a bit amateur. It was not unknown for Obree's home-made bike to shed vital parts at critical moments. He had a reputation (not entirely justified) for falling off. The image many cyclists wanted the world to see of their sport was that of the more glamorous Boardman. Not something that prompted their non-cycling mates to make jokes about washing machines.

By now, Boardman was riding for a French professional team, at the very top of the elite tree. Cheered on by the forces of conservatism, he was planning to retake the record. But the forces of conservatism had bigger guns than him. They had the UCI, the Union Cycliste Internationale. From its Swiss base, the sport's world governing body had its eye on Graeme Obree.

The UCI gave every impression of hating the Obree position, and – perhaps understandably – the fact that the unknown amateur had broken their glittering hour record using it. The record was the gold-standard in cycling, an account of the great champions and their abilities down the years. It was for the cycling aristocracy only. They were the only ones with the talent and the courage required. That was the way things were, and, I would imagine, the way the UCI wanted them to stay.

They'd missed the point. The glory of the hour is that it's just about how fast you can ride a bike. That's it, that's the only criterion, and with something that simple, you have to take whatever comes along. It's exciting when something unexpected happens. Fans all over the world were thrilled by Obree's ingenuity – the introduction of a big brain into a game traditionally solely about big legs. The problem is that sports administrators often come to view administration as being more important than the sport itself. And administration does not embrace excitement with much enthusiasm. Excitement makes life difficult and unpredictable.

The first time Obree broke the record in 1993, the UCI's discomfort was brief, because Boardman broke it again a few days later using a conventional position. When Obree took the record back the following year, he became something they didn't feel they could ignore. Other people were beginning to play with the position. Even Chris Boardman experimented with it, getting off the test bike and muttering something along the lines of, 'Oh shit, it works.' If they wanted to stamp it out, they were going to have to take action.

Shortly after Obree set his second record, his riding position was banned. The UCI decided that his saddle was positioned too close to the handlebars, and required that it be positioned further back. Everyone assumed that Obree would not then be able to get far enough forward to rest his chest over the bars. Everyone was wrong. Obree arrived undaunted at the World Championships, using the same bike, but with the nose of the saddle sawn off to fit within the new rules. The officials said he couldn't use it because it wasn't manufactured that way, so he produced a saddle from a child's BMX bike, and installed that instead.

Looking rattled by this ingenuity, the UCI apparently amended the rules about handlebars overnight – something Obree said was only communicated to him shortly before the race. It's hard to see it as anything other than a despairing 'anything to stop the Scot' rule, if it was a rule at all. Obree claimed there was nothing on paper, and that he was only notified of it verbally, in French and Italian. He spoke neither language. Since it was too late to make any changes to his bike, he decided to ride the race anyway. Inevitably he was disqualified.

I watched this strange event on a tiny black-and-white television in a small, gloomy hotel room in Paris. As Obree started his ride, blazer-wearing officials began to jump onto the track in an attempt to stop him. None of the commentators had any idea what was going on. For his part, Obree tried manfully to run the interlopers over, but they were more agile than they looked and kept dodging out of the way. It really was one of the most bizarre things I've ever seen – the cycling World Championships reinterpreted by *It's a Knockout*.

I was in Paris with Louisa, on what must have been our first holiday together. The August weather was cold and grey; it rained every day at some point. We had enough cash to get there, and to get a room in a dreadful little hotel somewhere off the rue de Rivoli, but not enough to actually do anything very much.

A couple of times we ate out; often we ended up eating bread and jam in the room, watching the cruddy little TV, which would only work for ten minutes at a time before it started emitting wisps of smoke. We walked for miles across the city each day looking for free museums and galleries. There were tears and arguments about whose stupid idea it had been to come to Paris.

I went to my very first bike race the morning after we came home, still feeling exhausted and depressed. The race was a suggestion of Louisa's father, who rightly felt that since I was doing a lot of cycling, I ought to put it to some greater use than mugging innocent cyclists in the park. I liked the idea – I'd been reading race reports in the magazines for months, and I wanted to see how I'd fit into this world.

This event was an individual time-trial in Bedfordshire, where the riders started alone at minute intervals, and simply went north on the A1 dual carriageway for 12.5 miles, turned round a roundabout and came back south for 12.5 miles, for a total of 25 miles or 40km. It was the kind of race that within a few seasons I would expect to win by minutes without really having to try. As it was, I was about ninth. Unlike the Parisian TV, I seemed unlikely to set the world alight. It had taken me slightly more than an hour to cover the 40km of the race. I hadn't really measured up to Obree's second record of 52.7km.

I'd had to get up at 3 a.m. to get there in time for my 6 a.m. start, only a few minutes after dawn. The race headquarters was in a village hall that still had debris from a wedding reception the night before strewn around it, and which stank of the embrocation that most of the riders – who were often surprisingly elderly – were rubbing into their legs.

This was not a glamorous sport.* I don't know that I'd really expected it would be; I knew that it was going to be a long way from the suntanned professional world. But I suppose I thought it would be more like, say, the couple of rowing regattas I'd gone to as a student. A bit of an occasion, friends and family out to offer support. As it was, everyone had gone home by 9.30 a.m. Almost no

---

* It was not an immediately welcoming sport, either. As I was getting ready, a short, middle-aged stranger limped over to inform me that 'We don't like newcomers here.' It was like *Deliverance* on wheels.

one looked as if they had enjoyed the experience. It was like finding a secret society for masochists.

It seemed extraordinary that events just like this one were where both the British hour heroes had started. Even the homespun Obree seemed an impossibly distant, exotic figure. Boardman might as well have been from a different planet. I was as likely to see a Lotus bike here as a flying saucer.

1994 was a big year for the hour record. The next attempts were from giants of the sport. In September Miguel Indurain broke Obree's record, riding a carbon-fibre bike made specially for the attempt and called, in a quiet, understated way, the *Espada* or 'sword'. He used the conventional elbow-rest position.

Indurain was exactly the kind of grand champion one might imagine the UCI felt was entitled to the record. From 1991 to 1995 he had won the Tour de France in an impassive, crushing style five times in a row. Yet his supreme physical ability, and all the help and support money could buy, only allowed him to beat Obree's second record by a fairly modest 327m, about 22 seconds.

Seven weeks later Indurain's Tour rival, Tony Rominger, demolished the new record. First, in a 'test run', he added nearly 800m, and a few days later another 1459m to push the record to 55.291km. It was profoundly impressive. It was the biggest step up in distance since 1894 – Rominger had moved the hour record to a new level. When I read about it in the paper I assumed the distance covered had been a misprint.

On a training ride with some friends from the university cycling club, as we howled along on a downhill stretch with a following wind, I pointed out that we had managed to reach – just – the same speed Rominger had sustained for an hour alone on the track. He seemed like Superman. Who on Earth could possibly do anything about that?

Well, Graeme Obree obviously. I mean, who else?

Obree had not taken the UCI's decision lying down. Even as he was being thrown out of the 1994 World Championships, he had a plan. The following year he was back, with a new position on the bike. Instead of the conventional low handlebars and short extensions, he used handlebars set only just below the level of the saddle and much longer extensions. His arms were now stretched right out in front of him, in a pose that was swiftly nicknamed the 'Superman' position. It looked, if anything, sillier than the previous tuck position. As you might expect, it turned out to be highly effective.

Graeme won the pursuit at the 1995 World Championships using Superman. The UCI commissaries stood about clenching their buttocks and thumbing through the rules, but couldn't find any that he was remotely contravening. The organisation had already taken a roasting from the press and public after the previous Obree debacle, and didn't have the nerve to institute any instant rules this time round.

Obree didn't get round to trying for the hour using this position; he was busy preparing for the 1996 Olympics, where in the end his chances were wrecked by illness. It was Chris Boardman who took that opportunity, on the newly built track in Manchester in September 1996.

It went sublimely well. When I asked him about it

several years later he said it had been his best performance ever. 'It was the only time in my career that I can't think of a single thing that we could have done better. It didn't hurt, I just had to sit there and wait for it to end. It was a fantasy ride, and it would be impossible to replicate.'

I wasn't there to see it, though I could have been. The friend who offered me his other ticket said that it was like watching a speeded-up film. 'No one,' he said, 'could ride a bike that fast. It was unreal.' The reception from the British cycling press was gushing: '[A] journey through the pain barrier to a realm mere mortals can only dream of,' said *Cycling Weekly*.

It seems a bit over the top now, but at the time? Well, look at it this way; when Rominger set the previous record, everyone thought it probably couldn't be beaten at all, not ever. Eddy Merckx was the greatest rider the sport has seen – a man who did things on a bike that should by any logic have been impossible – yet when he saw how fast Rominger had gone, he said that he felt like a 'very, very minor bike rider'. He didn't actually believe that, of course, but he was sufficiently impressed that he at least said it. Now Merckx had watched more than a kilometre being added to Rominger's distance. Boardman's fantasy ride was 56.375km. Almost exactly 35mph. To this day no one has ridden a bicycle further in an hour. It was – it still is – one of the most spectacular achievements in sport.

Some sympathy for Obree, who'd devised the position that allowed Boardman to do what he did. At least Obree had had the previous tuck position to himself. Now he'd had to watch Olympic medals being won and the hour being smashed by other riders who, having learned about Obree's genius the hard way, had been quick to adopt his new style.

The UCI had the solution to that. They banned the Superman position, on the basis its use was not in the best interests of cycle sport. Thoughtfully, they left intact the record Chris Boardman had set using it. Boardman had put the record on a high shelf, and the UCI had taken the ladder away.

Obree more or less gave up cycling – and I think so would anyone. He'd twice revolutionised track cycling, and twice the UCI had decided that they didn't like his way of doing things. On both occasions the official technical justifications for doing so were, at best, questionable. The rule change effectively put the hour record into hibernation.

I was still at Cambridge, writing a Ph.D. thesis. It was a very pleasant life. I had a small (tiny) flat entirely to myself in the north of the city, so for the first time in my adult life I could be sure the kitchen sink wouldn't silt up with dirty dishes while I was out, and that if I left milk in the fridge it would still be there the following morning. Most mornings I went cycling in the countryside for an hour or two after breakfast, then off to work in the library until early evening. Perhaps a visit to the college bar in time for last orders. I'm not really sure I've ever wanted much more from life, to be honest.

I was still on target for the academic career. I read academic papers over breakfast, I went to research seminars and did my best to understand the presentations of the other research students. I even asked intelligent-sounding questions, and nodded thoughtfully at the intelligent-sounding answers, before enjoying warm sherry and biscuits with the faculty members. And I don't mean 'enjoy' in an ironic sense; this was what I wanted to do, and warm cheap sherry was part of the deal.

I remained an enthusiastic but mediocre bike rider. I raced most weekends, and trained almost every day. I won a few races, including a British student time-trial championship in 1996, which at the time was the height of my ambition. I competed against Obree for the first and only time a few weeks later at the 1996 National 25-mile time-trial championships. I was so excited at seeing him in the flesh – I would probably only have been more excited by the arrival of Nelson Mandela, Elvis and the President of the European Court of Human Rights on a three-man bike – that I didn't really concentrate on my own ride and daydreamed my way around the course.

From the point of view of trying to race Obree, it wouldn't have made much difference. He stuffed people who stuffed people who stuffed me, and I finished a lowly forty-first. I wasn't too upset. I didn't think that bike riding was ever going to be much more than a hobby, so there wasn't much point in taking it awfully seriously. I gave a member of the University cycling club a lift to a race that summer, and when he said, 'Do you ever think of trying to turn pro?' I assumed he was taking the piss. (Given the forty-first in the National 25, I think he probably was.)

And that was more or less how life stayed for a couple of years. The hour record was dormant, and I was snoozing face down on a newspaper in the extravaganza of glass and steel that was the university Law Faculty.[*]

I finished the Ph.D. thesis in 1997, and got a job lecturing at Sussex University. Career nicely on track. The warm sherry was in slightly less lavish supply, and I had to work a bit harder. A lot harder, actually; for a year cycling took very much a back seat as I tried to cope with shifting mountains of paperwork, which Sussex University regarded as the principal function of a young lecturer.

Indeed, any attempt to teach anyone anything took a back seat to the paperwork as well, which was a pity since for the most part I quite liked teaching. Most of what I remember of the Sussex job is piles and piles of multicoloured carbon-paper forms, and hawking the bloody things up and down on the train to and from the London flat where Louisa and I were now living. I'd wanted to teach and research, but at least two to three hours of every day were consumed with tedious, repetitive filling in of forms that could equally have been done by a dog with a pen tied to its tail, for all the notice anyone ever took of them. It was a depressing time; I'd worked hard to get a career under way, but as soon as I got the job I'd wanted for so long, I discovered that I hated it.

The job in Sussex was a one-year contract, and I didn't try to renew it. A couple of years later I met a former

---

[*] The Law Faculty at Cambridge was designed by Sir Norman Foster, apparently using spares from the Stansted Airport terminal down the road. It had a few idiosyncrasies, including very small loos. Someone wrote above one of the urinals in the gents' on my floor, 'Norman Foster should come and have a pee here to see how uncomfortable it is.' The following morning someone had added, 'That's not architecture, that's gonorrhoea.'

student who told me I'd been badly missed, but then he spoiled it by calling me Dr Peterson. I went back to Cambridge to do more research. The only problem was that when I got there, there was not much research that needed doing. Plenty that could be done, but not much I'd get into trouble for neglecting.

Before Sussex had crushed the spirit from me, I'd have taken advantage of this to rustle up a few papers on whatever topics seemed appealing and simple, and hence ripe for being rendered off-putting and complicated by a thrusting young academic such as myself. But now I couldn't be bothered.

So I killed time by cycling aimlessly round south Cambridgeshire, Essex, Hertfordshire, Suffolk. Four or five hours a day, maybe, then a late lunch, then I'd go to the library for an hour or two. Usually I arrived there at about the point everyone else was going home. It still left me enough time to do the minimum necessary, and I sure as hell wasn't doing any more.

What I found was that lots of cycling, however aimless it felt, made me faster. A lot faster. I'd started to specialise in time-trialling, simple races against the clock, because I liked the idea that the fastest rider won. Like the hour record, there were no tactics or teams to worry about. You just got on your bike and rode as fast as you could. I started winning proper events, even beating some pretty good riders.

In the absence of a proper job, riding and racing were becoming less of a hobby and more of an obsession. Life was increasingly based round staying fit – I didn't go to the college bar any more, I stopped eating chips. When I started to add up the time I was spending in the gym, the time on the bike, and the time doing other weird stuff, like trying to breathe through the barrel of a Biro 'to make my lungs stronger', I was training for up to six hours a day. I was lucky not to inhale the Biro like a bit of spaghetti and choke to death, whistling towards my fate like a boiling kettle.

I still didn't see myself as more than a good local rider, though. I only went to the 1999 National 10-mile time-trial championships near Dorchester because I'd never been to Dorset before. I'd just discovered that Thomas Hardy used to live down the road from my flat in London and I was going through a sort of Wessex phase. Certainly I didn't go because I expected to do much at the race.

I thought I might manage the top twenty. I was second. You can tell you've caused an upset when they delay the prize-giving for half an hour to check repeatedly that they've worked out the timing correctly.

I followed that with fifth in the National 25-mile, and third in the National 50-mile. I won the season-long time trial series. After four years of making up the numbers, I was an overnight sensation.

By now I'd finished what I was doing in Cambridge, and I was jobless. It was worse than that really; not only did I not have a job, but after years of following a care-fully mapped-out career path, I didn't even know what I wanted to do. The only thing I was qualified to do was something I didn't want to go near. I was still doing a lot of training, and it was still for the most part because it was either that or watching daytime TV. There are guys in prison who end up with the ability to do 500 press-ups for much the same reason.

Then two things happened in 2000. First, I started off

on a new career as a pro cyclist. Second, the hour record came unexpectedly back to vibrant life.

First things first. The new career came about by luck. I happened to ring Dave Thompson, a vague acquaintance who ran a bike shop in the Midlands. One of his suppliers, the Taiwanese bike company Giant, and a mail-order company called MDT, which was run by a friend of his, were together looking for a UK-based rider to sponsor. It was unusual, in that they didn't want to sponsor a whole team, just an individual rider – most likely a time-trial specialist. So when the phone rang Dave was sitting there wondering who might like a small pile of money in payment for a little cycling. It was a done deal. I'd finally cracked it; I was going to get paid to do something I'd have been doing anyway, *and* I didn't have to look for another job. A very classy double.

Meanwhile, the UCI was probably beginning to realise that it had painted itself into something of a corner. Not only had no one broken Boardman's Superman record, but no one had even really tried. The general opinion seemed to be that it was impossible. After the frantic activity of the 1990s, it seemed that the UCI's rule changes might have killed the hour off altogether. Even when the mighty Merckx held the record, riders were at least prepared to have a go.

Chris Boardman himself was nearing the end of a career that had already begun to fade away. He was looking for some means of signing off with the dignity of a champion. Not surprisingly he started thinking about hour records. After all, that was what he was best at. But since the current record was inaccessible – and he should know, he'd set it – he had to think of something new.

What he and his team came up with was old and new. They would wind the clock back to 1972, when Merckx set his record. They were going to strip the technology away, abandon all the advanced aerodynamic riding positions, and attempt a record using an old-fashioned, drop-handlebar racing bike with a traditional frame made of round tubes. The kind of thing I and all my friends yearned for when we were kids. It was an idea of considerable elegance, a rather nice counterpoint to Boardman's reputation as the most high-tech cyclist of his generation.

The idea was not totally new. Both he and Graeme Obree had – separately – mooted it as a possibility in 1993–4. Obree even went so far as to suggest he'd like to have a go at breaking the hour record on the very same bike that Eddy Merckx had used.

The UCI, when they heard of this scheme, thought it was a simply splendid idea. (This on its own should be enough to make you suspicious.) So they took it over. They decided to rescind all the records set since Merckx's in 1972, on the basis that they had taken undue advantage of improving technology. Boardman could then attack Merckx's record, and the conservative order of things would be restored. The pesky Scot, the Superman position, and the high-tech wonder-bikes would simply never have happened. The 28-year hole that this would leave in the history of the hour record was not something that seemed to cause the UCI tremendous concern. It all seemed very unfair on a generation of champions who had suffered to set hour records, in good faith and according to the rules in force at the time, but who now, long after they had retired, had their records effectively annulled.

Out on the track, though, the new-old record was a triumph. Boardman started strongly, comfortably ahead of his schedule to beat Merckx. But after half an hour he started to slow down. He fell behind the pace. The capacity crowd cheered desperately; no one wanted to see a man synonymous with the hour record defeated by it at the last.

At 5 minutes to go, he was 52m behind Merckx. Not very far, but in the hour record the margins are dreadfully tight. Over just 5 minutes, that's quite a long way. Boardman continued to lose ground. With 3 minutes remaining, he started to wind up into a long, agonising sprint. With every fibre of his body screaming that he should stop, he managed to block it all out and just demanded more. These were the last 3 minutes of his career, and he was going out fighting. He started to claw back towards the target. With one lap to go, 18 seconds, he was still behind. Yet he managed it. He broke Merckx's record by 10m. That is the smallest margin in the event's history. It's about 0.8 seconds.

It was a striking contrast to the 1996 Superman record in every way. From high-tech to low-tech, from cool and controlled to last-gasp passion and a rage against failure. It was magnificent. Anyone who thought Boardman was a robot, who thought he lacked the guts of Obree, went to the bar to have a quiet pint and change their minds.

He was lifted off his bike, and he retired on the spot. The British cycling public fell in love with him all over again.

Just like the 1996 fantasy ride, I could have been there. I wasn't doing very much else, my season had ended and I didn't even have training to do. I listened to it on the radio, where the reporter had to scream to be heard above the roaring crowd. By now I'd met Chris, and he'd seemed nice enough, with a dry, self-deprecating sense of humour. I was pleased for him. And then, just as I had in Durham in 1993, I more or less forgot about it.

Over the next few years there were a couple of attempts on the record, the new-old one, which became known as the 'athlete's hour'. No one managed to get very close to it; indeed, the most high-profile of the attempts, by the Spaniard Abraham Olano, was cancelled at the last minute. (Though not before half the cycling journalists in Europe had travelled to watch it.)

My new career went better than the old one. I didn't turn into a superstar, but I made a reasonable living and enjoyed the racing. I managed to accumulate a very large pile of National time-trial championship medals over various distances – about a dozen of which were gold. I was the first rider to win medals in all the British championship distances from 10 miles to the 12-hour event, and I managed to do it in a single season.

What I didn't manage to do was break out of the domestic scene and get to the big time: the Worlds, the Olympics. The limited number of places available at big events, and the consequent need for riders to double up over several disciplines, meant that someone with my narrow specialisation was unlikely to get selected. I rode at the Commonwealth Games in 2002, in Manchester, but that was about as close to the top as I got. By the end of 2002 I'd won pretty much everything that was available to me.

So I found myself trying to think of something to do the following season. Something I hadn't done before. Something exciting. Something to which I could lend my talent for riding alone against the watch. Something that might lift me from the domestic scene to the world scene, and perhaps make me rich along the way. And damn me, I couldn't think of anything.

It was a cold, clear day in late November. I was driving back to London down the M6 from the last race of the year, the National hill-climb championships – it should have been weeks earlier, but it had had to be postponed until now because of the weather. In the passenger seat was David Taylor, a semi-retired cycling journalist.

He'd spent years on the staff of *Cycling Weekly*, but now just did the odd race report to fund an unquenchable urge to buy second-hand books and old jazz albums. (I was tempted to say an indiscriminate urge, but that's probably not quite fair. It just looks indiscriminate.) I often gave him a lift back to London. I enjoyed the company and liked his rather cynical view of the sport. He principally liked not having to catch three buses and a train to get home from the various desolate villages that cycle sport in Britain tends to revolve around.

He was trying to get to sleep, I imagine. Unfortunately I was keeping him awake – the adrenalin from a race takes a few hours to disperse, and in the meantime the athlete prattles on like a hyperactive but very stupid five-year-old. I was explaining at some length the dilemma of what to do the following season: 'Something different . . . exciting . . .'

After trying not to listen for several minutes, he cleared

his throat and said, 'Why don't you have a go at the hour record?'

I think he said it in the hope it would shut me up. I'm afraid it did exactly the opposite.

CHAPTER 3

LOUISA AND I MOVED HOUSE THAT NOVEMBER. THE new place was only a few doors down the road from the old, and in a typically skinflint mood I decided we could save money by carting our possessions from one to the other ourselves. I borrowed a small trolley, collected a few boxes and got to work. How hard could it be? Harder than it looked. It took days and days. I couldn't believe how much stuff we owned.

As my little trolley and I clattered to and fro, I had a lot of time for idle thought. In the back of my mind all the time was the idea of the hour. I couldn't get rid of it. There were a lot of reasons why it was attractive. It would be a challenge. The last couple of seasons had fallen into a well-worn groove, the same comfortable races against the same opponents, usually with the same result. There was a limit to how long I could do that. But most of all, the hour record could turbo-charge my career. I'd come to cycling late, and then I'd taken years to realise my potential. I was twenty-five years old by my first good season, most of a decade behind schedule. By now I was twenty-nine, I hadn't really achieved what I would have liked to, and I was running out of time. If I wanted to make the big time, I really needed a shortcut.

The hour was just such a shortcut. Most of the big events in sport are available only to a select few. However talented you are, you have to work your way up the ladder, through the system. Even if you are the most divinely gifted tennis player to pick up a racket, you can't win Wimbledon in your first season; they won't let you enter.

It's just the same in cycling. If you want to ride the Tour de France, you have to get into an elite pro team. Normally you only do that by getting into a lower-ranked pro team and getting the results, and you only get into that team by getting into a top amateur team and getting the results there. Each of these stages takes a year, usually more.

But the hour record? Well, it's different. Essentially you just decide to give it a shot. No team required, no extensive support systems. Anyone – really, honestly, anyone – can attempt the hour. You need a bicycle and an hour of track time, but that's about it.

You also, of course, need the kind of confidence (arrogance maybe) that allows you to believe you're going to break the record. That belief is the hardest thing of all. Anyone can dream about the hour record; I'd done it myself – the cheering crowd, the glorious last few laps when the record was in the bag. But to start seriously contemplating having a go at it in the real world was a little different. That kind of thinking is usually all it takes to put a fantasy back in its box. But the more I thought about it, the more I believed.

I kept retreading familiar ground. The hour record was

exactly the kind of thing I should be good at. I was a time-trial specialist, and this was the ultimate time-trial. It lasted for an hour, which was exactly the kind of length I liked my time-trials. It was on the track, a different environment from the road admittedly, but one where I had some experience. I'd even won a national title on the track the previous autumn – the pursuit title won previously by both Boardman and Obree. It all stacked up quite nicely. It began to look like the only logical thing to do with the coming season.

As winter wore on, idle thoughts began to crystallise into firmer plans. Instead of things like the national championship races, 2003 was going to be about the hour. Unfortunately, the hour-record plan could be expressed with all the detail it possessed in the phrase 'I'm going to have a go at the hour record.' Once I'd told you that, you knew as much about it as I did.

There was one problem in particular. Quite a big problem really. It struck me forcibly on a dull, windy New Year's Day at my parents' house in Northern Ireland, when I was suddenly face-to-face with the coming season and due to get back into some serious training. The problem was this: despite my growing self-belief, I had no real-world proof that I was actually good enough. Chris Boardman's record was 49.441km. I didn't know whether I could do 50km, or 49, 48, 47, 46 . . . Maybe not even that. I knew that I *should* be reasonably well matched to the requirements of the record, but that was all I had to go on.

I may have fallen in love with the hour record, but I was not so far gone as to forget that ambition can outstrip ability with effortless ease. When it does – as in most walks of life – you will finish up looking like an idiot.

The hour record, you see, is like nothing else in cycling. There are no long, solo events on the track, nothing that even vaguely resembles a national or world hour championship. The number of riders who have ridden an unpaced hour on the track, in the whole history of cycling, is probably fewer than 100. Yet it's the most important cycling record there is. That contradiction is part of what makes an hour attempt such a big event. Of course I'd never ridden round a track for an hour myself, because the only reason to do so would be if I was attacking the hour record, and I didn't know if I was good enough to do that (this is where we came in).

Comparing what I could do on the road was not a lot of use, because the UCI rules for the hour record meant throwing away all the aerodynamic refinements and riding in an old-fashioned drop-handlebar position. That would slow things down more than a little. But riding the track, made of smooth wooden boards, indoors and sheltered from the weather, was faster than the road. How these factors would balance out was anyone's guess.

There was really only one way to answer the question, and that was to take a bike to the track and ride it at 49.441kph. But that was harder than you'd expect. For one thing, I wasn't really very fit at the beginning of January. I'd only just started training again after a winter lay-off. If I was able to do an hour at 49kph plus in my untrained state, I would be able to break the record by kilometres come the summer, and even my most extravagant fantasies didn't go that far. I could get round that problem, though. The bigger difficulty, odd though it seems, was that I didn't have a suitable bike.

Don't misunderstand me, I had no shortage of bikes. One of the joys of moving to a larger flat that winter was that we could eat at the dining table again; in the old place it had been surrounded by nine bicycles of various sorts, and stacked with probably twenty wheels. There was a halo of unworn carpet round the table, untrodden for years because it was always covered in bikes.

However, now that the hour record had been time-warped back to the early 1970s, none of them was of any use to me. The record rules specified that all the tubes in the traditional triangular-framed bike had to be round and straight. Modern bikes are very rarely composed entirely of straight round tubes – they are often oval, or curved, or aerofoil-shaped because these are things that can make a bike faster, or more comfortable. All of my bikes had curved tubes, or oval tubes, or oval curved tubes, or some other twinkling facet of modernity. To get a proper grip on the hour record, I needed a bike that was cycling's answer to the Morris Marina.

I rang friends, especially old ones. I spoke to some traditional frame-builders who I thought might be able to lend me something that had been gathering dust since around the time I was born. No one had anything dated enough. I began to think I'd have to use something modern, and estimate how much it was saving me; a layer of guess-work that I really didn't like.

Then it came to me: the clue was in the question. Not just old-fashioned bikes: old-fashioned machinery in general. I had a friend from college, now an engineer of some sort, who drove some of the worst cars known to man. He bought them for £50 off men in pubs – making sure they had a full tank of petrol – and used them until they disintegrated, normally only a matter of a few months. You never knew what car he would turn up in, but you could always recognise it in the car park. He was a personal friend of every AA patrolman in Britain and the only man I have ever known who wore out a warning triangle. To Stuart Lemanski, a Morris Marina would have been a luxury conveyance. Of course he had an old-fashioned track bike, older than either of us, and in a lurid shade of 1970s orange.

Borrowing a bike off Lemanski carried with it certain risks; as a student he had been notorious for the regularity with which odds and ends fell off his bike. Wheels, gears, handlebars, things like that. At least with this bike there was not much to go wrong. Track bikes have no gears, and no brakes. You can't even freewheel; the single sprocket is fixed to the back hub, so that if the bike is moving, the pedals go round, just like a child's front-wheel-driven tricycle. The only way to stop is to push backwards against the spinning pedals. When supertanker captains want to make jokes about something being difficult to stop, they talk about track bikes.

Lemanski's laid-back approach to life meant that it didn't even occur to him to ask why I, of all people – a pro cyclist, remember – wanted to borrow his elderly track bike. Since I had no idea how difficult the hour was going to be, and there was considerable potential here for looking like an over-ambitious twit, I was keeping the infant hour project very secret. It was nice not to have to tell lies.

I took the carefully checked bike to the indoor track at Manchester Velodrome in the last week of January. There was a whisper of snow on the ground, and the sky was low and grey. Inside the building it was barely any warmer, and the economy-level lighting meant it was just as gloomy. The Velodrome is a barn of a place, with a high domed roof. A couple were playing badminton in the track centre, and their foot-squeaks and thwacks, and the rows of empty green flip-up seats round the outside of the track just made it feel emptier.

Indoor tracks are usually made of wood. In Manchester it's Nordic pine, laid lengthways in planks to form a lovely, fluid oval, 250m round, with steeply banked curves at each end. And I mean steep, about 45 degrees. It's much too steep to walk on. On a bike, the only thing that keeps you stuck to the track is the centrifugal force that you generate by riding quickly. The traditional analogy is a fairground wall-of-death. Too slow and you come unstuck and slide down the banking to land in a heap on the infield. If you do this in a race, there is a good chance you'll collect some other riders on the way down, who will explain your mistake to you.

Since I wasn't fit enough – or stupid enough – to ride for an hour, I was going to use a shortcut in the form of that sworn enemy of the UCI, modern technology. On Lemanski's bike I'd installed a set of cranks that, along with my speed in kph, recorded my power output (how hard you pedal multiplied by how fast you pedal) in watts. When I downloaded the data, I could find out exactly how hard I was working, and how fast I was going.

The idea was to ride at 49.5kph, just faster than the record average, and establish what power output I needed to do it. Since I had a fair idea of the power I could sustain for an hour, I would be able to see how hard the record would be. From previous races, I reckoned I could manage a little over 400 watts for an hour. It was all reasonably simple.

To give me a hand with the experiments, I'd managed to persuade Simon Jones to come upstairs from his office deep underneath the track. Simon was the British track-squad coach responsible for endurance events – anything longer than about a minute – and was in charge of a hugely successful group of athletes. You may have seen him on television at the last couple of Olympics, standing calmly by the track while the four-man team-pursuit squad thundered past at 60kph.

He didn't actually take an awful lot of persuading. He loved watching athletes operating at their limits, seeing just what those limits might be, finding the point at which a rider can simply give no more. Of course, if you're the rider in question, this is indistinguishable from sadism, but as Simon would be quick to tell you, that's just a matter of perception.

He arrived in the track centre with a bright, happy smile. 'This is going to be interesting,' he said. 'Chris was in agony when he finished his ride. *Agony*.' He grinned still more broadly at the memory, and took out his stop-watch with an air of expectation. 'Come on then,' he said.

I misjudged the speed of the first run badly. I was used to wearing a full carbon-fibre helmet that covered my ears. In a normal helmet, the sound of the wind rushing past and of my ears flapping in the breeze made me think I was going a lot faster than I was. The second run I pressed harder, until the wind was howling. Simon indicated that I was at the target pace. I managed only two laps before I thought I was going to heave my lungs out of my mouth and I had to stop.

Two laps, just 500m. Or about 1 per cent of the hour record. Okay, yes, I'd expected it to be hard, but not that hard. This was insane. I was sprinting flat-out, like one of those guys in baggy shorts and baseball cap that you see on television in the background of a marathon, trying to keep up with the leaders. They run wildly, clawing at the air, and they always fall back after a few strides. Meanwhile the elite runners might slide along effortlessly for another two hours or more.

The problem was not that I couldn't go fast enough for an hour; I could barely go fast enough at all.

'Told you it would be hard,' said Simon.

I'd been assuming that I'd be able to do this. It had never really occurred to me, not *really*, that it might be simply out of my league. When we downloaded the data from the cranks, the two laps had required well over 500 watts. It was a sobering moment.

But it just didn't make sense. Chris Boardman was good. Indeed, to British time-triallists he was a deity. But I wasn't *so* shabby myself. He wasn't so much better than me that half a minute was as long as I could keep up. The only time I'd ever raced Chris, at least I'd looked like I was in the same race. He'd beaten me convincingly, but not like this, not humblingly. I wasn't prepared to accept that the hour was impossible on the basis of the first test, because it couldn't possibly be right.

I was surprised by the unapologetic strength of my own conviction. I've never been a confident athlete, or indeed a confident person. I tend to work on the basis that I'll just do the best I can and see if it's enough – not actually a bad world view, since it usually stops me worrying about things I can't control. But the months of dreaming, then thinking and then planning had generated a real faith in my own ability. So Simon and I talked about what we might do to make reality match up to my own certainty.

The theory is simple. How fast you go is at the balance point between the power you put in, which speeds you up, and the resistance to motion, which slows you down. So, to go faster you need more power, or less resistance. More power was not a realistic option; I was already beginning to wonder if my legs were entirely capable of keeping their side of the bargain. On the other hand, the resistance to riding a bike fast is almost entirely aero-dynamic drag – which we could do something about. The challenge was to find some way of setting up the bike, and my position on it, that cut the power needed for record pace to 400 watts or less. What I started to do that afternoon was a painstaking, repetitive process of making controlled changes to the set-up, riding a few laps, then downloading the data from the cranks to see if the changes had made things better or worse.

Simon suggested moving the handlebars further forward, to try and give me a longer body profile. It helped a bit. It got the power required down from 550w to 510w. A lot too high, but at least we'd established that changing things would make a difference, and that if we changed enough things, I might still be able to do this.

Andrea Ingram wandered over, curious to know what we were doing. Well, she pretended to be curious, but I think she was just being polite. She must have known exactly what we were doing: the old-fashioned bike, the obsessive concern with 49.5kph. There was only one thing it could possibly be, and Andrea was not the kind of person who would fail to notice.

Andrea was the Velodrome's 'Track Development Officer', a catch-all job title that covered everything from coaching to editing the Velodrome newsletter, the marvellously named *Velodrone*. She was in her mid-fifties, I'd guess – though it's perhaps more relevant that the question of Andrea's age was something that had never occurred to me until this moment. She habitually wandered around the Velodrome in a pair of sports sandals, even in mid-winter, carrying a cup of coffee that miraculously was always half-full and steaming hot. I didn't realise it at that point, but over the next few months she was going to be very important to me.

Andrea spent a lot of her day supervising the groups of teenagers that local schools sent over to the track. It was hard to escape the suspicion that the schools only sent them to get rid of them for an hour or two. They were almost always unruly, often abusive, sometimes threatening. Any school would be improved by their absence. I didn't know it then, but in just a few months' time, at a testing session, one of them was going to steal my wallet and credit cards and set off on a spending spree in (of all the places you might go bananas with someone else's money) Argos. There is something profoundly depressing about that little honesty allied to that little ambition.

Andrea's patience with the kids wasn't inexhaustible – it couldn't possibly have been, for there were some whom Mother Teresa would have sworn a streak at – but it looked it. It made me feel pretty mean-spirited. And Andrea didn't just work with the kids. She looked after adult training sessions, come-and-try-it sessions, and anything else that came up, and while she grumbled about it half-heartedly almost all the time, she often ended up at the Velodrome for a 12-hour day at least semi-voluntarily. In her spare time she ran a cycling club and went to bike races and cycling festivals.

She was, and is, a *cyclist* in a way I never have been and never will be. I'm just a bike racer. She'd raced, especially on the track, since 1968, and loved the sport, lived the sport, while I just took advantage of it. To the extent that now, when she had an hour to go back to her office and try to sort through a bit of paperwork and have a biscuit with her bottomless cup of coffee, she couldn't resist the temptation to come and see how Simon and I were getting on.

We admitted it was an hour-record experiment. 'Can you do five minutes?' she asked.

'Not quite. More like thirty seconds.'

'You global superstar,' she said. 'So it's not going to be too difficult then?'

Did I forget to mention that Andrea's affection for cycling didn't blunt an edge of sarcasm and a slightly cynical world view?

We tinkered away for the rest of the hour's track time, but didn't make a lot of progress. We came to the conclusion that I needed to use a much longer bike, to get a more stretched-out position. What we were trying to do was to replicate the modern elbow-rest position I used in time-trials, but using traditional drop handlebars. I believed, or at least I hoped, that would make me faster. Against that hope was the certainty that it would be wildly uncomfortable, because instead of resting on my elbows, a very large proportion of my weight would have to be supported by the muscles of my arms and shoulders. It would be faster, but it might not be by very much, and it might well be impossible to hold the position for more than a few minutes.

Simon wasn't convinced that this would make much difference. 'I still think you'll struggle,' he said. 'A longer bike might help, but really you're on a hiding to nothing. Pity, it would have been interesting.' He headed back underground to his office.

This was clearly my cue to pack up and go home, give Lemanski his bike back and hope that he never asked what I'd wanted it for. But doing so was awfully difficult. I'd based my career on a scientific approach. But now, when I'd taken a lot of trouble to do a scientific test, I found I just didn't care about the result because it clashed with what I believed. I knew I could do it, I really did.

Andrea must have understood the look on my face. 'Look, if you want to keep working on this, I'll help,' she said. 'There are lots of things we can try; it's just going to take time. Get a longer bike built, and we can see where that gets us.'

Driving back south, I kept thinking about it. The tests weren't perfect; that much was clear. But they were the best evidence I had. Was it really wise to ignore them? If I pursued this, I was letting my heart rule my head. That would mean I wasn't quite the person I thought I was. But was that necessarily a bad thing?

It started snowing not far from Manchester, and the drive home took hours longer than normal. For 200 slow miles I tried to will myself into forgetting about the whole hour-record idea. But somewhere on the outskirts of London, in a jam behind yet another accident, I realised that I had no choice but to keep working at it. Otherwise I'd never find out, and I would wonder for ever. Even if I couldn't break the record, I needed to know. For once in my life it was time to go with what I believed, rather than what I could prove. Already I was wondering what would happen with a better bike, a better position, better wheels. I knew I would be going to return to Manchester again and again, to run test after test. To make riding 49.442km in an hour something I could do, metre by metre if that was what it took.

Over the next few months the testing generated hundreds of downloaded computer files, and pages and pages of notes. Since I always forgot to take any paper with me, they were usually on the back of other things: envelopes, track session signing-on sheets, hotel bills. They formed an untidy wedge of mismatched, folded, dog-eared paper that lived for months stuffed into the end pocket of my kit bag. I should have sorted them out, but I never did. I still have them, a bizarre diary of work in progress.

The importance of the hour over the years has been partly the result of a contradiction: cycling is not a sport where records are normally relevant. The heart of professional cycling is on the road, and road conditions vary too much for any records set there to have much meaning. Road riding is about beating other riders, pure and simple.

Yet any sport that revolves around speed begs for records. If you can go fast, you want to prove it in absolute terms, not just relative to your opposition. To say, 'I'm not just the fastest rider who turned up today; I'm the fastest there has ever been.'

The only environment controlled enough for worthwhile record-setting is the track. Even there, most of the racing is man-on-man, not man-against-watch. The kilometre race is a time-trial, the 4km pursuit is almost a time-trial, but that's it, and those events don't last for more than a few minutes. The hour is not just the most important record: it's the only record. If you compare it with athletics, it's all the long-distance running records rolled into one – then multiplied by the scarcity of attempts to beat it.* They are sometimes separated by years.

Most sports, from athletics to round-the-world yachting, have records that revolve around set distances. That cycling used a fixed time is part of the record's brilliance, because it means that its demands have remained essentially the same since the record began. If it had run over a fixed distance, the time taken would almost have halved by now, making it a rather different event. 'The hour' has a romance and a simplicity that no arbitrary distance could achieve.†

It can be traced back almost to the invention of the bicycle. Most of the very early hour records were set in England; the earliest record I could find was that of James Moore, who rode 23km on an ordinary bicycle (a penny-farthing) in Wolverhampton in 1873. He had also won what is generally accepted to be the world's first bike race of any sort, in Paris in 1868. His hour was unofficial,

* I am aware that this is not a very sound concept mathematically.
† I'll admit that the runners' mile comes close. But that had more to do with luck. The four-minute barrier turned out to be simple, romantic, difficult to do, but crucially not impossible. The give-away is that there is still probably more interest in Roger Bannister's miling career than there is in any contemporary race.

since there was no governing body to recognise his achievement. Unofficial records continued to be set in England, first on ordinaries, then on safety bicycles until the 1880s. Until the 1990s, and Boardman and Obree, this was the high-water mark for British hour-record success.

A fixed time was used simply because such challenges were much more popular then, though they were often over twenty-four hours, or longer. Both running and cycling had numerous six-day races – six days because that was the longest continuous period you could compete without racing on the Sabbath. God knows what they would have tried to do without this interruption.

Cycling has stuck to the fixed-time format for its record simply because there has been no reason to change. Since it is always attacked by a rider alone on the track, there is no need for a fixed finishing line. The rider simply completes the lap during which the hour expires, and his final exact distance is calculated as a proportion of that lap.

For the first record to be set under official, controlled conditions, cycling had to wait until May 1893, when Henri Desgrange set his record at the Buffalo track – so called because it was built on the site of Buffalo Bill's Wild West show. (The building of the track was financed by the Folies Bergère. I suppose it says something about the fashionable nature of cycling as an activity for the well-heeled in nineteenth-century Paris. I certainly can't see Peter Stringfellow sponsoring a cycle track now.) Desgrange rode 35.325km, and took a permanent place at the head of all hour-record tables. He's usually credited with inventing the whole thing.

Desgrange's genius was to get in first; he was not a man short on self-regard, but even by his own admission he was not an especially gifted cyclist. He just said he wanted to set a target for others. Fifty years later he recalled that he had hung a small bottle of milk from his handlebars to drink, and that after his ride he was so caked in dust, sweat, oil and snot that his supporters 'wouldn't touch me with tongs'. When he had cleaned up, they all went out for an extravagant meal to celebrate.

Desgrange's record was, as he predicted, short-lived. The following year it was broken by more than 3km, the biggest margin in hour history, by Jules Dubois. But as with so many things, it's the first man that is remembered. Just ask Buzz Aldrin or John Landy.

Desgrange had not finished erecting monuments. Ten years later, as the irascible editor of *Velo*, he dreamed up a cycle race round all of France as a means of publicising his magazine. That race was, of course, the Tour de France. The early editions of the Tour were savage, with stages of more than 400km, which often started shortly after midnight and lasted for more than twenty-four hours. By 1906 Desgrange was running his race over the high mountains of the Pyrenees – the Alps followed a few years later. These climbs are still feared today by cyclists on modern lightweight bikes with more gears than all the participants' bikes in an early Tour put together.

As in more recent years, cycling's early stars, like Oscar Egg and Lucien Petit-Breton, rode the Tour and attacked the hour. (Petit-Breton was not actually his name, but he was universally so called because he was a small Breton. The nickname also meant that he avoided his father finding out he was a professional cyclist.)

Desgrange kept a tight control over his race, constantly tinkering with the rules to try to ensure close racing, and to make sure none of the riders could get off with slacking. He was harshly critical of any whom he thought showed the slightest lack of commitment. He wanted to see effort and he wanted to see suffering. No coincidence that the grand tours, of which his was the first, and the hour record are the hardest events in cycling.

Meanwhile, back in the twenty-first century, I was in urgent need of an extra-long bike. Lemanski's bike was based on a fairly standard frame shape; the distance from the bottom bracket to the top of the frame was about the same as from there to the front of the frame. What I needed was something about 6cm longer than that. No one makes such a thing, because in normal use it would only suit someone about 7'3" in height with a 32" inside leg measurement – a rather limited market. I needed to get this made specially. That meant it was time to speak to the man who got me the pro cycling gig in the first place, Dave Thompson.

By this time Dave was my . . . well, it's hard to say quite what he was. He started simply as a friend, but on the strength of having done the deal with the Giant company that led to me getting paid a decent salary, he took to calling himself my manager. I didn't really argue. My reservation about the title was probably because he only dealt with sponsors, racing kit, that kind of thing. A lot of the rest of it – speaking engagements, race programme and the like – he left to me.

It would also be fair to say that he wasn't always unreservedly on my side, which might be perceived as a shortcoming in a manager. It wasn't entirely unreasonable in his case, since I didn't pay him (which might be perceived as a shortcoming in an athlete, come to think of it). What Dave liked best of all was a quiet life. He had a company of which he was the sole employee. It could easily have been a bigger company, but I guess small was just the way he liked it. The thing Dave hated more than anything else was trouble, of any description. While he was good at solving all sorts of cycling-related problems, he was not (and I don't think he'd disagree with me) your first choice in a proper crisis.

I had so far carefully neglected to mention the hour record to Dave. He, a bit like Andrea, was a real enthusiast for cycling. He adored talking about it; his customer service manner was much admired, because he would take hours to explain things to people. He wasn't going out of his way at all, he loved doing it. In fact it was often difficult to get a simple answer out of Dave, because he'd give me so much background information that after 10 minutes or so we'd both have forgotten what the original question was. If you asked Dave what he was having for dinner, he'd start by telling you where he bought the cooker.

I knew he'd love talking about the hour record. I knew this, because the happiest days of Dave's life (apparently) had been his time as a member of the famous Graeme Obree's support team. Quite what his role was has remained rather mysterious. Other members of Team Obree have various memories. The clearest on the matter is Graeme himself. When I asked him, he grinned broadly and cried delightedly, 'Dave! The chainring guy!' According to Graeme, Dave's role had been to deliver a chainring (the big front sprocket that the pedals use to turn the chain) to the team as they prepared to go to Norway for the first attempt. 'And he never really went away,' finished Graeme.

Dave tells of a rather more involved role. As usual I guess the truth – not that it really matters – is somewhere in between. The only thing for which I absolutely know he was responsible was the supporting of the left leg of Obree as he was hoisted aloft in celebration. I know this because Dave showed me a picture of himself doing just that. Though there is an unidentified pair of hands at the other side of the photo which have a firm grasp of Obree's other leg and look as if they are about to haul him off in a different direction, Dave is holding onto the rising star of Obree pretty firmly.

When I phoned and told him what I'd been up to, he could hardly contain himself. He didn't know whether to fantasise about me breaking the record, reminisce about Obree, or go all the way back to Francesco Moser, whose 1984 record Obree beat in 1993. Moser was a favourite topic of Dave's because of his disc wheels, almost the first examples of these anyone had used.

Dave tried to do all three at once. It came out as, 'Graeme, I mean Mike, I mean, I remember when Moser broke the record, and we all thought it was amazing when Graeme did it, and when are you going to do it, and where, and I remember the plane was late taking off, and I'd got the chainring . . .'

I kept quiet. Eventually his excitement would wear itself out, and I would be able to explain that really all I had was a plan for more experiments, and that for these I needed a frame built. I'd been a bit worried that this would put Dave off, since it would be a bit of a hassle to get it designed and built and paid for. But the momentum of his enthusiasm flattened any instinctive reluctance he might have had. After talking about Moser's wheels some more, he went off to sort out the frame with a frame-builder he'd worked with in the past.

So that was the technical side of 'Project Hour' launched. Next, the physical side. I had the chassis ordered; now I had to worry about the engine. That was me. Time for some training.

If you make your living the way I do, life revolves around training. You have to check your training plan before you can accept a dinner invitation, except for those months of the year when there is no point because you know you're just not going to go anywhere or do anything. I've missed countless friends' weddings because I had training to do. Some good friends of mine actually planned the date of their wedding to suit me. The vicar was, reportedly, speechless.

The concept of physical training – all physical training – is a simple one. You subject your body to a physical stress. It adapts to the stress, and grows stronger. In short, the more you do it, the better you get. However, for the hundreds of university exercise physiology depart-ments around the world to justify their existence, this simplicity has to be played down. In all areas of life, the more complicated it looks, the easier it is to get funding for it. (For instance, it's easier to get money to develop a stealth fighter than fund a health-care system. But I digress.)

Fortunately most of the difficulty that the physiologists deal with concerns why training works. If you're an athlete, you can trust that it does, and go back to keeping it simple.

For aerobic endurance events, from cycling to marathon running to long-distance kayaking, the basic model usually works like this. You spend a while doing long, slow to moderately paced training. The exact length of 'long' depends on your boredom threshold as much as anything else. I used to manage six- and seven-hour training rides, but as I got older I found I couldn't cope with that kind of thing any more.

Interestingly, cutting down the length of the rides didn't seem to make much difference to the response I got to them. Initially I found that a bit depressing; all those wasted hours. Then I met an exercise physiologist who assured me that the long, long rides were still part of the equation, they were still 'in my legs' as the traditional expression has it. An eminent physiologist recently came up with the notion that a major determinant of cycling ability was simply the number of pedal revolutions you had clocked up in your life. Naturally this embarrassingly simple idea was hushed up.

After a few weeks or months of the long, slow (dull) rides, you move into a phase of final preparation. Six to eight weeks before your major target you start what is often known as 'speedwork'. Total volume of training is reduced, but you incorporate faster rides. Often these are races, or sometimes 'interval' sessions, where you alternate riding hard and riding easy. How long the effort and recovery periods are, and how many efforts you make in total, are matters clearly liable to become quite complicated quite quickly, hence the enthusiasm for interval sessions in physiology departments the world over.

The speedwork, on top of the longer easy base, hopefully brings you to a peak of condition to coincide with the target, where you wipe the floor with the opposition and send them home, their bodies and minds destroyed. Hopefully.

It's not foolproof. The human body is a wilful thing. You never get the same response twice; sometimes the peak of fitness takes ten weeks of speedwork, sometimes four. Sometimes you can do three hard sessions in a week, sometimes only one. There is an art to training; to feel the fatigue levels exactly, so that you can back off before you overdo it, or know to press on when things are going well. Elite athletes, especially old, creaky ones such as myself, have to be able to read their body's signals. A scratch taking too long to heal, odd facial spots, dizziness on standing up suddenly – things like that are my alarm bells that I'm training too hard. Eventually I go deaf in my right ear, at which point it is definitely time to take it a little easier.

Now, though, it was winter, and it was long-ride time. Living in central London, that meant the 7-mile perimeter road round Richmond Park. For hours and hours at a time. That winter I rode 447 laps of the park. I'm not looking for sympathy, but I don't think I particularly enjoyed any of them.

Some did stand out; in early February I was forced off the road by a middle-aged woman in a Range Rover, who gave me an obscene gesture out of the window to make sure I knew it wasn't an accident. (The police are not interested in such matters unfortunately.) A few days later one of the park wardens threw a stone at me, which seemed a bit unreasonable. (He missed.) And in early

March I got propositioned in the public lavatories by a short bald man with a Lycra fetish.* I suppose the other 444 laps were okay, but I don't really remember much about them.

I've never been an enthusiastic trainer. There are some cyclists who just love riding a bike – they leap from their beds with a song in their hearts if they know they have a six-hour training session in front of them. Honestly, these people do exist. But to get me out of the door takes a damn good reason.

Once upon a time I was young and green, and I trained in what I look back on as a positive way: I selected my season's target and used fantasies of achieving it to fuel the long winter miles. I dreamed all winter about winning some particular race, what it would be like, how good the medal would look with my name engraved on the back of it.

Sometime in my first couple of paid seasons, I don't know exactly when, that view faded. I trained because it was what I did. Often weeks would pass in winter when I wouldn't think of the coming season's events. The training plan would say that on Monday I was to do a five-hour ride, so that was what I did. No bright picture of coming glory, just serving out time on the bike.

Racing changed too. It stopped being about hope, and started being about fear. Fear of losing. I'd won most of the events I wanted to win, and now there was nowhere to go but down.

* I don't mean to get on my high horse here, but I know the police would be much more interested in this essentially harmless little man than they were in the woman who ran me off the road.

In a bizarre twist, rather than my racing motivating the training, the training started to motivate my racing. I had to win; I'd put so much work into it. The new fear was that all those hours on the bike would be turned into a dismal waste of time because I failed to perform on the big day. The fear of ballsing it up because I was so scared of losing. Worst, absolutely worst: the fear of getting it exactly right and being beaten simply because someone else was better than me. I know there are plenty of cyclists faster than me out there, but I can't stand having it proven.

Where winning had once been a simple joy, it started being nothing more than relief. I'd managed to avoid being beaten. I'd got away with it again. I started to remember races where I was beaten much better than races where I won, because the pain was so much sharper than the relief. Winning is just winning; being beaten is something someone does to you. It's the difference between opening your front door and being burgled.

I suspect most successful riders are the same. I interviewed Graeme Obree in the Carlisle station buffet one October lunchtime. He told me his success in Norway was because he was so scared of failing that he would rather have died on his bike than have to go home recordless. 'And I don't just mean that as an expression,' he said, with a fierce intensity that drew half the buffet customers into the conversation, 'I mean it absolutely literally.' I completely believed him. He said breaking the record felt more like surviving a near-death experience than anything else.

Of course, you can't really say any of this. I'm blowing an unwritten code here. You can no more say that you're motivated by fear than you can go around shouting 'Bastard!' at anyone who beats you. (Well, you can, but it's frowned upon.) You have to stick to the presumed mores. The sporting point of view. We're all chaps here. You have to remember that the world is full of people who would like your talent and your job, but who have to try and fit riding a bike in around office hours or working on a building site, and then have you walk all over them at the weekend races.

The least you have to do is give the impression that you're having a good time. You can never admit that what motivates you is an obsessiveness that, had circumstances been different, could just as easily have made you an alcoholic or an anorexic. I hated losing. The day you get beaten and don't mind, you've taken your first step towards a normal life.

I make this sound like misery. It's not. It's a very satisfying way to make a living. You can point to some real achievements, with universal currency. It intensifies life – excitement, fear and relief are strong emotions. It's just that sometimes you do something remarkable, something that would make anyone else euphoric and that once would have made you euphoric, and all you feel is an unburdening. It can leave you a little empty. You can remember how it used to make you feel, but that's all.

In truth, it's nothing more complicated than losing your innocence. It shouldn't really be a surprise – loss of innocence is broadly what life is all about – but it is, because sport is still basically a game. It's supposed to be fun for its own sake. Sport is the last contact most of us have with childhood. It's not supposed to have your mortgage riding on it.

Yet when innocence gives way to a more experienced, and in my case slightly cynical view, it brings a deeper understanding of what's going on, and it's that deeper understanding that is the core of professionalism. It's about doing a good job, because that's what you do. And actually, that's something to be proud of. (And it's worth pointing out that it has nothing to do with money. Serious winners in grown-up sports have always been professionals.) It's just that you have to go looking for your lost youth somewhere else. I didn't want to go for the hour record because I imagined, in any way at all, it was going to be fun. But I hoped it would be something I could do well.

CHAPTER 4

IT WAS A LITTLE AFTER SEVEN O'CLOCK ON A COLD, dark March morning. I was back at the Velodrome in Manchester, sitting on a blue plastic chair in the track centre, waiting for Andrea.

I'm not a fan of early morning training; I'm normally still half-asleep. I have to pump myself full of caffeine, and even then I don't usually manage anything more profound than just looking like I'm awake. This time it didn't matter – I would have been wide awake whatever, because it was going to be an interesting morning. I had with me the longer bike that I'd had built.

It was a plain, slightly dull shade of yellow, and despite its unconventional dimensions, it looked reasonably normal. The give-away was that the wheels were a very long way apart. It was only about an extra 10cm, but I'd spent so many years living with normally dimensioned bikes that I found looking at this one a bit unsettling. It seemed to run slightly against the laws of nature.

I was nervous. On the drive up to Manchester the night before, the thought that I'd had this bike built on something of a whim started to gnaw at me. I couldn't even remember who it had been at the first track session who'd said, 'We need a longer bike.' Riding my wave of hour-record hope, I had just taken that thought and run with it. I was stressfully aware that this bike might turn out to be a complete turkey. And now I was sitting waiting, wearing full cycling kit, because Andrea was caught up in a traffic jam somewhere.

Eventually she appeared, wearing a fleece and a scowl, and clutching the inevitable cup of coffee. 'Bloody disgrace getting me up at this hour of the morning,' she said.

'And a good morning to you too.'

'Humph. It had better be worth it.'

Onto the track then. The first thing that became apparent was that the bike verged on the uncontrollable. The geometry of a bike frame – the length of the tubes and the angles at which they are joined – determines how the bike handles. Because no one had had cause to build a bike the shape of this one before, no one really knew how the geometry was going to work. The frame-builder had given it his best guess, but the net result was a bike with steering so extraordinarily stable that when it was moving it was almost impossible to turn the handlebars at all.

Unfortunately, turning the bars is how you keep your balance on a bike, tiny movements to keep the wheels below you.* I came very close to simply falling over

---

* Some time ago on TV I saw a scientist (well, a man in a white coat, which is normally enough for me) who maintained that it was the gyroscopic effect of the spinning wheels that kept you upright. To this end he got onto a bike arranged on two stilts positioned fore and aft of the wheels to hold them off the ground. He had an assistant accelerate the wheels using an adapted electric drill. [cont'd]

sideways before I realised that to steer and balance this thing, you had to treat the handlebars like the steering wheel of a bus. Any attempt at subtlety would be rewarded by being dumped onto the track surface. It was supremely awkward. 'It's like trying to do a slalom in a tram!' I shouted to Andrea as I struggled to bend it round the curves.

Occasionally the need to keep my balance fell at odds with where I wanted to go, and I'd suddenly lurch off in an entirely unexpected direction as if I was trying to avoid sniper fire. Standing by the track, Andrea gave the impression it was the funniest thing she'd ever seen. I suppose I'd cheered her up, at least until the bike – unbidden by me – turned sharp left in the middle of the home straight like a defective torpedo and headed directly for her.

I did get used to it after a while. It wasn't as unpredictable as it seemed, just different, and after a dozen laps I was 75 per cent under control. I decided to take a chance and wind up to record pace. Here was the morning's big news: it was immediately clear that the more stretched-out position on this bike had a major effect. When Andrea indicated I was on the pace, I was able to complete several laps comfortably; and when I stopped, it was because I thought I'd done enough for the first run, not because I was too exhausted to continue.

When the wheels reached full speed, he took his feet off the floor and put them on the pedals. He fell over instantly, with a wonderful flailing crash that could only have been born of supremely misplaced confidence. This was a man who absolutely believed he was going to stay upright. Watching him try to explain what had just happened was quite the funniest piece of television I'd seen for years. I'm only sorry I can't remember his name.

I couldn't have done it for an hour, not by a long way, but I could probably have lasted 5–6 minutes. That was a big step up from the sub-minute efforts that were the best I'd managed before, and it was now endurance riding rather than sprinting. Physiologically I was at least back on my own turf.

Back in the track centre, I sat down with my laptop to have a look at the data from the cranks, while Andrea rode the bike slowly round the infield, laughing at it.

You will doubtless recall that the original set-up using Lemanski's creaking bucket of a bike demanded 550w of power to achieve record pace, or (since I reckoned I could only manage 400w) more than one-and-a-third Michaels. On the day we bodged that down to about 510w. Now the long bike had got it down to 460w, one-and-an-eighth Michaels.

'We're on our way!' I shouted to Andrea, who was still trundling mirthfully around the infield.

She rode over and dismounted. 'For someone who's on his way, you still didn't look like you could do that for an hour,' she said.

I told her the details. She was less impressed than I was.

'It doesn't matter what the computer says; it's about riding that fast for an hour. You can't lose track of that, or you'll end up deciding you can do it based on a few three-minute rides, and then you might get a hell of a shock on the day. Maybe the UCI will let you break the record three minutes at a time. Like coursework rather than an exam.'

'Great. I'm going to have to attack the hour record through a barrage of sarcasm.'

I felt entitled to be pretty upbeat. After all, I hadn't

claimed I could break the record there and then, just that we'd come a long way. I may have been being excessively optimistic in Andrea's eyes, but as far as I was concerned making progress was a good thing. Maybe the early morning start was making her grumpy.

Yet even I had to concede that we'd played our joker, and there was still some way to go. There was no chance of a near-miss being good enough, because the body's maximum physical limits over an hour kick in abruptly. From previous experience I knew the very most I could hope for was 400w. That was all there was going to be, and no amount of passion or desire was going to change it. Indeed, at the back of my mind was the fear that, in the unfamiliar riding position, I might not even be able to do that much.

Back then to the process of tweak, test-ride, download and tweak again, with Andrea by the track with a watch, and me trying to keep my efforts as controlled as possible. We were attempting to shave off a few watts at a time with different arm positions, or different ways of holding the bars.

It was a dull, methodical process, and for the rest of that morning it was all the duller since, other than the saving we'd already found with the long bike, we didn't get anywhere at all. As we packed up, we still had 60w to go, and there was a good chance that it was going to come in 5w increments. When the margins are that small, you have to run the tests repeatedly to try to eliminate the elements of error that always creep in. This was going to take a lot of work, and already I was coming down off the initial high from the morning's first run.

But the testing process suited my personality. There

has always been a certain lack of carefree verve in my make-up. My parents possibly still have the school report that says, 'I've come across clever eight-year-olds, and naughty ones, but never really until now a boring one.' It was at about that age that I kept toy cars in different drawers according to their scale, and only played with them in matching sets. A year later I was put in charge of the class library (about thirty books) and agonised for so long about whether to use the Dewey Decimal or Library of Congress indices that the job was taken away from me and given to someone else. I was too boring to be a librarian.

Compare and contrast with Graeme Obree. His willingness to think highly unconventional thoughts allowed him to twice revolutionise track cycling. Imagine that the key issue – aerodynamic drag – is a boulder to be broken up. If Graeme and I both started at it with little hammers, after a while my approach to life might inspire me to try a slightly larger hammer. Graeme would tap half-heartedly with his hammer for a while, then go and get some explosives. As shards of rock whistled past my ears, I'd be muttering wistfully, 'Now why didn't I think of that?'

It was already clear that if I broke the record, I would immediately be classified as one of the less flamboyant holders. Sort of unswashbuckling. The ones that most of the world's cycling fans slightly resent. What cycling fans want is what most sports fans want: competitors who do it with style. Style is more important than success. Working at it is not stylish.

Consider for a moment Francesco Moser. An Italian champion of considerable charisma, winner of the World

Championships, the Giro d'Italia, and the hard men's spring classic, Paris–Roubaix. More than anyone else, he introduced the scientific approach to the hour. In January 1984 he went to Mexico City with an entourage of about twenty physiologists, biomechanists and cardiologists to attack the 12-year-old record of Eddy Merckx. He had researched the most aerodynamic clothing and equipment, and had special solid disc wheels built.

When he broke the record twice in a few days, Italian fans went wild. But elsewhere, the reception was rather cool. The former record holder, Jacques Anquetil, spoke for many when he said, 'The record was old, and Merckx had not lifted it to its proper level. You have to say that Moser prepared really well.' (A wonderful, double-edged attack – taking a swipe at Moser and clobbering Merckx on the back-swing. And don't go thinking that he might not have meant it that way.)

Another five-times Tour de France winner and all-round bastard, Bernard Hinault, was even blunter, 'This record doesn't impress me. Moser prepared scientifically and received the fruits of his efforts.'

While in most of his career he was a hero, somehow Moser's hour-record rides – there were many over the subsequent years, as we shall see later – mean that he is unfairly remembered as a super-dull, scientific rider who got to the hour record by a sort of legalised cheating. Much of the cycling world felt that the records had as much to do with his coach, Francesco Conconi, as they did with Moser. Indeed, Conconi wrote one of the world's most extravagantly boring books about Moser's record attempts, and it's clear whom he regarded as the senior partner.

Moser's predecessor, Eddy Merckx, was dull only in the sense that he won everything. He was an insatiable competitor; he simply loved winning bike races, dominating bike races, crushing opponents. If you got in his way, so the wags claimed, he ate you. Hence the nickname he hated, 'the Cannibal'.*

Even if you didn't like the predictability of Merckx winning things, you had to admire his style. When Merckx went to Mexico in 1972 to have a go at the hour, it was taken as read that he would set a new record, probably one that would last for two generations. He was expected to push the record to over 50km for the first time. He probably could have done, but (and here is all the insight into Merckx's attitude that you need) he decided that he'd like to break the 10km and 20km records along the way. These are records of aching triviality in the context of the hour, but Eddy wanted the lot, and that involved setting off like a stampede and keeping going as best he could. To put it in some context, he rode the first kilometre in 70 seconds. That was only 6 seconds outside the world record for riding a single kilometre, set on the same track. His time through 5km was world-class for that distance too.

He got the full set of records, but managed 'only' 49.431km for the hour. He had broken the record by a massive margin of almost 800m, but many thought he should have done better. I don't think anyone had the nerve to mention it to Merckx though, who had suffered in the ride as he had never suffered before. He was unable

* Note to Eddy's lawyers: there is no evidence, hard or circumstantial, of M. Merckx actually eating anyone, ever, at all, at any point in his career.

to speak for several minutes afterwards. When he did, he said, 'How I ache, I can hardly move. It was the longest hour of my career. It was terrible; you have no idea what kind of an intense effort it is until you have done it. The record demands total effort, permanent and intense. I will never try it again.' He never did. He subsequently said that he felt the hour had taken years off his life.

Moser, on the other hand, did a couple of laps to warm down, and got off his bike as if nothing much of note had happened. It might have been a 'better' hour, but it lacked the obvious passion and heroism that all fans want.

This is an essential problem with the hour. It is an event that rewards dull, methodical riders. The margins are so tight that doing it with passion will normally end rather badly. Precision works better. As the sport has become increasingly professional in its outlook, and media coverage and criticism have approached absurd levels, this trend has been reinforced. For the elite riders the stakes are now so high that the approach Merckx took is much too dangerous. You can't even try and do it in secret to take the pressure off, because it would be too great a waste of a publicity opportunity for the sponsors.

For example, the attempt of the Belgian Ferdinand Bracke, in 1967, would be utterly impossible now. He was a teammate of Merckx; indeed, the night before one Milan–San Remo classic he impersonated Merckx in telephone interviews with the press while his boss got some rest. His first ride on his record bike, and his first ride on the track he used in Rome, was on the morning of the attempt. Almost no one, including the press, knew the attempt was happening.

This was not a hopeful amateur we are talking about,

this was one of the world's top professionals. He would have won the Tour de France in 1968 had he not been overcome by nerves in the final time-trial. Yet the crowd at the track was composed of the idle and the unemployed of Rome looking for some means of killing a sunny October afternoon. If he hadn't broken the record, there is a good chance no one very much would have noticed or cared.

It has to be said that the tall, grey-haired and very, very thin Bracke was just the kind of man you would want to see break the hour record. He was universally reckoned to be a clean rider – and given the openness of doping in the 1960s, there is every reason to accept that this was true. He was modest and dedicated. That he married late in life because he couldn't bear to leave his widowed mother was, perhaps, overdoing the Monsieur Nice Guy routine just a little, but you get the idea.

From the fans' point of view, as a record-holder I would offer the worst of all worlds: if I was going to do it at all, it was only going to be by working at it – and I couldn't compensate for this lack of style by being a real star. I was a star only if you didn't look beyond the UK for your results, which is indeed the way most UK cyclists see the world. (Except in Yorkshire, of course, where they don't look beyond Yorkshire.) If I managed to better Boardman, it would certainly be seen as at least a partial devaluation of the record.

With a bit of luck, the gloss that I was going to rub off the hour was going to stick to me. I wasn't really trying to make myself a star, but if I did break the record I wanted to cash in with personal appearances, exhibition races and the like. To do that I needed to maximise the interest in my attempt. Pretty much since I'd first thought of doing the hour record, I'd envisaged the attempt taking place in late June or early July to tie in with the start of the Tour de France, the annual high point of interest in matters cycling.* By coincidence there was a track meeting at Manchester on 2nd July. Since Andrea was organising it, I didn't have much trouble getting the attempt scheduled to open the meeting.

So, now I had a date, and the project was beginning to fall out of my head and into reality quite neatly, almost without conscious effort. (And boy, shouldn't that have made me suspicious!) I was working through the technical issues. I'd been training pretty consistently for a couple of months and was making steady progress. It was all under control. When I got back from Manchester I put a big exclamation mark and a little cartoon bicycle in the space for 2nd July on the calendar Louisa kept in the kitchen, where I would see it every day.

By now the racing season in the UK had started. While

---

* Given the extensive TV coverage of the Tour, there is always a good chance that anyone in the news will crop up regularly when commentators are stuck for something to say. The quiet of a stage's early hours can often bring on considerable idiosyncrasy in commentators. Eurosport's admirable David Duffield, for example, regularly sets off on sweeping digressions into unexpected topics, like the competing merits of various French regional cheeses. He has a huge fan-base among people who are not much interested in bike racing, but who simply adore the sound of a man on his own in a commentary booth for six hours. Occasionally they're treated to periods of lengthy silence while David wanders off for a pee, or get to listen to him answering his mobile phone. For David, commentating is almost a retirement project; in his younger days he held the Land's End to John O'Groats tricycle record, and, while a manager at Halfords, provided the bikes for a notorious Queen video that featured a hundred naked women cycling round a running track. The bicycles, by the way, went back into stock.

my season was aimed at the record, I still needed to make sure I justified my existence to my sponsors. I might have started to fancy myself as a Tour de France support act, but I had rather more mundane events to deal with first or I'd lose my job.

My first race that year was a time-trial round the lanes of the Sussex–Surrey borders. Early season races are normally pretty low key, but they can still be hard work. The roads are often very muddy and gravel-strewn after the winter. If you're lucky, the weather is just cold; more often it's wet and windy too. When I lived in Cambridge the season used to kick off with a race out on the fens, where it's so flat that if you stand on a chair you can see the curvature of the Earth. There was always a wind that came from the Russian steppes without having encountered anything that might have warmed it up or slowed it down. On headwind legs of the course, the wind could bring riders almost to a standstill.

The Surrey race was more heartsome than that. Pretty villages, country pubs, red phone boxes and the like. England as seen by a Hollywood set designer. It's an affluent area and the gardens and verges were awfully nicely trimmed, but it didn't really compensate for the crappy roads. Clearly everyone who lives there has a nice lawnmower and a 4×4. At least on the Sunday morning in question, the weather was acceptable. I got round without falling into any potholes to win easily, by something like 5 minutes.

I'm afraid it didn't really get the adrenalin flowing; I'd known that I was going to win (assuming nothing went wrong), and I won. To get a buzz from winning, you have to feel you're properly up against it. In the end, for me the exciting bits of a racing season usually boiled down to a handful of national championship events in late May and June. The Surrey race reminded me why, after the previous season, I'd been so keen to find a new challenge.

But because it was an early season race, it got a bit of publicity, and it reassured my sponsors that I was on the job – at this point in the year they'd been paying me for five months, and for all the evidence they'd seen to the contrary, I might as well have been spending the time laying down blubber like a seal. More importantly, it reassured me; I'd ridden pretty fast, almost as fast as I ever had on that course, and I knew that while I was a long way short of the sort of form needed to break the hour, I was not bad for that time of year. I had a good base on which to build. I went home happy.

I might have gone up in the time-trial world – to the point where I could win races and then have the effrontery to claim it didn't get the adrenalin flowing – but the races were still the same as the first one I'd competed in seven years before. Time-trials have remained more or less unchanged since first contested.

They work like this. They are usually based in a village in the country, miles from the nearest traffic light – though often close to a main road, where the racing happens. The village hall is the normal centre of proceedings, where the organisers go to organise, the riders get changed, and where those family members who've been dragged along as 'helpers' can enjoy a good sulk and a cup of tea. The halls usually have a dusty wooden floor bearing fragments of a long-ignored badminton court, and often a small stage painted to form the set for a

Gilbert and Sullivan opera. Always there are piles of plastic stacking chairs, signs asking people to turn out the lights, and noticeboards titled 'Mothers' Union' and 'Bridge Club'.

Even after years of tramping in and out of these places at bike races, they always take me back to my days in the Scouts, presumably because traumatic incidents from adolescence are hard to shift. The only thing I was any good at was pioneering, a Scouting skill that consisted in its entirety of tying sticks together with string. My diagonal lashings were much admired. As a social skill, however, there is a limit to how far it gets you, and I remember my days in the Scouts as consisting mainly of being laughed at for no reason I ever fully understood.

Sometimes you don't get an HQ as such, just a result board set up in a field or by the roadside. The circuit of Windermere had its HQ at a public lavatory for several years. (If they'd asked me, of course, I could have knocked them up a village hall out of sticks and string.)

The races themselves give every impression of being just like the village halls, thrown together after the war to try and cheer people up, and not much altered since. The normal format is for riders to start at minute intervals over a period of two hours, and race for distances of up to 100 miles, or for periods of twelve hours or (occasionally) twenty-four hours. Many events are held early on a Sunday morning, to try to use the roads while they're quiet. It can mean starting at anything from 5.30 a.m. in mid-summer, maybe getting up at 2 a.m. to get to the course. It's often perfectly possible to get up, race and be home before anyone else has woken up.

Spectators are almost unheard of; even at national

championship events a ratio of one spectator for every two competitors is rarely exceeded. Prize-giving ceremonies are rare; normally everyone just goes home when they finish and the prizes are sent out with the result sheet some time later. And the rewards are very small; £75 would be a big race, and I've often received £10 or £15 for a win – only a little more than the entry fee.

Sometimes an organiser makes an effort to give their race a bit more pizzazz; a commentator might be employed, sometimes a few advertising banners are put up, or a prize-giving is held, with a podium. But it never really works as planned. Usually the commentator is a bit green, and can't think of anything to say except, 'And here comes Hutchingson, going really fast . . .' He will say this as soon as he sees me, and run out of steam quite quickly. By the time I pass the group of three or four spectators, there will be only a screech of feedback from the speakers. The advertising banners are rarely accompanied with any actual money for the event; normally they have just been borrowed to make the place look better. And the podium will have been knocked up out of plywood in someone's garage the previous afternoon, and will be so small that the winners have to hold onto each other to keep their balance, like a motorcycle display team.

For all its homespun character, it's a bigger branch of the sport than you would expect. There are 10,000 competitors in the UK, many of them racing dozens of times a season. There are numerous websites devoted to it, and even some press coverage. And it's a lovely sport. It's friendly and relaxed. It is – and I mean this totally sincerely – uncontaminated by money, and it's one of the few branches of cycle sport without any drugs scandal, or even drugs rumours.

It is a long way from the continental elite races. There, thousands of fans line the closed roads, dozens of police escort the riders, and television helicopters follow them to provide footage for many hours of live coverage. In France, Italy and Spain cycling is the second most popular sport behind football, with all the attendant money and glitz that that suggests.

The stars of this scene are paid millions of euros, and do all the things that sports stars do: date models, drive Ferraris, release ill-advised records. They have a cosseted life, driven to the events in specially fitted-out buses, with mechanics, chefs, masseurs and a dozen other varieties of team staff to look after them.

But (and it's a big but) when it came to the hour, I had an advantage over the big stars. The teams who pay them millions also keep them on a tight rein. I was paid rather less, and in compensation I was left pretty much to look after myself. I could make the attempt whenever I liked, and I could base the rest of the season on making it the best attempt I was capable of. No one was going to tell me suddenly that I had to do a particular race, or that I had to do a photo-shoot for a sponsor's latest ad campaign.

Hour rides have often suffered from coming at the end of a long, hard season, dropped in as an afterthought in the quiet months of autumn when the rider is still fit, but when there is not so much going on. As we know, Merckx didn't do himself any favours by the aggressive way he attacked the hour. But on top of that, he was at the end of a nine-month season that included 129 races, an average of a race every two days. (He won an astonishing 40 per cent of these, including the overall classifications of the Tours of Italy and France.) While the normal rules didn't really apply to Merckx, it's hard to believe he wasn't more than a touch tired by the time of the attempt.

Another five-times Tour de France winner, Miguel Indurain, had it even worse in 1994. At least Merckx had been keen to attack the hour; Indurain gave every impression of having been forced into it by his team. He won the Tour de France in July, which was really all he wanted from the season. But he had to keep fragile form and falling motivation together for another six weeks until the hour. This was a lunatic bit of planning; six weeks was too long to hold form, but not long enough to rest and build up again. Almost any other interval you name, longer or shorter, would have been better. If Indurain had been as strong-willed as he was strong-legged, he'd have told the team where to stuff this schedule. He seems to have been too nice.

It's a testament to his simple physical ability that he still managed to grind out over 53km to break Obree's second record by the slim margin of 327m. But that was in the context of a rising panic among other hour hopefuls that Indurain, by a mile the best time-trial rider of his generation, would push the hour record out of reach for decades. Credible commentators predicted that he would do 56 or 57km, or even (a touch of hysteria here) 59km.

There was a substantial minority at the time who challenged the view that Indurain had performed poorly. They felt he had simply demonstrated the quality of the British amateur record-breakers who had immediately preceded him. Pete Keen, Boardman's coach, said of Indurain's ride, 'It's a good record. I don't see people screaming past.'

Two months later Tony Rominger screamed past on his way to over 55km. There was a stunned silence from the cycling world. Indurain had beaten Rominger by more than 2 minutes in a Tour time-trial in July, most of 2km in hour language. But while Indurain had won the Tour, then struggled on towards his record, Rominger had pulled out of the Tour, taken the time to rest and regroup, then focused on preparing for an attempt in November.

It's been clear down the years that the best rides, from a subjective point of view, come from careful training and preparation. That's what I was trying to do. Despite the so far inconclusive testing, everything was now aimed at 2nd July. I'd worked out the training programme backwards from that date, and I was going to make sure the equipment issues were sorted out well in advance of it. I had the whole thing quite clear in my mind.

The only thing was that . . . well, July seemed a very long way away. I may have had this glittering target to work towards, but day-to-day reality was the same old stuff. Long training rides in the park . . . and while the weather in March was better than it had been in February, it was still often uninviting. The park traffic was no respecter of athletic class, and every ride I did there felt like a battle. But the alternative was riding on the home trainer in the kitchen, sweating by the bucket and trying desperately to think of things that might keep me entertained: CDs, the radio, even a book on a music stand. If you think riding an exercise bike down the gym lacks stimulation, try doing it for five hours a day for a week, while the rain beats against the kitchen window. It was stupefyingly dull.

I was also worried about the finances of the project. I could make all the pretty plans in the world, but they weren't going to count for a lot if I ran out of cash. While the sponsors had paid for the amazing unsteerable test bike, I had no real assurance that anyone was going to pay for anything else. All I could get were some vague promises that it would all be covered if I sent in a proper expenses claim after the record attempt.*

For the moment it was all coming out of my bank account: track time, travelling expenses, hotel rooms and various bits of specialist kit. I was having to spend money like I got it for free, and the total in my current account was thundering downwards like the altimeter on a crashing aeroplane. Since I was more used to cycling causing money to flow into my account, this was not an experience I was enjoying. If I broke the record, then fine, I was going to make a lot of money. But whatever I got, my sponsors would do better, and I didn't like the idea that they might end up getting it for nothing. I disliked even more the idea that if I didn't break the record I'd be left holding the bill.

At least this was by a long way the cheapest hour attempt in living memory. That was some comfort. The opening of Manchester Velodrome in 1994, the first covered track in the UK, made a huge difference to British track cycling. Obree may have built his own bike,

---

* In fairness I should say that everything was indeed paid in the end. I didn't know that at the time, though.

but he still had to get it to the track, and the track was in Norway. I think Boardman estimated the cost of his first attempt at more than £20,000, a lot of which was spent on trips to the track in Bordeaux, the nearest suitable indoor facility.

My mission statement, on the other hand, was along the lines of: 'To push back the boundaries of human physical endeavour, so long as it doesn't involve any significant expenditure.' I refer you also to my family motto, 'Higher, faster, cheaper.' If there was a record for kilometres per hour per pound, I'd have been a long way in front already.

By the next trip to Manchester it was getting towards April. For the first time it was sunny, and if you stayed in the sun it was even most of the way to warm. The skylights at the top of the Velodrome's domed roof caught the morning light and gave the wood of the track a warm glow. For the first time in months the building was bright and welcoming.

Andrea arrived for the session carrying a dog-eared copy of *Sporting Cyclist* magazine from 1958. It had a three-page article about Roger Rivière's second success-ful hour-record ride that September, written by the then doyen of cycle journalism – in English at any rate – René de Latour. He was a proper Frenchman who wore the stereotypical striped jersey that I assumed was only worn by Frenchmen in cartoons. As well as reporting on Rivière's ride, de Latour was a member of the French star's support team. He was responsible for preparing the crucial lap-by-lap schedule for the record attempt, as well as for riding a motor-scooter to provide Rivière with pace in training sessions and warm-ups.

(He did the same for Jacques Anquetil nine years later.)

Andrea was more interested in the pictures. 'Look,' she said, 'the handlebars are set pretty high, only just below the level of the saddle.'

Last time, I'd set the bars on the test bike pretty low, for no other reason than that was how they were on my road bike. That wasn't a good enough reason not to try something new, so we moved the bars up.

The most striking consequence of this was to make an uncomfortable bike even worse. Now my elbows were bent at almost 90 degrees, with my forearms close to horizontal. It was like an upper-body version of the unsupported chair exercise. Within the space of the half-dozen laps I rode, my arms and shoulders began to ache. But it was a good call from an aerodynamic point of view; it shaved about 15w off the total.

When we put the bars up another few centimetres, we found that the same two things happened again. Faster, but harder to sustain. We decided to focus on the positive. Andrea was terribly pleased with herself. 'Old Roger knew what he was at,' she said gleefully, 'who'd have thought it.'

For my part, I resolved to be more respectful of riders who, after all, had spent their whole careers riding bikes like this one. It's easy to confuse 'more modern' with 'smarter'; 'new' with 'better'. I was forgetting that there was a good chance the best way to do something old-fashioned was the old-fashioned way. It's a particularly cretinous mistake to make when you're involved in the time-warp technology of the athlete's hour. Rivière had ridden almost 48km in 1958, which was something that I didn't reckon I'd be able to do this early in the project, even with the advantages of forty-five years of development. He must have been doing something right.

By now the bike looked less like a lean racing machine, and more like something for doing a paper round *circa* 1976. All it needed was a basket, and maybe one of those horns you worked by squeezing a rubber bulb on the end. (I had a dream a few nights later where I was trying to break the hour record on a bike with handlebars that had both a basket, containing a sea-lion, and a whole row of these horns, which were being used by the sea-lion to play 'The Internationale'.)

Doubtful aesthetics aside, it had been a good morning's work. Crucially, I felt I was now within reach of the magic 400w; better wheels (when I got around to organising them) might well now be enough on their own to get me there. It was obvious that the progression towards being able to break the record was a fitful thing; there were going to be no major breakthrough moments. As epiphanies went, this might be as good as it got. We packed the bike and the computer up, and the sun shone through a skylight onto the track in a big golden square.

Instead of going straight home, I took my road bike out for a ride. Out of the city to the east, and over the Pennines towards Holmfirth. It was a ride I'd often done after morning track sessions over the previous few years, and I loved it. Up the long climb out of Mossley, past the reservoir. The air got colder as I approached the top. From the empty road across the green hillside I could look back at the grey-brown sprawl of Manchester and imagine I was seeing the industrial revolution as it happened. I continued on up, and over the bleak, grassy plateau of Saddleworth Moor.

I was on a high. The session had gone well, spring was on the way, and the hour record was getting closer in all respects. Andrea's yellowing magazine article had helped. De Latour's writing had dated, like a Pathé newsreel, but it communicated a sense of enthusiasm that felt as if it came straight from Roger Rivière himself. He was twenty-two when he set that record, and it was clear he knew he was at the height of his powers, and that he loved it. He wasn't attacking the record because he felt he had to, or because it was a good career move; he was attacking it because he knew it was something he was bloody good at.

There were other reasons to do it, but for me part of the hour record was supposed to be about trying to get a bit of adventure back into cycling, and there was no point in adventure – walking unaided across the Arctic, rowing the Atlantic, whatever – if you didn't look up from time to time and feel what it was like to be doing something extraordinary. The article didn't gloss over the difficulties they'd had. But it retained beautifully a sense of joy.

That was a contrast to the coverage of the more recent attempts, from Merckx in 1972 into the 1990s. Those articles focused on pain and suffering. They told with relish of wrecked athletes being lifted from their bikes and being unable to walk for days afterwards. It didn't sound like the same event.

Rivière, of course, didn't finish his career with the hour record. After he took it to more than 47km – but for a puncture towards the end of the ride, he might well have been the first past the 48km or 30 miles mark – he focused on what was expected to be a great road racing career. He was fourth in the 1959 Tour de France. But in the 1960 race he went downhill rather badly; the man whom de Latour said 'has a fortune at his winged feet' crashed into a ravine on a mountain descent and broke his back. A doping product had left his hands too numb to pull the brake levers. (He subsequently admitted that he'd also used drugs to break the hour record.) He was paralysed and confined to a wheelchair, and died of cancer aged just forty.

I'm glad I didn't know about any of that until much later. I rode back through Manchester towards the Velodrome with a real sense of enthusiasm for the record, for the piecemeal process of breaking it. I'd always known how important it was, but now I could feel it.

Whatever I went on to after the hour, it was unlikely to be a career in road racing, at least not in its more technical sense. Road racing is not simply racing on the road – I did plenty of that – it means bunched racing. Probably what most people think of when they hear the words 'bike race'. (It's called a race 'in line' everywhere else on the planet, which is rather less misleading.) I'd done a fair few road races, but it wasn't something I enjoyed very much. Tactics are very much part of that game, and I intensely disliked the idea of being the strongest rider in a race, yet failing to win because I made a tactical mistake. I'd put this into tediously regular practice in my first few races.

The tactics, of course, are what makes it interesting for most riders and spectators. Despite claims from riders and fans, they're not usually blindingly complicated; from a detached viewpoint, it's a long way short of the usual cliché about 'high-speed chess'.* But it can be very hard to read what's going on when you're in the middle of a race. I wasn't instinctively good at it, and I didn't have much inclination to learn. In spite of myself, I did get better at it over the seasons, but I never liked it.

Perhaps it stems from coming to the sport late, or from a lack of real ambition to get to the top of cycling, but I was quite happy with specialising in what came easily to me: time-trialling. It opens you up to a certain amount of abuse, though, because road racing is the senior branch of cycling, and it's where the real glory is. There were many who regarded me turning my back on it simply because I didn't enjoy it as wasting my talent. Some of them were remarkably unembarrassed about telling me what I ought to do, and to hell with what I might think.

In the UK there is the most peculiar hostility between riders who prefer road races and those who prefer time-trials. Even riders who do equal numbers of both find they get put in one slot or the other. The peculiarity of the hostility is most apparent in its asymmetry; the road riders abuse the time-triallists ('testers' is the pejorative term), who normally suffer the insults with a combination of defensiveness and stoicism. ('You're probably right, but it really doesn't bother me.')

It's a further eccentricity of the relationship that if you do a road race, and win, the roadies are still not happy. I did a few road events in my preparations for the hour,

---

* I have previous in the chess arena; at school I was entered in the Irish chess tournament for (I think) under-thirteens. There were several hundred competitors, some of whom were quite bad in their own right, but that didn't stop me finishing flat last. My interest in any activity that is billed as 'chess on . . .' is limited.

including a race that I won in Hampshire. As road-racing testers tend to do, I won it on my own, having ridden away from the bunch with a few miles to go. Everywhere else in the world of cycling the solo break is the most romantic, swashbuckling way to win. In the UK it's seen as a technique favoured only by the kind of pervert who enjoys racing up and down a main road at six o'clock in the morning.

When Eddy Merckx won a stage of the 1969 Tour de France by almost 8 minutes after a 130km solo break across the mountains, he was a hero. If he'd done it in Hampshire, he'd have been a 'fucking wanker tester' and someone would have threatened to punch his face in at the HQ afterwards. That's my experience of the matter anyway.

Like all good prejudices, this is an echo from the past. Let me take you back to 1893. We were there in the last chapter, of course, but then we were in Paris for the first official hour record. Across the Channel in Britain, the first national body for cycling was the National Cyclists' Union.

The NCU did not care for racing at all. It feared such an undignified brouhaha would bring the respectable, indeed downright posh pastime of cycle touring into disrepute by association. In any case, cycle racing on the highway had been stopped by the police because it was frightening both horses and early motorists. But the competitive spirit of the riders was too strong to be so easily damped down. Place-to-place record-breaking on the road crept under the radar of both organisations. Since it only involved one bicycle it manifestly couldn't be racing.

It was obviously a small step from place-to-place record-breaking to time-trialling over fixed distances. It started as an underground movement, with riders wearing inconspicuous black clothing and setting off at minute intervals, prepared to swear blind to any interested constable that they were just out for a bit of fresh air. Courses were identified only by secret codes, so that even if the police heard about a race they still wouldn't be able to find it. (The secret codes are still used to identify courses today.) But in the end the constables were not much bothered by the solitary riders. Horses were on the way out, and by now the motorists were frightening the cyclists. Gradually, time-trial racing became legitimate. Meanwhile those who wanted to ride mass-start races, like everywhere else in the world, were reduced to cycling grumpily round aerodromes, presumably cursing the testers all the while.

The revolution came on 7th June 1942. Percy Stallard from Wolverhampton had been campaigning for permission from the NCU to run a mass-start road race for some time, but was roundly ignored – probably on the grounds of class as much as anything else. But the NCU had seriously underestimated him. In his frustration he decided that if they were going to ignore him, he was going to ignore them. In purely practical terms all he needed was the cooperation of the police, which he secured by offering to donate the profits from his proposed race to a police benevolent fund. I think the common term for this is 'a bribe', but I don't suppose that really matters after sixty-four years.

Stallard's race frightened no one, and was counted a great success by all except the NCU – which suspended everyone concerned from membership, including those who just went to watch. The response from Stallard's followers was the British League of Racing Cyclists, the BLRC. By November 1942 the two sides had dug in for the long term. The NCU, *Cycling* magazine and the time-trial riders on the side of the cycling establishment, versus the Leaguers.

Cycling was torn apart. New clubs formed, old clubs split apart, families argued, old friends stopped talking to each other. The sides grew factions, and the factions grew factionettes. People were banned from one or other or all organisations pretty much by whim. Even Percy Stallard was banned from the BLRC. It was how communism would have been if anyone had ever tried it properly in Britain, except with more Loyal Toasts.

Eventually, though, the BLRC more or less won the argument. Apart from anything else, the Leaguers were able to forge links with continental racing, and to compete successfully abroad. And as Britain headed into the 1950s, the Leaguers were cool, with dark glasses and colourful jerseys. (Well, okay, really only cool in a British cycling context.) They built up a critical momentum.

Yet there is resentment to this day about the way the BLRC was amalgamated with the NCU in 1959, which the Leaguers regarded as a takeover. The new British Cycling Federation didn't exactly roll out the red carpet when it banned many of the BLRC's best riders from amateur competition. There is a folk memory of the bitter divisions, and it takes its clearest shape in the tensions between roadies and testers. Road racing and time-trialling in the UK are still run by separate organisations, fighting over a dwindling pool of riders.

And despite being in the majority, it's the roadies who still nurse the stronger resentment on behalf of the old BLRC.

This persecuted majority still provides most of British cycling's international stars, simply because international racing is based around mass-start events. Meanwhile, it has been an acute embarrassment to British time-triallists that whenever one of their champions goes abroad to compete in their specialist event, they get beaten by margins that could be measured as effectively with a sundial as with a stopwatch. Seeing bloody testers getting stuffed is, of course, a source of considerable satisfaction to many of the road fraternity.

This gripping story of class warfare and sports administration eventually intersects with the hour record in a flash of irony. With no British rider having held the record in the 100 years of its existence, when Obree and Boardman came along within six days of each other they were both from a time-trial background.* The testers had finally found heroes of their own who could stand at the top of international cycling.

This whole ridiculous, backbiting history was another reason why I wanted to succeed. Time-trialling is an obscure and put-upon branch of cycling, but it is one I

---

* It's interesting that the BLRC's poster boy of the 1950s and '60s, Tom Simpson, had a long-term interest in the hour record. This is not something about which one hears a great deal, possibly because of the politics of the sport at the time. He attempted the amateur hour record in November 1958, but missed by 275m. He also considered an attempt on the professional record in 1964, using an innovative small-wheeled bike made in the UK by Moulton, but was unable to reach a financial arrangement with them to cover the loss of prize money that would be involved in the specific preparation. At the time of his death, during the 1967 Tour de France, he was planning another attempt.

love. I agree with the roadies that road racing is more exciting, but I'm not a very exciting person. I didn't ever go time-trialling because I thought it was going to be intrinsically exciting.

I did it because there is a purity about riding a time-trial that appeals to me, something of much more value than it is normally credited with in Britain. To measure your effort perfectly over the length of a ride, to go as fast as possible using nothing but your own skill. I wanted to do the hour, the ultimate time-trial, because it was really worth something.

CHAPTER 5

I SAT ONE MORNING ON MY ROOF-TERRACE – NOT AS posh as it sounds, I could just as well have said 'roof' – having breakfast in the warm sunshine. Spring had finally, well and truly, arrived. I was nervous. And here's the thing: I had no idea why. I had the empty feeling in my stomach, the slight tightness in my chest, and the fast, thumping heartbeat, all for no reason. It was just an ordinary Tuesday morning.

As I had a second cup of coffee and contemplated the day's training, I was able to enjoy the sight below me of commuters sitting stationary in their cars. This was normally a very satisfying contrast. Today it was accompanied by the feeling of dread that you have when you wake up on the morning of something nasty, the details of which you haven't remembered yet. This time I didn't remember anything. Nothing interesting or exciting was lined up – not today, not this week.

It took me about half the morning to work out what it was: it was spring. The sunshine, the warmth. Only a couple of weeks ago, 2nd July had seemed a very long way away, a different season, a different world. Suddenly it had come closer, because 2nd July might look just like this.

The day's training was not too demanding; the previous day had been hard, so today was recovery. It was sufficiently early in the year that the park was still reasonably quiet, and I had plenty of time to think about the hour. Suddenly there seemed to be a lot to do. Up till now it had all been rather cloistered; just Andrea and me in the quiet, echoing Velodrome playing around with a bike and a bagful of components. It wasn't really a secret, but no one had ever taken much notice of us.

As I clocked up the miles, it was clear that there was a long way to go to get the attempt onto the track. I could imagine what it was all going to look like, and I possessed almost none of the components. I couldn't believe that I'd been so relaxed – so complacent. I was preparing for a moon-shot by firing a washing-up-liquid bottle into the air with a rubber band and fantasising about what moon-dust would look like close up. When it came to making a list of things I didn't have, without trying I could think of: bike frame, front forks, wheels, tyres, skinsuit and helmet. If I stripped them away from my mental image of 2nd July, the only thing I had left was me, naked, and a large expectant crowd. This was not an image I liked.

I was tempted to ignore it all, and just hope the dull feeling in my stomach would go away. But I counted the weeks out on the calendar, and found it was only twelve till the attempt. It was time for action. It was time to prioritise.

I decided the first things to sort out were the frames. I had, as you know, the unsteerable one. I would need something that provided the same riding position, but with the geometry adjusted so that it handled properly. This was where having a bike manufacturer as a sponsor was a mixed blessing. While Giant were happy enough that I use a test frame built by a UK builder, for the actual attempt they had insisted on me using something they had built themselves. That meant a custom-build in Taiwan, and shipping to the UK. Previous experience of this process suggested that twelve weeks was some way short of generous, particularly since I wanted a chance to ride the new frames before I had to use them in anger.

I rang Dave Thompson, this being his area. I hadn't been speaking to him for a while, and he was excited to hear that the hour project was going well. It was a little difficult to navigate away from a general conversation about it, to the more specific issue of frames. When I managed it, all he said was, 'No hurry, Mike, it'll only take a couple of weeks.'

I wasn't at all convinced about this, and said so. Dave and I had conversations along these lines regularly. He was convinced, for some reason I never fathomed, that a 'just-in-time' approach was the apogee of professional-ism. It was certainly not how he treated customers of his company, who were amateurs and consequently got fast service. But when it came to team matters, things often arrived with moments to spare (though never actually late), and Dave would swell with pride and explain that this was 'always how it is in the pro teams, Mike'.

This time I insisted I wasn't prepared to settle for a planned delivery of 30th June. Even if the frames did turn up then (which they might well – Dave had never been responsible for something failing to turn up at all), I didn't want the stress of worrying about it, to add to what I could see was going to be a pretty tense few days. Nor was I prepared to believe that it was only going to take two weeks to design and build the frames, and forty-eight hours to get them to me.

Dave failed totally to understand that for me to be at my best on a race day I had to be as relaxed as possible. That meant avoiding last-minute panic, not going looking for it. Cool, organised, efficient. Repeat it like a mantra. Eventually I battered him into submission.

'Okay, okay, we'll try and sort something out,' he conceded. 'More or less the same as the last one, but with more responsive steering?'

We talked steering geometry for a few minutes. I'd love to explain how it works, perhaps with some diagrams and equations – sadly, space does not permit. But we agreed on what changes we needed to make, and Dave said he'd get onto Giant immediately. I'll be honest and report here a suspicion that he wasn't going to do anything of the sort, but would put his notes in a drawer and pass them on at some moment of his own choosing. I didn't have the nerve to accuse him of this. In the end you have to trust people. Looking back at it, this suspicion was probably unworthy of me. As I've said before, Dave was sometimes a bit reluctant to get moving, but when he said he'd do something, it got done. If he'd been planning to pull the wool over my eyes, he'd have caved in a bit faster.

I was probably feeling a bit shifty myself. I hadn't really wanted to have that conversation at all until after I'd done a proper trial ride on the track. The traditional test is to do 20 minutes at hour-record pace. If you can do that in training, then on the night when the pressure is on and the adrenalin is flowing, you can do the hour. That's the theory anyway. This test in one form or another has been part of almost every hour-record attempt for 100 years, and it's rarely been wrong. I'd wanted to do that early, to get a clear idea of where I stood.

That was a sound idea, but I'd reckoned without the amount of work needed on equipment and position. I was weeks away from a set-up sufficiently close to optimum that a trial would be a helpful thing to do. If I did it now I'd be miles off, and I'd learn nothing. It wasn't so much that I had doubts, more that I wanted to be able to prove myself objectively. It was part of the careful scientific approach; I wanted to document and justify everything. I still wanted to have an attempt that was underpinned by evidence rather than faith. I was beginning to realise that this was sometimes going to be difficult. Indeed, in many respects the whole thing was already based on faith.

I'd expected that organising the frames would make me feel a bit more relaxed. It didn't. By late afternoon the dull feeling in my stomach was still there. In the same way that the coming of spring had brought the attempt closer, getting the frames under way had made the whole thing bigger. There were other people working on it, more money being spent, more expectation being aroused. I'd been worried before that Andrea and I weren't enough. Now I was worried that Andrea, me, Dave and the combined forces of Giant Bicycles were rather too much. It had all become just a little more serious. If something that's only on the horizon looks huge, you know that when you're toe-to-toe with it it's going to blot out the sun.

I supposed I'd better get used to the idea, and went for an afternoon nap. Being a full-time athlete was not, I reflected as I dozed off, without its compensations.

The whole season was beginning to gather momentum. I was training hard, about twenty-five hours a week at this point. There were now races every weekend, which added to the workload, and travelling to them, which reduced the effectiveness of my recovery. The races were not for the most part terribly important, but somehow a race effort is always harder than a training one. Living in central London didn't really help; even a 'local' race usually involved leaving in the middle of a Saturday morning and getting back in the early evening. Sometimes I ended up racing on Sunday as well, when the races are always early in the mornings, so an even earlier start. By a few weekends into the season, Louisa and I would feel as though we hadn't seen each other for months.

In the middle of most weeks I took a trip up to Manchester for training or testing on the track, normally split into two sessions over Tuesday and Wednesday, with Tuesday night in a cheap but tropically over-heated hotel down the road from the Velodrome, where I could lie in sweaty wakefulness and listen to the PA at the greyhound racing from the Belle Vue stadium next door. The carpet was sufficiently synthetic that if you walked to the bathroom too fast, you got an electric shock when you touched the door handle.

Even days at home in London, with no travelling anywhere, usually involved four or five hours on the bike, and maybe a session in the gym. The routine of travelling, racing, training and testing was a bit relentless. My kit bag was packed on a permanent basis, and wherever I was, I felt as if I was always getting ready to leave.

The racing season gathered pace. I rode one of the few international road races in Britain, the Archer Grand Prix in Buckinghamshire, where I fairly conspicuously failed to cover myself in glory. I just sat at the back of the bunch all day. That I finished without difficulty when more than half the field gave up suggested that I might have managed something a little more ambitious, but somehow I couldn't be bothered. I'd entered it with a view to getting a hard work-out, rather than with any more competitive ambitions, and I followed through with that approach. By the time I'd finished and trundled back to the HQ, I was feeling pretty sheepish. It wasn't a very professional way to ride.

I didn't want to hang around the HQ making excuses for myself. I went straight from there to Manchester for a session the following morning, arriving just as it was getting dark. I had lunch on the way, a chicken sandwich that, when I thought back to it, hadn't really tasted quite right. At the time I was just hungry. As I carried my bags across the hotel car park, I felt a little odd. As if my stomach was distended with water. I had trouble keeping my balance as I opened the door to the building. I checked in, feeling less and less happy, and found that filling in the registration form was nearly more than I could manage. The reception desk began to swim in and out of focus.

The first thing I did when I got to my room was vomit explosively into the loo. The second thing I did was to repeat a similar process with the other end of my digestive system. Surely, I thought, this must have created some sort of vacuum? I didn't get to think about it for very long before I was sick again.

I'd had food poisoning before, but for sheer violence this was something else. It was like getting beaten up. I continued to retch long after I had anything left to throw, and every spasm was like a punch in the stomach. I had a raging thirst, but I couldn't even keep water down. In the calmer moments I seriously wondered if I was going to die. It would, I felt, be an undignified end: killed by a sandwich in a cheap Manchester hotel room. But I couldn't even make it as far as my bag to get my phone and summon help, because the entire contents of my body were being evacuated through the nearest exit. It was sheer panic in there.

As my body weight plummeted, I began to get delusional. Somehow the whole thing got bound up with, not the dodgy sandwich, but the morning's race. This was what I deserved. I was being punished for a display that wasn't even as good as half-hearted. I was convinced that the ghost of Henri Desgrange – the first record-holder – was trying to kill me. I'm totally serious about this; it's not a bit of fantasy I invented to make food poisoning sound more interesting. I really believed he was there in my hotel bathroom in some shimmering form, torturing me to death. Not for pleasure, but because he felt it was necessary.

At the time it made some kind of sense; when he was race director of the Tour de France, Desgrange was notoriously unforgiving of any rider whom he felt had not given his all. Now, in view of my poor morning's work, he was going to ensure I didn't lay my unworthy hands on his record by killing me by desiccation, here on the floor of a hotel bathroom. God knows, I thought, he could have found some less extreme way of keeping me off the magic list. But Desgrange did not do things by halves. The Tour de France was not the work of a man given to moderation. He was going to kill me, and he was going to kill me good.

Eventually I fell asleep, exhausted in every sense. I don't remember it, but I made it to the bed. I slept like I was dead. Finally Desgrange left me in peace, assuming his work was done. Maybe the ghost's eyesight was failing, and he couldn't see that I was still breathing.

I woke up the following morning, which was only the first surprise. The second was that I felt fine. A little thirsty, a bit shaken, but by the standards of the previous night, I was just dandy. It was bizarre. I went downstairs and tentatively had some breakfast. I stayed fine. I'd never had such a short, violent illness before, and I really didn't believe it had gone. My recollections of the previous night were similar to those from the late stages of a mighty drinking binge, yet this morning I hadn't a trace of anything like the appropriate hangover. It was like a memory from years ago.

I sat at a table by a window and had a coffee and tried to read the paper, but I couldn't concentrate on the page because the whole Desgrange delusion began to trickle back to me. It was unsettling to know I'd believed in something so ridiculous.

Unsurprisingly I was late getting to the track; I arrived more than halfway through a two-hour session that I'd planned to use for some detailed equipment testing. Then I couldn't find Andrea immediately, and then I had difficulty getting the computer to work. In the end, instead of a nice relaxed examination of several options, I only had time to charge through testing three sets of front forks, and even then the runs I managed were not at a very consistent speed, which compromised the usefulness of the data collected. I'd driven to Manchester to be violently ill, waste two hours of precious track time and drive home again. I was very frustrated by the whole thing. I could have stayed in bed for the previous twenty-eight hours and I'd have been substantially better off.

I had a coffee with Andrea before I went home. I felt pretty crap again. I don't think my condition had actually deteriorated; it was just that my expectations of health were higher than they had been when I woke up. As I blew on my coffee, Andrea examined one of the pairs of forks I'd been trying to compare. The forks were made of carbon-fibre, and the legs were a deep aerofoil shape rather than the traditional round or nearly round section.

'Are these allowed under the athlete's hour rules?' she asked.

I really didn't want to talk about this. I just wanted a hot drink and a biscuit. 'The rules don't mention forks,' I said. 'They only deal with the main frame. I'm taking that to mean I can do what I like with forks, and I like those.'

'I wouldn't like to have to depend on that interpretation,' she said. 'I'm sure you're right. But the UCI commissaires are a bit prone to interpreting rules in a restrictive manner. There's a good chance you'll get one of them trackside on the day who'll look in his little rulebook and tell you that you can't use these.'

'If the rules don't ban them, there's nothing they can do.'

Andrea set the forks down on her desk and looked at

me. 'Michael. Get this straight. At the moment you are in charge of all this. When the attempt comes, you are not in charge. The UCI is in charge. If the commissaire says you can't use these, then that's the rule. You might be able to argue about it for months afterwards, but that won't help you on the night. There is every chance that they will ban them, because they don't look the way they will expect the forks on a traditional bike to look. You're a lawyer, so you look at the rules first. I've always suspected that Commissaires go with their instincts and look at the rules second. And on 2nd July, you'll have to do it their way. If you want to break this record you are going to have to get that into your highly qualified, but nonetheless surprisingly thick, head.'

I felt as if I'd been told off. I had been told off. I had that hot flush that I associate with sentences beginning, 'But sir . . .', which attempt to shift the blame onto someone else. In the end I just said, 'Okay' and finished my coffee. My head was throbbing, and I really couldn't put together a coherent defence. It's as well I didn't. I had an unwise tendency to forget that Andrea knew a lot about the way track racing worked in the real world.

Certainly Chris Boardman had used a fairly conventional set of forks, and Andrea was absolutely right that a commissaire might decide that the athlete's hour rules were, for all practical purposes, 'ride a bike just like Boardman's'. And there was a dilemma anyway. If the idea of the athlete's hour was to create as level a playing field as possible, was it entirely reasonable of me to try to exploit the rules to their fullest extent? Was the lack of a specification for the forks a deliberate omission, or a mistake?

It's an inherent problem whenever anyone tries to devise a rule with the intention of avoiding experimentation and development. There will always be gaps, and the possibility for deviation between the spirit and the letter of the rule. The certainty that not everyone who contemplated an attack on the record would take a principled position meant that the clear temptation was to work to the edges of the written rule.

In the end the dilemma was resolved when I watched a film made about Boardman's athlete's hour. There was a segment about fork testing, and among the forks he tried out was an aerodynamic pair similar to mine. Granted he didn't actually use them, but I decided that his mere possession of them meant that Boardman had had no principled objection, so I didn't need to have one either.

You don't spend an evening like the one I'd just had without some lasting effects. By the time I arrived back in London I was very tired. I slept for fifteen hours, through two alarm clocks and a ringing phone. When I finally sat up in bed, my battered stomach muscles protested so sharply I thought I was going to be sick again.

I decided it would be wise to abandon my training plans for the day. I never liked doing this; as you know, I'm an obsessive man at heart, and I considered any shortfall between the training I had planned and the training I did to be a very serious personal failing.

The other side of the coin is that on days when I'd decided that I really was too tired to train, instead of relaxing and getting the full benefit of the rest, I would fret and pace around the flat, worrying that I ought to be doing something more constructive. I'd think the decision through again and again, try to work out whether I should train after all or maybe do half a session, all the time knowing that if I (of all people) had decided I needed a day off, then I really did need a day off. Because I'd planned to train, and mentally I was committed to it already, the urge to just *do* something was almost impossible to damp down. The only way around it was to do something else.

On this occasion the something else ought really to have had nothing to do with the hour record. I should have gone to the cinema, or read a novel. I was in serious need of a break from the damn thing, but already it had expanded like foam to fill the entire space inside my head. I thought about it pretty much all the time I was awake: the testing, the equipment and my physical condition. I was also aware that even if I thought I was thinking about something else, my subconscious was still all about the hour.

I felt distinctly hassled now; I was worried about getting the frames made, I'd had a truly rotten last trip to the track, and was now behind on the testing programme. Worst of all, I'd had a lecture from Andrea on the Real World of the UCI, which, while perfectly well intentioned, had left me feeling chastened and rather naive. How could I be the model of cool professionalism if these were the kinds of things that happened to me?

It seemed that the instant the project started to accelerate, as soon as it became much more than a private dream, I was destined to lose control of it. Circumstance and other people would take it away. Since my whole approach to it had revolved around keeping it under control, I found this pretty unsettling. I'd never thought of myself as a control freak, but at base that was what I was. If I'd managed to keep a bit more distance from it, I'd have seen that none of it mattered all that much, not at this point with the attempt still so far away. There was time for everything. But I had my nose hard against the hour record and it was all that I could see.

I don't think the idea of trying to forget about the hour for a while even occurred to me. I decided that instead of taking a deep breath and spending the afternoon watching cartoons, I'd go looking for more hassle and worry and start on another equipment issue, that of wheels.

This was something that had been bothering me. At the risk of stating the terribly obvious, the wheels on a bicycle are important. For a time-trial, they are probably the most important equipment issue of all. There are practically endless ways of doing it, from the traditional shallow rim and numerous wire spokes to solid carbon-fibre discs, via every conceivable point in between. I saw a prototype bike a few years ago that dispensed with a front wheel altogether, and used a rollerblade. I wouldn't have liked to try and make it stop in a hurry.

The recent history of the hour record is closely bound to the development of the wheel because, for the UCI, the rescinded modern, technologically tainted records began with Francesco Moser's ride in 1984, and the clearest technological shift was his use of disc wheels. Otherwise there was not much about his equipment – apart from lots of shiny chrome – to set him apart from his predecessors. Up till then the record had been attempted exclusively on what anyone would regard as normal spoked wheels.

Moser's big, shiny disc wheels became the covetous fantasy of time-triallists everywhere. Testers take wheels seriously, and in an instant the pub debate had moved on from everyone's favourite brand of spoke to where they could lay their hands on some discs.* I know of one rider in the 1980s who, when he finally got one, slept with it. Moser's discs were the start of something more profound than a wheel revolution, because although they were aerodynamic, they were heavy. Really heavy. Early discs could be more than twice the weight of normal wheels, yet they were a lot faster.

Since the dawn of cycling, riders have been obsessed with reducing weight. Yet on a flat track or road weight is of almost no consequence. Once it's moving, it will keep moving. Isaac Newton cracked that one in the seventeenth century. But his work has never been as popular among cyclists as it might have been, and in the 1970s and early '80s the British time-triallist saved weight by using a Black & Decker to perforate repeatedly his bike's handlebars, seat post, and even frame. A top-flight 1970s time-trial machine looked like Swiss cheese and whistled 'Land of Hope and Glory' on a myriad of holes whenever the breeze got up.

The clear superiority of disc wheels finally convinced cyclists that weight was not the last word in defining a fast bike. The new buzzword was 'aero'. As in 'You're looking pretty aero, Mike!' This acceptance allowed the development of all the high-tech aerodynamic frames,

---

* In practice, in anything except the most windless of conditions, a disc wheel in the front of the bike leads to catastrophically difficult handling. I discovered this one day wheeling – not riding – a track bike with a front disc across a car park. A puff of wind caused the bike to turn sharply into my legs, and resulted in a classic prat-fall as I went straight over the bike and landed in a puddle. Needless to say, these things never happen when no one is looking.

helmets, skinsuits and the like that distinguished time-trialling and the hour record in the 1990s. Which, of course, led to the backlash from the UCI. There is a splendid irony in the fact that the last straw so far as they were concerned was not the result of a team of white-coated technicians beavering away in a wind-tunnel, but the intuitive leaps of Graeme Obree.

Clearly the athlete's hour demanded some sort of old-fashioned wheels. And here is where I reckon the UCI fluffed it. Well, it's one of the occasions I reckon the UCI fluffed it anyway. They could have specified something just like Eddy Merckx used. Or perhaps just like the best technology of his day – Merckx's wheels were on the robust side. That would have involved simple box-section wheel-rims, and twenty-four or twenty-eight normal round spokes per wheel.

Instead the UCI specified 'Spoked wheels with a minimum of 16 and a maximum of 36 spokes; the spokes may be round, flat or oval, providing that none of their cross-sections exceeds 2mm . . . Shallow, unelongated, non-profiled rims; shallow rims are understood to be rims whose cross-section fits inside a 2.2cm square.'

This is not the most helpful of regulations. Even if you get past the obvious mysteries (What on earth might a 'non-profiled' rim be? Is the spoke count for one wheel or two?), it allows the modern hour aspirant a considerable advantage over 'gold-standard' Merckx. A wheel with sixteen flat, bladed spokes is a very different thing to one with twenty-four big, round ones. Imagine, if you will, driving in a car at 30mph. Wind the window down and hold sixteen round spokes so that they poke out into the airstream. That's the drag you can save by simply throwing away eight spokes per wheel. Add the further amount you save by making the remaining ones flat (it will more than halve the resistance). Now bear in mind that every 10 grams of drag you can shave off will add about 45m to the distance covered in an hour. It's instructive to reflect that Boardman broke Merckx's record by 10m, which probably comes down to a couple of spokes.[*]

Crucially, however, the wheels will *look* just the same as Merckx's. It suggests that the UCI's motivation for the whole athlete's hour thing was essentially aesthetic.

If Merckx himself had tried using wheels built to the minimum spec demanded by the rules, chances are they would have fallen apart. Only advances in rim and spoke technology make such skimpy wheels possible. Even so, they're weak and flexible, and prone to breakage. Riders of Merckx's generation would probably have rejected them outright as just not being tough enough. But if such wheels would make me faster . . .

Given my angle of attack on the record, I was prepared to sacrifice pretty much all the structural stiffness. As long as they didn't actually disintegrate, I didn't really care if the wheels were a bit wobbly. My plan was to have a pair made with the absolute minimum of sixteen spokes per wheel (which I assume is what the UCI meant), and to use flat, bladed spokes, the weakest but most aerodynamic of the flat-oval-round options.

---

[*] The wheel regulations were the result of protracted negotiations between Boardman and the UCI. Boardman originally wanted to use simple disc wheels, on the basis that he wanted to establish a new record with minimum technological input, and he rightly reckoned there was nothing as 'standard' as a flat disc with a minimum specified weight. The UCI wanted to continue from Merckx's record, so it needed to specify spoked wheels of some sort.

I started by ringing Dave, who firstly knew a bit about wheels, and secondly had a decent wheel-builder among his contacts. However, it turned out that the wheel-builder had vanished without trace a few months previously, and Dave was too cautious to express any opinion on the matter himself.

So I started working my way through the various master practitioners of the UK wheel-building industry. This was not a process that took long. There was a consensus that my proposed ultra-light specification would result in the back wheel flying apart in many directions as soon as I made a full-on starting effort. The UK wheel-building industry was quick to remind me that even Chris Boardman had used eighteen bladed spokes in the front and twenty oval ones in the back. And, as they were indelicate enough to point out, I was fatter than him.

Michael: Well, I'm just kind of bigger. I wouldn't exactly say 'fat'.

UK WBI: We would.

In the end I settled on ordering a pair with twenty oval spokes in the rear wheel and sixteen bladed spokes in the front. Because they had to be made on a bespoke basis, even down to buying blank rims and drilling the spoke-holes in them, they cost a fortune. The hubs alone were going to cost more than my first racing bike.

As a final flourish, the UK wheel-building industry offered to conceal my nipples.

'Pardon?'

'Concealed nipples, like. Chris Boardman had concealed nipples.'

'I'm sure he did, he was always a model professional.'

It turned out that nipples are the little adjustable nuts that join the spoke to the wheel. Apparently it is possible to gain a small advantage by putting these inside the rim, though it makes building the wheel a little more difficult. (And a little more expensive, but by this point I didn't care.) They would be ready in a couple of weeks.

I make it sound like all that was the work of half an hour. Actually it took nearly three days of leaving messages, waiting for people to get back to me, arguing about specifications, them going to source components, getting back to me again – when I'd be out, so they'd have to leave a message, so I'd have to get back to them – and of course arguing about the price. I was left feeling that these had better be the God-damned finest pair of wheels ever to grace a bicycle.

Easter was late that year, and it was a relief when it arrived. I had a heavy racing programme, which meant I was going to have to set aside the various essential-but-distracting logistical issues and concentrate on my body for a couple of weeks. My physical ability was my greatest asset in attacking the record, but I knew there was a danger of my taking it for granted, when in fact it needed to be worked at. Being forced to spend the Easter period putting in some quality mileage was very good news.

The other attraction to the race programme was that by planning so that it took me to the North of England, then Scotland, then Northern Ireland, I could work my way back to my parents' house in County Down for a sort of training camp in the week after Easter. It was perfect. In the morning I could go on training rides down the coast to the Mourne Mountains, return for a late lunch, and spend a quiet afternoon in the garden with a book. The weather was as kind as it was ever likely to be in April, and my responsibilities ran to nothing more taxing than wriggling out of helping my 70-year-old father with his latest gardening earthworks. It was a simple life of good training, resting and eating properly. I imagined I could feel myself getting physically sharper by the day. I was as relaxed and confident about my cycling life as I'd been since the start of the year.

Surprisingly, I managed to keep the happy bubble intact all the way back to London. I smiled indulgently at the children running wildly around the ferry, fuelled by excitement and Coke (the children that is, not the ferry, though it's a nice idea), and when the traffic ground to a halt on the M6 at Birmingham for an hour, I listened to the radio and made a few non-essential phone calls in a mellow frame of mind. I was like a new man, laid-back, worry-free, and back in tune with the cool, professional method. All of this didn't mean there weren't things to be done, just that now I was going to do them in a new, chilled-out manner.

Item one was, like last time, wheels. I had still only got this problem half-licked, literally. You see, I needed two bikes for the record. (If you were paying attention earlier, you will have noticed I referred to getting 'frames' built.) The rules require a spare bike. This is – they tell us – in case of any mechanical mishap. They wouldn't want me to be disappointed if some terminal failure meant that I had to abandon the attempt.

It was nice of the UCI to take steps to prevent this sort of emotional trauma. Not every sports governing body would be so pro-active. However, the chances of a track bike, a very simple machine with no gears or brakes, suffering the kind of mechanical failure that would demand a whole new bike are vanishingly small. You might get a puncture, but that would only demand a spare set of wheels. Even then, I think it would be reasonable to let the rider take the risk.

I try not to be cynical about the UCI's motives, honestly I do. But sometimes I lapse and find myself wondering if this rule might only exist to keep the cost of the hour up a bit. It's sure as hell hard to square with one of the prime justifications for the introduction of the athlete's hour record, that of reducing costs. In truth, it seems to me that if that was really what the UCI had wanted to do, the athlete's hour is a turkey. If they had allowed the use of normal track pursuit bikes – well, I had two of them in my collection already, with carefully worked-out equipment and position choices already made. Getting hold of shiny new, but essentially obsolete, kit meant getting things built specially. And you have to duplicate it. And then you have no chance at all of selling any of it unless you're lucky enough to meet another hour-record hopeful, because it's not the slightest use for anything else.

Frames hadn't been a problem – since my sponsor was providing them, I just asked for two. Wheels were different. Given the uncertainty I had about whether anyone was ultimately going to pick up the bill for all this, they were effectively coming out of my depleted bank account. I'd already blown the whole budget on one pair. They were, I felt, going to be the best possible choice for the job. The amount of money I'd spent meant I had to feel that. But I still needed serviceable spares – not to use, just to put into the spare bike and wave bad-temperedly at the UCI on the night. Given the lack of a second-hand market, it suddenly struck me that Chris Boardman might still have some.

So I sent him an e-mail:

Chris, as you may well be aware, I'm planning an attempt on your athlete's hour record in July this year. I'm having trouble with some of the equipment issues, especially wheels. I was wondering if there was any chance you would be prepared to lend or sell me a pair? It will probably be too little too late, it's bloody difficult to ride that kind of bike that fast! Thanks, Michael.

I thought it struck an appropriate compromise between business-like and obsequious. I got a reply almost immediately. He was equally business-like, if less obsequious. No, he hadn't heard I was having a go at the record, and no he wasn't going to help. He'd had to do it on his own, and he couldn't see any reason why I shouldn't do the same. He was generous enough to wish me all the best, and said that if he could he would try to get to the track to watch on 2nd July.

In the following weeks, as the attempt approached, a couple of people asked me if I'd been in touch with Chris. When I told them about this correspondence, they were surprised that he hadn't wanted to help. I wasn't. It was his record, and there was no reason why he should help me. I'd certainly rather he didn't, if he didn't want to. He'd even gone so far as to wish me the best with it, which is more than anyone attacking a record of mine would get from me.

I suppose the people I spoke to felt it was just a little out of keeping with the image the hour record has acquired. The idea fostered by the holders is that it's being on the list that counts, not being the current champion. I'm unaware of any other sporting record where, whenever it is broken, the press always present the full historical list.

One of the traditions of record attempts during the 1990s was Eddy Merckx turning up to watch, and to warmly praise a successful ride. When Rominger broke the record in 1994, he said, 'Seeing Tony ride today, I suddenly feel that I was a very minor rider. He reflects the ideal of perfection and motivation.' I suppose we could all be that self-deprecating if we knew no one would believe us, but you get the idea.

Francesco Moser wrote the foreword to Obree's book. He makes it sound as if Obree's breaking of his record was the best thing that ever happened to him. In turn, Obree said that he was perfectly happy for Miguel Indurain to break his 1994 record: 'I've failed in an hour record attempt. I know what it's like, it's awful. I wouldn't wish that feeling on anyone. A great champion like Indurain doesn't deserve that.'

It hasn't always been such a mutual admiration society. The hour record's first real red-blooded rivalry was the Berthet v Egg duel from the early years of the twentieth century. The relatively unknown Frenchman Marcel Berthet broke the record in 1907, at the Buffalo Track in Paris. He was a track specialist, and he prepared for the record attempt with considerable care. His record lasted five years, until August 1912, when the Swiss Oscar Egg broke it, also at the Buffalo.

Unlike Berthet, Egg was something of an all-round cycling star. He won races on the road, including arduous stages of the Tour de France in the days when it was a real man's race. (He won the titanic Brest–La Rochelle stage in 1914, 470km in 16 hours and 13 minutes, then won the following stage as well.) He won on the track, too, in the old style, non-stop six-day races. Photos show him looking relaxed and rather handsome, with a slightly crooked smile.

Berthet was not overly impressed with Egg as a rider in the six-day events. Egg was apparently not much impressed with Berthet as a human being. Berthet broke Egg's record in August of the following year, 1913. Egg reclaimed it fourteen days later, only for Berthet to take it back after another four weeks. These exchanges were conducted in an atmosphere of considerable enmity between the riders, with their attempts much hyped in the press, thousands of spectators coming to watch, and track promoters prepared to pay top francs to get the next attempt at their meeting. It was like the heavyweight championship of the world.

As you might expect, Egg and Berthet were milking this for all it was worth. They were, after all, professionals. It's been suggested that they took care not to break the record by an unmanageable margin, to ensure that the other had the chance to take it back and keep the whole show going. Appearance-fee negotiations were conducted with a hard edge.

Berthet and Egg did not have the whole thing entirely their own way. In July 1913, shortly before the pair joined battle for their lucrative summer of record-breaking, the German Richard Weise spoiled the duopoly by breaking Egg's record, in Berlin. Or so he thought; he reckoned without a certain bloody-mindedness – not to mention chauvinism – on the part of Oscar Egg.

Egg was unwilling to accept that his record had been broken by a rider who was not part of the exclusive group based in Paris, and he didn't like the inconvenience of having to get the record back from this interloper by the traditional means of riding further. Instead he personally remeasured the Buffalo track where he'd set the 1912 record. As luck would have it, the lap was actually 1.7m longer than had been thought. This upgraded Egg's record from 42.112 to 42.360km. Since Weise's ride had been only 42.276km, his ride wasn't ratified.

Egg's administrative triumph didn't last long; Berthet's first 1913 record was only eleven days after Weise's ride. Since Berthet rode at the Buffalo track, Egg's tape measure wasn't going to help him this time. But, as we shall see, he obviously didn't throw it away.

The final act took place on 18th June 1914. On a beautiful spring evening in Paris, before a huge crowd, Egg took the record to 44.247km. Berthet was planning an attempt later in the summer – and under the circumstances there is no reason to suppose it was not going to be successful – but before he could do so, war broke out. Egg's record stood for nineteen years, making it the most durable of all hour records.

Egg continued racing through the war, and Berthet picked up his career afterwards. Egg continued to be successful on the six-day circuit until his retirement in 1926. The last record I can find of Berthet as a professional was in 1923, though he won only one post-war race, a six-day in Brussels in 1921. The old rivalry was apparently over.

After he retired, Egg opened a cycle shop in Paris and grew wealthy. He retained an interest in his record, and went so far as to put up a 10,000-franc prize for the first rider to beat 45km.* He wasn't in a tearing hurry to hand over the cash – to discourage aspiring record-breakers, he was fond of telling anyone who would listen just how agonising his last hour ride had been.

Attempts came and went, some of them by very talented riders like the Italian Alfredo Binda in 1929. He'd won almost everything there was to win, including three World Championships and five Giri dell'Italia. He was the Merckx of his day, but he couldn't beat the fifteen-year-old hour record, which even by then seemed to have come from a different age. Oscar Egg must have glowed with pleasure. There was another near-miss in 1932 when Maurice Archambaud exceeded the distance in Algeria, but couldn't get the record ratified because he'd failed to have the correct officials in place.

Eventually, in August 1933, Jan Van Hout of the Netherlands broke the record, and the 45km mark. Egg rushed to the Roermond Velodrome to offer warm congratulations and hand over the cash in non-sequential used fifties. Well, almost. Actually, he rushed to the Roermond Velodrome with his trusty tape measure, climbed over the wall round the locked track and indulged in a bit of stealthy remeasuring. It will not be

---

* One contemporary source says the prize was simply for beating his record, though it would seem uncharacteristic of Oscar Egg to make life so easy.

tremendously to your surprise to learn that the track was short, wiping enough off Van Hout's ride that not only was it under 45km, it wasn't even a record. Five days later, at the nearby Saint-Trond track, Frenchman Maurice Richard finally, unambiguously, broke Egg's record. By the track, his good friend and helper Oscar Egg led the celebrations. Since the new distance was only 44.777km, he got to hang onto his 10,000 francs a little longer as well.

Then it started to get complicated. A track is measured round the datum line on the inside. But unlike, say, a running track, there is no kerb to stop a cyclist riding inside this. If there were, riders would be forever hitting it and falling over. The problem with Van Hout's record was not that the track was short, but that he rode inside the line. This was no secret – the cycling press had shown photographs of him doing just that. Egg had taken full advantage of this mistake, and used his tape to chart the shortest rideable lap, fully 30cm inside the datum line, and almost on the grass.

While Richard and his supporters celebrated, a rather undignified argument broke out between Egg and the Dutch Cycling Federation, which insisted that Van Hout's record was legitimate. They took exception to Egg breaking into the track, and to the way he'd measured it. Eventually the track was measured again, at a point that was reckoned to be close to where Van Hout had actually ridden, and he was credited with this intermediate – not to say indeterminate – distance. It was given as 44.558km; more than Egg's old record, but less than Richard's. Van Hout had broken the record after all, even if he'd held it for just a few days.

Unfortunately for Van Hout, by the time this was worked out, no one cared. Van Hout was omitted from most of the official lists for years afterwards. The wider turmoil by then surrounding the hour record was the problem. Even Maurice Richard was not finally credited with the record until almost a year later.

The story of the hour in the 1930s is of two strands twisted together. The particular story I've just told turned out to be the more important, and it's the strand that became part of hour history. It didn't have to be that way. The discarded strand began in 1933, before any of the Van Hout, Richard and Egg shenanigans, when one Francis Faure rode 45.055km on a machine called a Velocar. It was the first recumbent bicycle, with the rider lying back with the pedals out in front of him, and it was in all respects a faster means of transport than the traditional, upright bicycle.

The UCI dithered, and dithered good. They decided to give the hour record to Faure, then said this was provisional on the UCI Congress the following year making a decision. The UCI Congress decided to pass the problem on to a special committee. Finally the UCI's committee decided that the Velocar was not a bike after all, and shifted Faure's record into a special class for records set by things that were not bikes. Maurice Richard at last got credited with the record and was given a medal by the UCI to apologise for the chaos. The hour story continued along the upright bike strand, and the recumbent was left as a bit of a curiosity.

The UCI committee's decision was influenced by the appearance of machines with an aerodynamic shell. The first was ridden by Marcel Berthet, of all people, out of retirement at the age of forty-five, and determined to be the first to crack 50km. He got to within 80m of doing so. His Velodyne was just a normal bike, surrounded by a huge oil-paper shell. He looked like a man riding a bicycle inside a tent, and it was as hot and sweaty as that sounds. Oscar Egg – who else? – came out of retirement as well, and built himself a recumbent that he planned to enclose, combining the best of the Velocar and the Velodyne. An increasingly flustered UCI placed Berthet's record in another new category, for aerodynamic things that were not bikes.

It was not so much the ordinary recumbent that the UCI was worried about, as where these potentially enormous machines might take them. The idea of a group of them racing was compared to 'tanks advancing across the Somme'. It was not just that they were faster; they would have changed the whole basis of cycle sport. The UCI wanted to keep competition machines close to ordinary, everyday bicycles. The enclosed machines of the 1930s were impractical, and even the open recumbents had had a very limited take-up outside the serious enthusiasts. It might have been a slightly Luddite decision, but it was not as irrational and self-interested as modern recumbent fans claim. (Recumbent riders' ability to bear a grudge suggests they would have fitted right in at the UCI.)

As a postscript, it's worth saying that the committee's fears were unfounded. The aero-shelled vehicles in fact got smaller and smaller, and faster and faster. The current hour record for a human-powered vehicle is almost 90km. I looked at the possibility of an attack on this record using a machine called the Mango, built by

Kingcycle in High Wycombe. When I went to see it, I assumed the machine they were showing me was a scale model, until they opened it up and invited me to get inside. It was like being in a suitcase full of bicycle components. They had to sit on the lid to get it shut. The plan fell through for lack of funds. It didn't help that the machine was subsequently written off in a high-speed crash; the steering was something they never really managed to make work.

After the dust had settled, the 1930s saw several successful hour rides. Seven in total, if you count the 1942 ride of Fausto Coppi that drew to a close that era of records, and which lasted for fourteen years. Like Egg's 1914 record, it was preserved for long enough by war and its aftermath for an aura of impregnability to grow around it. By the time Jacques Anquetil broke it in 1956, it was the modern era. The record was in colour, and a lot of the cast are still alive. But somehow nothing seems as exciting as the black-and-white Berthet–Egg battles. The hour has never really had another rivalry like it, and there have been few characters that resonate quite like Oscar Egg. I ought to have measured the Manchester track as a tribute to him.

CHAPTER 6

I WAS ONE OF THOSE SCHOOL-KIDS WHO TOOK TO heart the endless lectures about preparing a revision time-table. It is possible this will not be a surprise. It is also possible that I took it a little too much to heart, since I was left with the conviction that the sole secret to exam success lay in the preparation of the perfect revision timetable.

To this end I bought a sheet of A2 paper and marked out on it the days to the exams, and then the date, time and location of each paper to be sat. I also bought nine coloured felt-tips, carefully selected to represent a subject each. I felt it was important for quick and easy reference that each subject should have an intuitively appropriate colour. (It took some days to be sure the colours were correctly partnered to the subjects. I coloured in cards and left them around the house where I might find them unexpectedly, to see whether I thought, 'Aha! Chemistry!' or whatever.)

Then I had to work out a mathematically perfect means of completing the timetable, so that the only random element was the scheduling of the exams. Equal time per subject, with equal cumulative time between the revision sessions and the exam to which they related. It was complicated; I had about twenty-five individual papers to sit. I'd found a real-world application for algebra before I finished. But it was a masterpiece. I pinned it up over my desk, and my friends came round to marvel at it.

I am telling you this because sometimes to see to the heart of someone's personality you need to examine them in times of stress, and there are only so many occasions of what I would call 'set-piece' stress in a lifetime. Exams and driving tests are the ones that spring to mind, getting married maybe and, for some of us, sporting events. Things you know are coming, for which you should prepare. Broadly, I think we respond to each of them in a consistent way. I prepared for my driving test by memorising the Highway Code rather than by learning to drive.*

It is clear that, in times of stress, I try to distract myself from the actual nub of the problem. I don't ignore the problem altogether. So far as school exams were concerned, that would have meant listening to something mournful on the stereo and reading some of Thomas Hardy's less cheerful writings. I showed no such wilful blindness; I just ran full-tilt at a side issue, because it was easier than dealing with the exams themselves.

* I passed first time, though in part because I did my test on 2nd January, and the examiner was very clearly still suffering from a hellish hangover. When he asked me to do an emergency stop, he offered the expected instructions, then added, 'But there's no need to go mad.' After that he just sat there and I drove him round Ballymena for an hour. He didn't even ask me any questions about the Highway Code.

I had a to-do list for the hour record. Meticulously neat, revised every day, and at one point numbering 126 items, it took the form of a sheaf of index cards so that I could keep track of the progress of each item and make useful notes like phone numbers, where they would be easily to hand. It was a frankly perplexing contrast to the rough handful of scrap-paper that constituted the testing records. (Though one of the items on the to-do list was 'rationalise testing notes'. It never did get done, possibly because it was only priority 4α. The α meant it was important but the 4 meant it was non-urgent.)

I was sitting on the stairs down to my front door one morning in my cycling kit, contemplating one of these cards with nothing more helpful than 'Tyres – 1α' written on it. I should have been training, but a rain-shower had come over just as I was about to leave, so I had fifteen minutes to spend worrying about how to solve this one. I needed the lightest, most supple and consequently most fragile tyres possible. The best were the ones Boardman had used, made in tiny quantities by an obscure company called Dugast, but I had not so far, despite a lot of phoning around and Internet searching, been able to find any. Their expense, coupled with a short life expectancy, made such tyres of little interest to most riders.

As I stared at the card, Andrea rang me.

'I've got some tyres for you, if you want them,' she said.

Whoa there! Could she read my mind? From Manchester? 'What are they?' I asked, though I already knew the answer.

'Dugast.'

I was a little freaked out by this. 'I've been looking for some of those for weeks.'

'Well, you should have asked me.'

Her timing was immaculate. A few days later I was going to the track to test the new wonder-wheels. Andrea's Dugast wonder-rubber would be the perfect partner for them. To speed things up a little, I had the wheels sent directly to Andrea at the Velodrome. Unfortunately I forgot to tell her about this. When I banged on the door and walked into her office, I found her glaring at me over an improbably large cardboard box.

'What's this?' she demanded. 'It's addressed to you. Am I a post office? I thought it was a bomb!'

'Bombs don't arrive by courier with a tracking number and a return address.'

'You seem to know a lot about it.'

'Anyway, it's got the quality mark of the UK wheel-building industry on it: two crossed spokes and a scowl.'

She tried to keep glaring at me, but couldn't manage it and laughed instead. 'Come on, let's see what all this money you've been complaining about has bought.'

The wheels were beautiful. I'm not normally too bothered about equipment aesthetics – I like my kit to work properly, and beyond that I don't really care. But these were stunning. They made every other bicycle wheel I'd ever owned look heavy and crude. When I held one by the axle and set it spinning, the light sparkled off the spokes, and the almost frictionless hub bearings meant that it just kept spinning. I got tired of holding it long before it even looked like it had started to slow down. It felt alive.

To say I was pleased with them was an understatement. But for the moment they were a toy without batteries; I needed to put the tyres on them, and tubular racing tyres have to be glued into position and the glue allowed time to dry. I'd have to wait until the following morning.

For the moment I had another session booked on the track, and I was going to use it to make Andrea happy by doing an extended ride. So far I hadn't ridden the hour bike for more than about 5 minutes at a time, either in testing or in short training efforts. Andrea's suggestions that I really ought to try riding it for a period more in keeping with the grand plan had become rather more forceful of late, and had frankly begun to fringe into nagging.

I was aiming to do 45 minutes at a speed that was short of record pace, yet hard enough that I would see how uncomfortable the position on the bike might be when things got tough. I knew this was an issue, but investigating it was something I'd managed to put off. My excuse was that I hadn't finished tweaking yet, and there was no point in trying a longer ride until I had a final position. Andrea's riposte was that the position was already getting too extreme, and I ought to check that I could ride it as it was before letting it get still more outlandish.

Up onto the track then, with the current best set-up. I settled down into the position, and began to unroll lap after lap at a pace I knew I could sustain. Riding the track in an economical manner is a skill; it takes practice and concentration. It was not something that had come naturally to me, and I was still prone to regular lapses.

For the first 10 minutes or so I was fine. Then it began

to get dull. I hadn't really thought of that as a potential problem. I didn't suppose it was going to be a problem on the big night, but for the moment riding repetitive solo laps of the track could have been designed to be boring. It was hard enough that your mind couldn't wander, but not interesting enough to be – well, interesting. It reminded me faintly of something. I'd done something just like this before, but a long time ago. I didn't try to remember too hard, because it was a welcome distraction, and I didn't want to use it up too soon. After about another ten minutes it drifted back: it was just like writing lines. Round and round, same careful shape each time, each lap almost identical to the previous one, on and on.

Apart from the boredom, it was fine. I rode for 45 minutes at about 47.5kph, and suffered no ill-effects. My back and neck were a little sore, because unlike on the road there was no chance to move around a bit and relieve the pressure, but it was certainly nothing that would get in the way of breaking records. My arms, where I'd expected the most trouble, had almost no discomfort at all. Andrea was gracious at being proven wrong.

I stayed at the track for an hour or so, to put the tyres on the new wheels. The glue used to do this was pungent, and better used in a space larger than a hotel room. In any event, when I glue tyres onto wheels it tends to result in a thin coating of glue on all surrounding surfaces. Since my last visit to the hotel had been for a night of not-always-accurate vomiting, I felt it would be wise to avoid also gluing the remote control to the bedside table, or myself to the bathroom door-handle.

I sat down on the concrete floor at one end of the track

centre with the wheels, the tyres and a small, old-fashioned-looking pot of glue, which came complete with a little brush, and set to work. I was cheerful, and doing an easy but necessary job. Given that I almost never had real time off now, it was as close to relaxing as I'd come in a while. As I sat there carefully brushing glue onto both tyre and wheel rim, Andrea was supervising a group of local cyclists who had come in for a training session. They weren't taking it too seriously and I laughed easily at the wisecracks they shouted to each other as they rode. It had been a good day.

The following morning was good, too. The combination of the wheels and the top-grade tyres felt phenomenally fast. When I got out of the saddle to accelerate onto the track, I'll admit the wheels felt pretty flexible, but down in the racing position I just flew along. I didn't need the data download to tell me this was good, that this was not a marginal improvement. When I did look at the data, I found that the power required for 49.5kph had dropped to (incredibly) 385w, a saving of about 30w on the previous wheels, about twice the amount I had let myself believe possible. The magic 400w barrier was demolished. Over the course of the hour, the wheels would gain me about 1.5km. We did a couple more runs just to make sure, but there was no doubt.

The sum that I couldn't stop myself from doing was to add the 1.5km to the 47.5kph at which I'd ridden the previous day's 45-minute trial, and get 49km. Only half a kilometre to go! And the previous day had been well short of a flat-out effort. It was a thrilling thought.

When I'd started out at this game, the effort required

to ride at record pace was beyond anything I could imagine being able to do, and my continued interest in the record had been an uncharacteristic act of faith. Now, by diligently experimenting, looking for the best equipment, and making an endless number of short test runs on the track, I felt I'd got the record within reach. It wasn't just that I'd done what I set out to: it was the way I'd done it. The dull, painstaking way. No heroics, no leaps of intuition. I felt as if, given enough time and computing power, I could do anything I wanted.

In fact the only thing stopping me from thinking the hour record was easy was that I knew it couldn't be. Whatever the numbers on my computer screen said, the hour record was not a trophy that could be taken home without a fight. But at that moment, the evidence suggested it was a very long way from impossible.

I went to shower and change. I needed to get back to London, and I knew the roads were going to be crowded. Already my mind had drifted away from the success of the long ride and the wheels, and back onto the problems. I felt again the gnawing worry that I carried everywhere now. My mobile rang just as I got out of the shower. It was Dave Thompson. I contemplated declining the call, but I was going to have to speak to him at some point and he would keep ringing until I answered.

'Hi, Mike, urgent problem here . . .'

'What?' That was the end of my serene morning all right.

'Giant want to know what colour the frames are to be painted.'

'And . . .?'

'Well, that's it.'

'Don't *do* that to me.'

'Do what?'

I told him I didn't care, as long as the paint dried quickly so that they could ship the frames soon. Dave started telling me that all paints dried at the same speed, and I had to explain that had been kind of a joke. I could barely articulate how little I cared about the colour of the frames. I was angry that I was having the conversation at all, and it nearly brewed into a row before it dawned on me how silly that would be, and I made an excuse to end the call.

By the time I had spent four hours driving home, the initial elation of the wheel testing had worn off, and a depressive hangover had kicked in. The record had seemed so close, before Dave reminded me how much there was still to be done. Now the record felt as far away as ever.

You see – and I'm going to have to admit to this sooner or later – I'm superstitious. Really quite superstitious. I haven't mentioned it before, because I'm somewhat ashamed of it. (The appearance of Henri Desgrange in a Manchester hotel room may have given you a clue.) It is a serious aberration – it does not fit at all with what I like to think of as my character.

I want to be clear that this is not about 'touching wood' or avoiding walking under ladders, but a firm conviction that taking things for granted means they'll be spirited away. Even when I've arrived at a bike race as the hottest of hot favourites, I can't bear to hear anyone tell me it's in the bag. That means I'll puncture, or crash. I've been reduced almost to tears by over-enthusiastic fans predicting great things for me. Once or twice I've come near to running away from them. I'm sure I've managed to appear close to lunacy, abruptly changing the subject of a conversation from a championship race that starts in 15 minutes to the fact that the wall outside the race HQ needs repointing.

Back home, I didn't even let myself tell Louisa how well the wheel-testing had gone; when she asked I mumbled something about 'All right, but I need to do more work.' I refused to discuss it further. I was in denial about how possible it all seemed. And when Andrea's number flashed up on my mobile the following morning, I didn't answer, because I knew she would be upbeat and I wouldn't be able to cope with it. You win races by always being scared, always being hungry. Always demanding more. Training hard, preparing carefully, racing like you mean it. Complacency comes to be something you're petrified of.

To atone for the moments of confidence, I started thinking about the testing programme again, as if the magic wheels had never entered my life. I spent hours that could have been used for training and building up my confidence leafing through old cycling magazines looking for helmets – my new obsession – and worrying that if I couldn't find exactly the right one, the whole project would crumble away.

Headgear is a thorny issue for the aspiring record-breaker. The problem is that helmets have to address three issues that are to a large extent mutually contra-dictory: protection, ventilation and aerodynamics. To provide protection they need some bulk, but that makes them terribly hot, hence the need for ventilation. But a helmet with big vents that suck in cooling air and swirl it round your head creates a lot of aerodynamic drag. In fact a modern cycle helmet is just about the least aerodynamic thing you could put on your head. (Well, I imagine a sombrero would have its limitations, but I've never actually tested one.)

So to deal with the aerodynamic issue, time-trial riders wear special aero-helmets. They have no vents, just a smooth shell, and a point at the back that eases the airflow onto the rider's back and shoulders. The heat will slow you down less than the aerodynamics speed you up.

The athlete's hour rules, on the other hand, demanded a protective helmet with 'no devices or shapes added to or moulded into the helmet with the intention of or having the effect of reducing air resistance'.

A considerable challenge. Anything designed for speed was out, but in practice anything not designed for speed was designed for ventilation and hence enormous drag. I needed something designed with no regard for matters aerodynamic, and with equally little regard for ventilation. A worst-of-both-worlds helmet. Not surprisingly no one seemed to manufacture such an object. Certainly if they did, they didn't advertise it. Boardman had solved the problem by having his helmet sponsors make him a one-off unventilated version of his normal racing helmet. This was a solution open only to the biggest stars, but I wasn't even convinced it had been a good one. The helmet had been smooth-shelled, but it was still quite bulky and looked to me like an unaerodynamic shape.

Of all the equipment issues, this seemingly simple item turned out to be by a big margin the most difficult. I ended up dreaming about bloody helmets. With everything else, I knew broadly what I wanted and I just had to find it. On this I didn't even know what the dream solution was. The first glimmer came when I was riding back from training, down the New King's Road in Chelsea. I stopped at some traffic lights beside a woman on a bike with a child on a trailer-bike tagged on behind. The child was wearing a smooth, round unventilated helmet. I actually tried to persuade her mother to let me try it on. She said no, and if I'd been her I'd have said the same (and much more) to the sweaty stranger who, when he got home, noticed a big bit of snot adhering to his nose.

The idea was a good one, though. I went looking for children's helmets. The problem was that they were too small – who'd have guessed it? – and it was only helmets designed for babies and toddlers that had the shape I wanted. Older children apparently cared passionately about adequate ventilation.

The issue came to a head one Tuesday evening. I was going to Manchester the following morning, supposedly to test helmets and skinsuits. I hadn't found any helmets that seemed to be worth trying, even on an off chance, and all I could think of was to work my way through the Velodrome's supply of hire helmets.

This particular Tuesday had already been hassled; I'd waited in for a courier to deliver some chainrings, and of course the courier hadn't ever turned up. I spent the morning and most of the afternoon pacing about impatiently, before finally admitting it wasn't going to happen and trying to stuff some training into the too-short gap that I had left before a friend arrived for an after-work dinner.

I got back home just in time to let Tony in, and left

him to appraise my CD collection while I had a shower. Then we opened the bottle of wine he'd brought, and he had a glass while I drank a sports drink with ice and a slice of lemon, in an effort to look civilised. While we waited for Louisa to make it home I told him about the hour-record attempt.

He was, I think, the first person not directly involved in my hour that I told about it. I certainly remember I was anxious to hear what he thought. He was a cyclist of much longer standing than me and much more steeped in the history, and many cyclists take their history awfully seriously. I'd come to the sport later than most, and I sometimes felt like an impostor. I was worried he might think that somehow I was being disrespectful towards the record. Telling him was testing the water for the probable reaction when I made my plans public, as I was shortly going to have to do.

Tony was delighted with the idea. 'I always thought you should have a go at that,' he said, 'but I didn't like to mention it. I thought you might think I was taking the piss.' I could tell he meant it, he looked properly like a man who'd heard something he liked. In fact his enthusiasm rapidly started to scare me. 'How much are you going to break it by?' for example. To dampen him down a little, I started telling him about the problems, including the helmet issue.

'Have you tried one of those small round helmets that the skateboarders use?' he asked casually.

It was brilliant. I knew exactly what he meant, those neat helmets that come down to the top of the neck. Ventilation isn't really an issue, so they have an almost unbroken surface. As a bonus, given the demographic of skateboarders, there was a good chance they were cheap. The question was where would I get one?

'Well,' said Tony, 'Halfords might do them.'

There was a Halfords superstore a couple of miles down the road. I passed it regularly, and I knew it closed in 10 minutes. I don't think I actually grabbed Tony by the hand, but I hustled him out of the flat and into my car so fast he didn't have time to set down his glass. When Louisa got home a few minutes after we left, she found that not only had I not locked the front door, I hadn't even closed it.

The small grey skateboard helmet that we bought while the shop staff turned out lights all around us was, when tested the following morning, a great success. Chris Boardman later complained that I shouldn't have been allowed to use it, on the assumption that since it wasn't designed for cycling, it couldn't have offered the level of protection required by the rules. Well, it was made to the same recognised standards as many bike-specific lids. And here is the irony; it was manufactured by Giro, Chris's own helmet sponsor. I can't claim it was as advanced a bit of parallel thinking as Graeme Obree might have managed, and it wasn't even my idea, but for once Team Hutch had got one over Team Boardman.

While the helmet was good, the test session itself ended in frustration. I'd forgotten to recharge the battery in the computer that controlled the power-measuring system. While we got good data on the helmet, when I came to do similar skinsuit tests, the system ran out of juice. It was a clunking, stupid mistake and I was angry with myself. Perhaps it showed the stresses of the record were beginning to get to me. Normally I'd have been pissed off, yes, but I'd have been repressed enough to bottle it up. Not any more. 'FUCK IT,' I screamed, 'FUCKING PIECE OF CRAP!' It echoed round the building. It's not the kind of thing I usually do, and on the rare occasions when I am that angry, I'm pretty repentant almost immediately. This time I paused, then swore some more.

That was the end of the testing session. I did a couple of 10-minute efforts at about record pace; we called them 'training' – in reality they were just something to do to kill the hour. Their physical benefit was negligible, and anyway my pace judgement had gone to hell. I was still so cross about the empty battery that I couldn't think straight, and I started the efforts far too fast before fading away.

After I'd packed my stuff into the car and slammed the door, I came back into the Velodrome to see if I could book some extra track time in the next few days. As I was leaning over the reception desk trying to read the booking diary upside down, Andrea walked past, and we said goodbye. A moment later she came back.

'Tell me you're not booking the track,' she said.

I said I was hoping to get back up in a couple of days.

'Just don't,' she said.

I said I needed to do the skinsuit tests.

'Don't. You'll lose more than you'll possibly gain. Listen.' And she explained some things that should have been obvious. That I'd already put myself in a better position than I'd imagined possible. The previous week, after the wheel-testing, I'd been grinning like an idiot, dreaming about a record I had felt sure I was going to break. Nothing had changed since then, apart from having suddenly convinced myself that it wasn't enough after all.

'The set-up you have is good enough,' she said. 'Why can't you accept that?'

'Because it could be better.'

'Some people are never happy.'

'Yes.'

'You are one of these people.'

'Okay, yes, fine. Have you finished?'

The testing had been a shiny, silvery, sparkly thing to look at instead of contemplating the difficulty of what I was trying to do. A mobile over a baby's cot, to save junior from the horror of worrying about growing up, losing his virginity, getting a job and trying to repay his student loan. It was so simple. Just one magic number to work on, with nice clear results and an immediate reward for getting it right. It was something I could measure, something I could control, and because of that I'd become obsessed with it.

Take the skinsuit tests for which I had been trying to book track time. I had only one suit to test. Given that I had no alternative, this was the suit I was going to use for the attempt. Whatever advantage it might offer was the best I was going to get. Yet I wanted to make a 12-hour round trip just to see how good it was. To see what effect it would have on the magic number. Not because it would make a blind bit of difference to the hour attempt itself.

The record was about how far I could ride in an hour. It was not about staring at a computer screen, fretting about whether to move my handlebars up or down a centimetre. And anyone watching over me the previous few weeks would have been hard pressed to work that out just by looking. I was exhausted from the constant trekking to Manchester to chase smaller and smaller improvements in the set-up. I had devoted hours of mental energy to worrying about the most obscure details – would there be any aerodynamic benefit to shaving my arms? – rather than working towards a calm perspective on what I was trying to do. It was time to start concentrating on the record, the big picture, and on preparing myself for the ultimate test of riding ability.

I had to stay away from the Velodrome for a while, get back to basics. No more testing. Andrea was right: the current set-up *was* good enough. On my next trip up I would face up to the hour record, the traditional hour record, and do what I knew I needed to do. The 20-minute test was the next staging post, and it would tell me more than any amount of computer data. It was time to get real.

CHAPTER 7

Don't listen to anyone who tells you about an exerciser's 'high'. There's no such thing. It's just a lack of oxygen to the brain caused by trying too hard. You can get the same effect by half-strangling yourself – though at considerably greater risk of embarrassment or death, or both. If a high is all you're after, drugs are quicker, and probably cheaper than gym membership fees.

Even sex is a better high, and God knows that's not cheap or easy to lay your hands on. Arnold Schwarzenegger said that getting a good pump in his muscles was better than an orgasm. Trust me, he was lying. Just because it has shock value doesn't make it true. If you've been lifting weights for years, waiting for the big O, I'm sorry to disappoint you.

Exercise is no more fun for full-time athletes than it is for everyone else. We're still more or less the same as the average gym user, a figure normally driven by fear. Fear of a beer-gut, fear of cellulite, fear of getting old. Training is something you have to do, because if you don't do it, something bad will happen. You'll get fat. Or old. Or, in my case, lose. Training itself can be very satisfying, but that's about as good as it gets.

The other problem with training is that its marginal benefits drop sharply. If you want to keep improving, you have to keep increasing the training load. Between 1999 and 2000 I moved up from the silver and bronze positions in national championship events to the top of the podium, just a handful of seconds faster. To do so I had to double the amount of training I did, to more than thirty hours a week. Training rides often lasted six or seven hours, maybe followed by an hour or two in the gym. It was a lot, though there are long-distance triathletes doing fifty hours a week who would regard my thirty as a holiday.

On the whole, training is dull. The interesting bits of an athlete's career are the performances, not the practice. The contrast between racing and training is probably at its most stark in sports like rowing, where every four years the Olympics roll around and for a few days everybody knows their lightweight four from their coxless pair. Then the Olympics finish, and the poor bloody rower has to go back to getting up at a spirit-numbing hour each winter morning to do the first of the day's work-outs on a cold, dark river while everyone else is still asleep.

But to win, you must train, and because I knew that, I always managed to drag myself out of the house each morning and do whatever the training plan said must be done. But it's hard. Each day is like all the rest. In winter I could take a week off, a month off, and nobody would know. Nothing bad would happen for weeks, until the racing started. By then I could blame it on something else. But I didn't do this, I couldn't. You can't fake it –

you are fit, or you are not. And you are all there is. The piercing honesty of it means that you have to give it everything or nothing at all.

It's like any other obsession: the real world fades away and your personal demons turn up the volume. Just like the guys down the gym who get hung up on having huge arms and a six-pack stomach, you want to be fit, want to be fast. Over time the connection between training and result becomes an almost unconscious work ethic. Training comes to be something you just do, for hours at a time, without thinking once about why you're doing it. This sort of instinct towards hard work is a good thing, allegedly.

As with any other obsession, what you might actually gain materially from training is not what it's about. Winning races is nice, but it's probably not, on its own, worth the work. If I wanted money, there are easier ways. It's about self-image, about being in control of who and what you are. Just ask a recovered anorexic; the heart of an eating disorder is not usually anything so simple as a desire to be thinner. The harder I worked, the faster I went, the better a person I became. Maybe if I broke the hour record that would be enough. I would have defined myself, and I could go home happy.

There is a dirty secret about training – one that no one tells because it undermines a fundamental modern belief. It is this: you *can't* be anything you want to be. Not so far as sport is concerned anyway. You have to train, but for all except a lucky handful it's not enough. The greater part of athletic ability seems to be genetic rather than trained.

A very rough guide to endurance athletic ability is a

thing called VO_2 max: it's a measure of how much oxygen you can use at full stretch, and it indicates the size of your endurance 'engine'. It's expressed in terms of millilitres per minute, usually per kilo so that you can compare athletes of different sizes. An average for my age group and sex would be about 50. My highest measured value in the hour-record season was 83ml/m/kg.

Training does not have all that much of an effect on VO_2 max. For most people a 15 per cent improvement is as much as they can hope for. If we do the obvious sums, we find that the average man of my age might make it to 57.5. Meanwhile, if I had never started training at all, I'd still probably have a figure of 70ml/m/kg. I could turn up to a national championship after a year off and have a good chance of making the top twenty.

VO_2 max is a nice simple measure, but it's not the whole story. There are issues like efficiency: a bit like fuel economy, a question of how much energy you can produce for a given amount of oxygen consumed. Some people adapt better to training than others. But these appear to be largely genetically determined as well. Most people could do the same training I did, or any top athlete did, but they would not be as good. It works both ways: there are plenty of cyclists in the world a lot better than me, and pretty much whatever I do, they will stay better than me.

Enough science. Here is what I'm talking about. In May 1995 I did my first 10-mile time-trial, and recorded a time of 23 minutes something. Pretty reasonable for a first go. Second time out I'd got the hang of it, and did 10 miles in 19 minutes 44 seconds. I beat thirty club riders who had been hammering away at it for years.

Since training will only get you so far, there is an obvious temptation to try something a bit more direct. No book on cycling can really avoid the topic of drugs. The sport is so closely linked with drugs that my downstairs neighbour once came banging on my door late on a Friday night because he was having a few friends round and wanted some dope. (I think he'd misunderstood the nature of competitive cycling.) Drugs, cycling, cycling, drugs. And let us be clear: the drugs do work. If drugs can make you dance for days on end, does it not also seem likely that they can make you ride a bike faster?*

I don't make this assertion from personal experience. I was, and am, clean. That probably makes me an idiot, but I'm happy with that. At least I'm an honest idiot. I was never even in an environment where it was an available temptation, so I never had to make any real decisions about it. I can't claim the moral high ground of a Graeme Obree, who said that he had walked out of his only pro team when he was asked to subscribe to the drug-buying kitty.

Still, I guess I could have cheated if I'd really wanted to. You can order anything on the Internet, though there is a cautionary tale of Italian pro Dario Frigo. He bought a drug called Hemassist that way, and collected it from a

---

* On the form you fill out when you give a sample to dope control, there is a section where you are invited to give details of any medications or supplements you are using. It's wise to fill this out in detail, since if something you used was contaminated and produced a positive test, it would help your defence. One dope-control officer told me about a rider he'd tested the previous week who in the first column of this section, asking for details of the product, wrote, 'Blue pills' and in the column asking why he was taking them, he wrote, 'To make me cycle faster.'

shady individual at a Milan airport. His £500 turned out to have bought him a bottle of saline solution. I'm only sorry he didn't buy more.

In the end, most drugs that make you go faster are also able to kill you. There is no race on Earth I'd like to have won enough to die for it. When riders started using the now famous EPO (erythropoietin) in the late 1980s there was a series of 'unexplained' deaths, mainly of Dutch riders who just died in the night. EPO works by increasing the number of red blood cells, hence the amount of oxygen that the blood can carry. It also makes the blood thicker. When it reaches the strawberry-jam stage, the heart can no longer cope with pumping it.

Death usually came at night, when the pulse dropped close to its minimum and the thick blood flowed slowly. The solution was to keep the blood moving, by getting up regularly in the night to take some exercise. A college friend came back from a holiday a few years ago and complained that he'd been woken several times by members of a cycling team jogging up and down the hotel corridors.

Would you risk dying if the battery in your alarm clock gave out? Why would anyone? Because EPO makes a rider faster, and in a big way. It's not like a training shortcut. You can exchange yourself for a whole different athlete. The rate of oxygen delivery to the working muscles is the major performance-limiting factor in aerobic sports like cycling or running – that's what determines the VO_2 max. More red blood cells means more oxygen means more speed. Much more speed. In a 40km time-trial, a race I might complete in 48 or 49 minutes, EPO would probably make me 2 or 3 minutes faster. Maybe more. In hour-record terms, it would probably mean more than 3km further. It makes all my position- and equipment-testing look pretty silly.

EPO's popularity was enhanced because it was very difficult to detect (apart from the bit where you're found dead in the morning, and your suitcase is full of phials with 'EPO' written on them). To try to stop riders killing themselves, the UCI instituted a 'health check' that prevented riders competing if they had an unusually large number of red blood cells. Since cell count is only a symptom of EPO use and not proof, they couldn't be disqualified. They were simply required to sit out for a period, and were allowed back to competition only when their cell count was more normal. It was for the athlete's own benefit, and even cynics like me would admit that it probably saved lives. But it didn't stop EPO use; it just set a limit on it.

There is now a test for EPO, though its reliability seems doubtful, given a number of confessed users who weren't caught, including the Briton David Millar. Just in case, as always, the cheats move on. The 1980s precursor to EPO, blood doping, was briefly back in vogue. Blood is taken from the rider, stored until his body has replaced it, and is then reinjected. As with EPO, it increases the number of red cells available. There is now a test for that too. But there will be something else. There always will be. There always has been. Hell, even the ancient Greeks were at it, with various herbs and plants.

Cycling has such a big problem because drugs are part of the very texture of the professional sport. There was never a golden, Corinthian age of cycle racing. The heroes of the sport have always been professional, and where money is involved, every advantage will be sought, legal or not. Certainly the use of drugs was well established among racing cyclists by the 1920s, and probably long before. Indeed, if it weren't for the use of drugs through the sport's history, the races would probably not be as gruelling as they are.

The hour record and drugs is a topic that will not make the lawyers of Yellow Jersey Press happy. Certainly, drugs have featured in the hour. Most famously, 1956 record-holder Jacques Anquetil's views on doping were well known: 'Put the needle just here, please, nurse. Mmm. That's the good stuff.' Lest you think I'm just taking my libel-law-constrained frustrations out on the dead, Anquetil was the man who said you couldn't race on mineral water. In a similar vein, when Fausto Coppi was asked if he ever used drugs, he replied, 'Only when necessary.' To the obvious follow-up, when was it necessary, he said, 'Almost always.'

Anquetil was a cold, calculating rider, who rode in a style designed to be both dominant and economical. He was a superlative time-triallist, a talent that underpinned a long career and was the foundation of his five Tour de France victories. His approach to his job was rational, and untainted by any hint of romance. If doping was part of bike racing, it was part of bike racing. If that was what was needed to win, he would do it. He led a protest against dope controls on the 1966 Tour.

He took part in a famous experiment with Ercole Baldini – the man who broke Anquetil's 1956 hour record – where they agreed to race a time-trial (the Grand Prix de Forli) without chemical assistance. They were the favourites by miles, so they could afford to take the chance. They were first and second, but reckoned they were about 1.5kph slower than they should have been. They agreed it should be the last such experiment.*

Anquetil didn't ride the 1967 Tour; instead he gained himself considerable notoriety with outspoken comments on his own drug taking, other people's drug taking and (for completeness' sake) bribery in professional cycling. He would have known about these things; he was *Le Patron*, the biggest of the big cheeses. His revelations shocked fans and angered riders.

It was partly to atone to his sponsors for this lack of discretion that he went for the hour again in 1967, eleven years after he first broke the record. He used a very large gear to grind his way to a new best distance of 47.493km. Then, so far as atonement was concerned anyway, it all went spectacularly wrong.

Anquetil and his team had been warned in advance that this would be the first hour attempt subject to dope control. Yet when the appointed doctor approached Anquetil in the trackside 'cabin', he was angrily, and physically, ejected by Anquetil's team manager, Raphaël Géminiani. He was told that Jacques was not giving a sample at the velodrome. The champion was not at the beck and call of a lickspittle doctor. If the whole thing was so important, he could come to their hotel, 20 miles away. On the basis that this was outside the regulations,

---

* This story is quoted in Les Woodland's *Yellow Jersey Companion to the Tour de France* (2003). Les is clearly a man of parts, since his other books include a manual on sound recording and a guide to the public lavatories of Norfolk. The Baldini–Anquetil story was questioned by a journalist I know, who covered the race in question, and said they both looked as stoned as usual.

the doctor declined. He waited the prescribed time at the track, but Anquetil left long before him.

A few hours later, in a sudden change of heart, Géminiani rang the velodrome, to see if a sample could still be taken. He was much too late. Anquetil did take a test, but only two days later, after he had returned to Normandy. It showed that, by then at any rate, he was clean. It was no help to him. The UCI refused to recognise his record, and banned Géminiani from attending any bike race for a year. (This was not an entirely new experience for him: he had already been banned from races in Italy after a violent confrontation with officials there.)

The UCI decision was big, big news. There were many – riders, officials and fans – who felt the record should be ratified. After all, the record he had broken, that of Roger Rivière in 1958, had been set using drugs. Everyone used drugs – Anquetil himself said so. It was not fair to expect him to attack the hour record unassisted.

The UCI had made a choice between the integrity of its hour record and the integrity of its new anti-drugs stance. It chose correctly, and the tide was turning. Drugs had been responsible for the death of Tom Simpson on the climb of Mont Ventoux in that year's Tour de France, when amphetamines had combined with the hot conditions to bring on heart failure. Now there was this row over the hour. There was clearly a problem that the UCI could not ignore any longer.

But the affair did little to dent Anquetil's popularity with the fans, and he was received with wild enthusiasm at subsequent races. The magazines reporting his 'disgrace' carried on the same pages adverts placed by Anquetil's equipment suppliers, keen to be associated with the non-record. He was still a hero.

The argument was made obsolete four weeks later when Ferdinand Bracke, who was universally agreed to be clean, exceeded both Rivière's and Anquetil's distances in Rome. According to *Cycling* magazine he provided a negative sample 'with a smile on his face' (possibly more detail than we need).

Whether Anqetil was actually doped is, obviously, unknown. Rivière was not only doped, but provided details of what he had used – his own special amphetamine mix – and claimed that he had had to take tablets during the ride itself because the effects wore off too quickly. As a harbinger of the 'designer steroid' scandal of 2004, in a 1967 interview Rivière claimed there were drugs being manufactured for sportsmen about which the testing authorities knew nothing.

Rivière and Anquetil provided the hour's biggest drugs scandals. There has been no shortage of innuendo since, but nothing more solid than that. Other holders have actually failed tests, but not at a record attempt. Eddy Merckx failed one at the Giro d'Italia in 1969. He was thrown off the race and received a one-month ban. This would have involved the sport's biggest star missing the Tour de France. The UCI may have had this in mind when they rescinded the punishment – though not the conviction. It is worth noting, however, that Merckx always denied any wrongdoing, and claimed there had been a conspiracy to prevent him winning the race. Certainly, preventing Merckx winning races when he was in his prime would usually have required a conspiracy.

Another five-times Tour de France winner, Miguel Indurain, was found to have used a proscribed asthma treatment shortly before his hour record, but was cleared when his doctor confirmed he had asthma. You can tell a lot about the sport's doping culture from the issue of asthma. I have no reason to question the case of Miguel Indurain, but in the late 1990s I knew spectacular numbers of non-asthmatic UK riders who used asthma treatments, protected by a doctor's exemption from the doping regulations. It was easy; they memorised the symptoms of exercise-induced asthma from a website, went to their GP, recited the symptoms and got a prescription.

In the vast majority of cases this was cheating. But it was easy to do, much more so than using anything stronger, and sporting morality had taken such a battering over the years from doping scandals that most of the cheats quite genuinely didn't think they were doing anything wrong. Eventually the regulations were changed, and you now have to get your exemption from a specialist. Still pretty easy to fake if you know what you're doing.

Of course, the whole thing is infused with chauvinism. The French celebrated Anquetil's hour record regardless. Belgian news reports of the Merckx affair in 1969 could have culminated in a declaration of war on Italy without it looking out of place. When the British rider David Millar admitted taking EPO to win a world championship, I wrote an article for *Cycling Weekly* wherein I suggested that this was cheating, and should be regarded as such. At the next bike race I went to, in southern England, no one would speak to me. To many British cyclists, Millar was a victim rather than a cheat.

None of this is anything new. In 1898 William Hamilton became the first and only non-European to hold the hour record, the first rider to break 40km and the first rider to make an attempt at altitude – in Denver, Colorado. Naturally the debate in Europe concerned none of these things, but rather the question of whether a gang of hicks in Stetson hats could be trusted to time an hour, count laps, measure a track and perform simple arithmetic. The weight of opinion seemed to be behind 'no', but as the Europeans couldn't prove anything, they had to live with it.*

The best doping product of all was champagne. Used on and off for most of the last 100 years – British sprint-king Reg Harris was a fan – it seems to have fallen out of favour now. That is a great pity, since it was as pleasant as it was legal as it was ineffective. And I would have enjoyed billing my sponsors for a few bottles to help me prepare for the hour record.

As it was, no champagne. No drugs. Just training. By the end of May, hard training. I'd fought the boredom of the long, cold winter miles. I'd made the transition into faster riding and racing in the spring. Now, in early summer, almost all the riding I was doing was executed at speed. Speed is the killer. Anyone can ride a bike for hours on end if they want to badly enough. Winning races, of any length, means going fast. And to race fast, you must train fast.

* Incidentally, Hamilton's hour ride was the only one ever staged outdoors at night. He had a moving light shone onto the track in front of him to provide pace. This practice has now been banned, though not before Miguel Indurain looked at using a laser for the same purpose in 1994.

The target was 2nd July. That meant now, in late May, I was doing some of the most severe training I'd ever done. Just for a start, I had a race most weekends, and at this time of year most of these races were important in their own right. The day after the race, I would do just a couple of hours of easy riding. That constituted my day off; the sickest joke your body plays on you is that it recovers from hard efforts better with some exercise. Just at the point when you feel most like spending the day in bed, you have to go cycling again.

The racing wasn't the worst of it. The worst of it was the three days of the week when I felt like I was doing my best to kill myself, Monday, Wednesday and Friday – the double-session days. In the morning I did three hours on the road, at a steady pace. I then spent the afternoon dreading the evening session, on the home trainer in the kitchen. I tried to keep some variety in the evening training – it was always easier to cope with it if there was at least some element of novelty, but whatever it was, it revolved around the well-worn principle of interval training. Ride fast, ride easy, ride fast. Repeat until you are sick over your handlebars.

At its most simple, minute intervals. Ride fast for one minute. Hard enough that your legs are burning after 30 seconds. Every pedal stroke after that is a big effort. You must keep the cadence high, 120rpm. You fight the urge to stop twice a second. Finally you can stop, spin easily. I took only a minute off. Then another minute of long effort just like the last. I used to force myself to do fifteen efforts like this. It's a horrible way to spend half an hour.

At least that session was simple. The worst session of all was what I called the 20/10 session. This sounded innocuous: 20 seconds at about the same pace I could sustain for a minute. 10 seconds at about the same pace I would use in a 90-minute race. It was hell. My pulse would just climb and climb as the session went on, sometimes staying at over 190bpm for 10 minutes. My absolute maximum pulse is only about 196bpm. This was hard.

I used to do two 20-minute periods of this, separated by about 10 minutes. The session was suggested to me by a coach, whose standard instruction was to take as much time between the efforts as you felt you needed. He subsequently told me about a conversation he'd had with a member of the national squad.

Coach: How did the 20/10 session go?

Rider: It was fine.

Coach: How long did you leave between the efforts?

Rider: Three months.

You can only cope with sessions like this if you are very motivated by some goal or other, or if you have the obsessive mindset that refuses to accept failure to meet a target you've set yourself. Extremes of hope or fear. In truth, that session was probably too hard. It had too much to do with taking a pride in hurting yourself, and not enough to do with rationally assessing the damage you are doing to your body and your mind. After that session I had to take a cold bath to get my body temperature down enough that I could go to bed five hours later. Otherwise I would just lie there feeling feverish, with my pulse racing and my mind spinning.

The days between the hellish kitchen sessions were like

winter days: longish steady rides. Except it wasn't winter any more, and in London it was hot. The air was heavy and stagnant. Drivers were bad-tempered. You had to concentrate, because if you didn't, someone would bundle you off the road. A few hours that might have been an escape from the stresses of the record now became a source of stress in themselves. I'd rather have been torturing myself in the kitchen.

Looking back at it, by this point it was beginning to get on top of me. The training was difficult and it absorbed a lot of physical and mental energy. But that wasn't half of what I had to deal with. Barring extreme accidents, I would have two legs come 2nd July. There was no such certainty surrounding the rest of the equipment. I was still very worried about whether the bike frames were going to materialise. Dave had assured me repeatedly that it would be fine, but I'd long ago ceased believing him. Apparently, on the far side of the world, they were being lovingly crafted. I didn't care about them being lovingly crafted, I just wanted them *here*. I was nervous about the forthcoming 20-minute trial which would decide whether I gave the attempt the final green light. I was working out the details of the attempt itself, making sure that the relevant formal paperwork was being dealt with.

All these things were spilling into my training diary, a dull-as-dust document concerned with training done, weight, resting heartrate and numbers from 1 to 10 summing up how I felt, mentally and physically. There was not much editorial content. It said things like: '75kg, 45bpm. Physically, 6. Mentally, 5. Morning: 3 hours steady, OK. Evening: 2×20 minutes 20/10. Not nice, very hot, heartrate over 190 for most of second effort. Took a long time to cool down.' So far so normal.

Then it swerved into: 'No word on frames, no reply from the UCI. Pissed off with the whole thing. Would anyone like to give me a hand? Course not, every bastard too busy with own head up own arse. He wants to break the hour record, let him sort it out.' This would be crammed into the margin, because it wasn't supposed to be there at all. But the frustrations were boiling over, and they had to go somewhere.

Worst of all, I was beginning to worry about my physical readiness. The training was hard, and it was going well. But usually when you start to approach a peak of form, you feel good. Tired from the training maybe, but mentally sharp; there is an impatience to get to some races and start walking over people. You know the way top 100m sprinters strut? Like that. Me, I just wanted to sleep all day. The 1–10 scores fell consistently through May, and were still heading south into June.

Time was the enemy in more ways than the obvious. Sixty minutes to ride. Five weeks to try and get ready. The same five weeks to try to keep myself together. It couldn't come soon enough: it couldn't take long enough.

As Andrea had suggested, I'd stayed away from the track for a couple of weeks. I got a bit of peace and some consistent training, without tiring drives and sleepless nights on sparsely sprung hotel mattresses. I just abandoned the testing I'd planned; it seemed unlikely to produce a net gain. But I couldn't avoid the 20-minute record-pace trial. Assuming I managed the trial, I would make the attempt public. Backing out after that would not be a private disappointment, it would be a public humiliation.

I'd asked Simon Jones if he'd come and help me, which was a little disloyal to Andrea. I wanted him there because he had a degree of detachment. I didn't trust myself with dispassionately judging the outcome of the trial if there was any degree of ambiguity. I also wanted desperately to impress him. He coached the highly successful national squad riders. He was not used to standing by the track watching bad bike riding. I really didn't want to fail in front of Simon. Fear of failure: Michael's little helper.

This was important – it was my first encounter with the hour record proper. This kind of trial was such a hallowed tradition that it had become part of the record's texture. This was the start of the path described in all the old magazines, or shown on the films. After months of quiet preparation, following my own instincts, I was throwing my lot in with everyone else who'd ever been serious about the hour. And in 20 minutes, I would have a very clear idea if I was to be a man of the record, or not.

I tried to replicate how I imagined the real record attempt would be. I warmed up on a home trainer. I drank the same energy drink, and wore the same kit I planned to use, even down to the sunglasses. Simon had prepared a schedule: I had 23 seconds to complete the first lap from a standing start, then 18.2 seconds for each lap thereafter.

The first 10 minutes or so were fine. Simon was indicating that I was slightly up on schedule, and riding steadily. It looked good. My breathing was in its fastest rhythm, but it was steady. I was in control. I began to feel rather pleased with myself. Through halfway; no problem.

Then, quite quickly, it got hard. Now the fast breathing rhythm wasn't giving me enough air, but any faster and my breathing would be out of control. I tried to keep a lid on it, to stay relaxed, to focus on riding a nice economical line. Another couple of laps. I still felt like I was drowning. (And I was supposed to be able to manage this for another 50 minutes?) I was on the edge of hyperventilation, and there would be no getting back from there. So I had to slow down. Next lap Simon was showing I was behind pace. Next lap he was showing a long way down. Then he gave up – it was clearly pointless. I stopped at 16 minutes.

I did several warm-down laps. Not that I really wanted to; I just didn't want to have to talk about what had happened. When I finally did stop, neither of us knew quite what to say. It looked like the end of the road. Finally I said, 'Well, that went badly.'

'Yes,' said Simon. 'Sorry it didn't work out.'

'That's it, you reckon?'

'Yep.' He picked up his few things and headed back to his office.

Andrea had appeared from somewhere, and we were left together in the track centre. I felt embarrassed at all the work she'd put into a project for which, when it came down to it, I didn't have the legs. She shrugged and said, 'Never mind. Good try.' She left as well. No one ever knows what to say when things like that happen.

I started to take the wheels off the bike, to pack up and go home. Just why the hell had that been so hard? Okay,

I know it's dangerous to make big extrapolations from limited evidence, but the testing we'd done had been pretty comprehensive. So what was going on? I stopped what I was doing and looked dumbly at the track, as if maybe it had grown longer. I decided to download the ride data to my laptop, just to have a look at the numbers. At least I could give my hour-record plans some sort of an autopsy.

The file looked as I'd expected. The lines on the graph representing power and speed were steady till 10 minutes, then fell away a little, then steepened into a dive. What was curious was that the speed line during the steady part of the effort was at just over 49.4kph. That was fine, it was record pace. Except that the Velodrome was cold that morning, only about 18 degrees. And you go slower in cold air than in warm, because warm air is less dense (that's what keeps a hot-air balloon aloft), so the aero-dynamic drag is lower. The difference between 18 degrees and the 26–7 degrees that I'd expect for a record attempt equated to about 0.6kph, or in terms of distance, 600m.

Normally you take account of this, and make a suitable correction to your target speed. Herein was the cock-up. I had assumed Simon would make the correction when he worked out the schedule. He assumed the target speed I'd given him was already corrected. A scenario broadly familiar to anyone from NASA who has ever watched a multi-million-dollar satellite crash into the ocean. Was 0.6kph enough to make the difference between what I expected and what I got? I had no idea, and there was no way of working it out now. It was a stupid mistake – I should have checked – and now I had learned nothing from what should have been the most useful test of all. But at least it was a spark of hope.

The only thing I could think of was to do the trial again. All I needed to do was to scrounge 20 minutes of track time from someone. I left my kit where it was and went to see what I could find.

I managed to have another go the following morning. This time the pace was right, but I was too tired from the previous day's exhaustive effort to hang onto it. I finished the 20 minutes, but I fell behind in the second half. It was no more use than the first go. I was so frustrated I wanted to scream. The hour record attempt was bearing down on me. Now I had to make a final decision about whether I was going to go public with the attempt, whether I was prepared to face the explosion of interest and expectation that would provoke, without really knowing whether I was going to be able to do it. It was the situation I most wanted to avoid. The whole strategy had been based on not letting this happen.

I knew Simon reckoned that 0.6kph one way or the other didn't make any difference. So far as he was concerned, that was only the kind of safety margin I should be allowing anyway. I hadn't asked him to come to the second test. I hadn't even told him it was happening. So far as he knew, I was back in London preparing a classified ad: 'Complete hour-record kit. Everything for the aspiring hour record-breaker. Only used for 16 minutes.'

Simon's unambiguous opinion should have brought an end to the whole thing. But I realised I couldn't let go. The project that had begun as a cool, rational way to prop up the last stages of a creaking career had got its claws into me. I'd put so much work into it that I couldn't just walk away and go back to the normal season's grind. That was why I hadn't told Simon about the second trial. No one was going to stop me, not now. On 2nd July, the attempt was going to happen.

It was a funny feeling. It wasn't the exhilarating rush of a successful trial. It was more an acceptance that I was going to finish the job. And what I needed now was for the planets to align in whatever way meant the next few weeks were organised and hassle-free. Really, really I needed that.

I had the National 10-mile championships that weekend, in Warwickshire. Was this a handy distraction or an extra burden? I think in the end it just about qualified as a distraction. If nothing else, it allowed Louisa and me to stay in the least accommodating hotel in history.

The hotel was a doleful-looking, low building in shades of grey and brown, somewhere near the end of the M45. Presumably it had been built by someone who didn't know that the M45 was destined to be the quietest motorway in Britain. Unusually for a hotel at 3 p.m. on a Saturday, it was locked. During the week I suppose 80 per cent of its rooms contained lonely sales reps trying to balance sorting out their orders and watching porn. At the weekend it didn't even have any staff. You had to get someone from the service station next door to give you a key. At least *Fawlty Towers* had a bit of life about it. This place was like one of those ghost villages abandoned after the Chernobyl explosion.

To complement the world's worst hotel, next door was the world's worst restaurant. In a moment of stupidity I asked how the Cajun Chicken was cooked. 'I'll ask the chef.' A moment later, 'The chef says he doesn't know, he just takes it out of the bag and warms it up.' In common with some outlying districts of Louisa's family, here I suspect that warming things up counted as home cooking. Since they had run out of baked potatoes, I ended up ordering the thing; it was vile.

The following day's race was not great. I don't even remember much about it. The hour preparations meant that I wasn't able to rest before the event, and in the end I was too tired to make much of an impact. (Yeah, yeah, excuses.) I tried hard, though, and the focus drove the hour out of my head for an afternoon, which was the best thing I got out of it. But as soon as I crossed the finish line, my mind skipped back to its default setting.

In the end I was second, 17 seconds behind Stuart Dangerfield. I was only surprised that he hadn't won by more. I sent an e-mail to one of the sub-editors at *Cycling Weekly* suggesting an appropriate headline would be 'Dangerfield Bad, Hutch Even Worse'. I think in the end they went with 'Dangerfield Beats Hutch Yet Again'.

The National 10 should have been more than a distraction. It should have been a crucial part of the build-up, a chance to show off my heightened physical powers. And despite the excuses, a man planning to break the hour record should have won. It should have stirred up *something*.

On the way back to London, Louisa said, 'You're very quiet. Are you annoyed about the race?'

'What race?' I replied. The hour record wasn't a race, what could she be talking about? As recently as the previous season, I'd won the 10-mile title race and it had been one of the year's big results. Now I'd had my title taken off me, and I'd forgotten about it before I was 20 miles down the motorway.

When I got home, I shaved my head. Not as a penance – I'd forgotten about the National 10, remember – but because it was the next stage of the hour. For years I had worn my hair in a pony-tail. For the hour there was an aerodynamic penalty to hair flapping about. A subsidiary benefit, and the reason for the shaving rather than something closer to my mother's idea of a nice-young-man's haircut, was heat loss.

As we know, you need warm air, but ideally a cool rider. In his record attempts Chris Boardman was sprayed with a volatile alcohol solution, which produced the same effect you get with a finger that's been dunked in methylated spirits, except without staining him purple.

It's funny that I find myself thinking about Boardman being stained purple. Hidden from the sun for so long, my scalp turned out to be a pale-blue colour. I could feel the air swirling round the back of my head as I walked. I tried to convince myself I looked tough, and ready for action. It didn't work. What I looked like was Sinéad O'Connor, and not in a good way. My new look was cool all right. But only in the temperature sense.

It's easy to be flip about this. The kind of man who breaks world records shouldn't care about his appearance. But shaving my head felt like a sacrifice, in a way that all the trips to Manchester, all the time and effort spent training, just hadn't. I'd given up a part of me for the record, something that I wasn't going to get back whatever happened. It wasn't an arm, or a leg, or a finger.

Or the years of life that Merckx once said he felt the hour record must have cost him. But it was a real commitment. In a very palpable sense, there was no going back now. I just had to feel the top of my head.

CHAPTER 8

HUTCH TARGETS HOUR RECORD, SAID THE HEAD-line. This much, and so much more, you already knew. But it was the first that anyone else had heard about it. The article covered most of the first news spread in *Cycling Weekly*, accompanied by a pleasingly speed-blurred photograph of me on the Manchester track. There were details of where and when the attempt would be, and what I had to beat. The article went on: 'A shot at the record – whether it succeeds or not – is sure to propel Hutchinson from his relatively humble status as a UK "tester" into the limelight of the world cycling stage.'

I was playing with the big boys now.

It was a sudden change in context. I'd been used to being a rider on the UK time-trial circuit, but that's not really the big time. Even in its most modern incarnation it's still rooted in post-war austerity, in black and white.

This is not necessarily a bad thing. British time-trialling has a sense of community that you'd be pressed to find in the big-money, big-ego worlds of tennis or football. British cycling's own Roger Bannister was a guy called Ray Booty, who in 1956 was the first person to ride 100 miles in under four hours. Time-trialling was in its heyday, and 'the Boot' was a big star. Yet he quite commonly finished a race, got out his camping stove and made tea for anyone who fancied a cup. Not perhaps too unusual in 1950s Britain, but I could have done the same thing after I too broke the 100-mile record, in 2003, and no one would have been awfully surprised. (Except that I could just have crossed the car park to the race HQ and got everyone tea there.)

I was leaving all that behind me. There was a list of former record-holders: Coppi, Anquetil, Merckx, Boardman. And there was me apparently putting my hand up and saying, 'I can beat these guys. I can ride faster than Merckx, or Anquetil, or . . .' That wasn't me at all. I'd only been thinking of beating a number: the magical 49.441km. Where the number came from was not my problem. I'd managed to leave the personalities out of it. Now here, top right, was a picture of Lance Armstrong – much smaller than the picture of me – and a caption saying that he was also rumoured to be going for the record later in the year, and would it be Hutch he was trying to beat? To me it all looked about as realistic as the 'Michael Hutchinson. Wanted: Dead or Alive' poster that someone gave me for my tenth birthday.

Like the poster, though, the idea of it being real was exciting. Who wouldn't rather be a Wild West desperado than a Northern Irish schoolboy dreading games on a wet Thursday afternoon? Hutch head-to-head with Lance? You bet. And it was kind of real. I hadn't broken the record – yet. If I did, this would be my new environment. In the meantime it was provisional stardom. I was pretty thrilled by the thought that all over the world bike fans were looking at pictures of me on websites as a probationary world contender, rather than an obscure British champion. In some ways, like the magazine article said, win or lose – life would never be quite the same. I was going to measure myself against the very highest standard, and everyone was going to come and watch.

Not all riders have been so excited by a bit of press attention. As with other sports, the most celebrated competitors have found their fame to be double-edged. The bigger the star, the greater the danger.

The Italians have, over the years, bestowed the title of *Campionissimo* on several riders, but for most the title belongs only to Fausto Coppi, the man who dominated the world of cycling in the years after the Second World War. He set his hour mark early in his career, riding 45.848km in Milan on 7th November 1942 to break the record by 81m. That is not much of a margin: it's only about 6 seconds.

It was not the crushing record you might expect of a man who is the only serious challenger to Merckx for the title of best cyclist ever. But for an attempt put on at short notice in war-time, in a city that was, in the words of *Cycling* magazine, being 'seen to' by the RAF, it wasn't at all bad.

To get the record was more than Coppi really hoped for. He was short of training and racing, and he said before the attempt that he would have a proper go at it sometime in the future. He never did, possibly because of what he put himself through that morning in Milan. An athlete in top form can give easily of his best. An undertrained rider may go almost as fast, but will suffer and suffer for it. Coppi had a hellish time, and he was almost unconscious as he was helped off his bike. He heard the lap bell still ringing in his head for minutes afterwards. Like Merckx, Coppi felt the hour was something that, having done once, he had no desire to do twice.

Coppi was already in the army when he broke the record, and the army didn't care if he was a star. He was shipped to North Africa with his infantry unit a few weeks later, where he was swiftly captured by the British and spent the remainder of the war a prisoner. The British, naturally, had never heard of him.

The war knocked a big hole in Coppi's career. When he got home in 1945 he was twenty-six, and should have been halfway through his career. Instead he had barely started. He still had time to win the Tour de France twice, and the Giro d'Italia another four times (he'd won a war-time Giro in 1940). In 1949 he was the first to win the Giro and the Tour in the same year, and he repeated the double in 1952.

He was, as Merckx would be, a dominant rider. He didn't just win, he won in such style that race promoters had to increase the value of second prize to keep the other riders interested.

Coppi was much more than just a cyclist. Simply to list his cycling achievements only tells half the story, maybe less. He was an icon. He represented the modern, the casual and (scandalously) the secular. He had a blind manager, Biagio Cavanna, who added an element of the mysterious. It was not by chance that Coppi was the hero of so many rebellious members of the British League of Racing Cyclists. Coppi was Italian style and post-war cool.

Coppi married shortly after he returned from North Africa, though he spent many weeks hanging around in Naples before eventually cycling and hitching north to his betrothed, which suggests that he might have been less than enthusiastic about it. Then in 1948 he met Giulia Locatelli, the wife of an army doctor, who became infatuated with him. Giulia's husband was a cycling fan, and initially was quite keen on the friendship, even asking Coppi to their home or to accompany them on outings. Eventually he made the mistake of letting them out on their own, to a Harlem Globetrotters basketball game. Giulia later reported that Coppi had not taken his eyes off her all night.

So an affair began, and Coppi was immersed in scandal. The story broke after a race in 1953, when Coppi was pictured embracing an unknown woman (unknown in so far as she was known not to be his wife) in a white coat. She became the 'woman in white'. Post-war Italy was a conventional place, and when Giulia left her husband to move in with Coppi, they quickly moved beyond the scandalous and into the truly shocking in a way that is almost beyond modern comprehension. They were thrown out by Coppi's landlord, and when they bought a house of their own, it was raided by the police at midnight to see if they were sharing a bed.

They were, and in what seems more like a scene from 1753 than 1953, Giulia was taken to the cells for a few days, to encourage her to reconsider. She stuck with Coppi. Eventually, after a trial, she and Coppi received suspended prison sentences for desertion and enticement respectively. (She did not, by all accounts, take much enticing.) The financial settlements Coppi finally reached with Giulia's husband and with his own abandoned wife were complicated and rancorous. One begins to see why Coppi never found time to return to the hour record.

Italy, and the wider world, was divided over Coppi, between the conservative forces who saw him as an adulterer plain and simple, and those who felt he'd been ill used by the undoubtedly manipulative Giulia. The Church was predictably outraged; the Pope refused to bless the Giro d'Italia because Coppi was a competitor, and wrote to Coppi personally to tell him of his displeasure. The exact contents of the letter remain a mystery, since Coppi burned it.

The papers followed all of this in detail, and dispatched the early paparazzi to follow them. It's a modern story set in a less forgiving time. Today a sports star would emerge from such a storm reasonably unscathed to launch a lucrative book. Coppi was destroyed. His physical form suffered so badly that his competitors had to push him up hills to save him from humiliation.

He seemed unable to retire; he raced on and on, getting worse and worse, towards his fortieth birthday, destroying his reputation. By the end of his career he spent most of his time riding only exhibition races, because he could no longer cope with real competition. Even then, the organisers of these races had to drastically reduce the distances involved just so that he could finish.

Coppi couldn't even die without getting swept up in controversy. In 1959 he went to an exhibition race in Upper Volta, now Burkina Faso in sub-Saharan Africa. The group he went with was a stellar one, containing Jacques Anquetil and Roger Rivière, hour record-breakers of the 1950s, and a generation younger than

Coppi. After he returned, he complained of flu-like symptoms, and Giulia said he was yellow-looking. In France another member of the party, Raphaël Gémaniani, had the same illness. The French quickly diagnosed and treated malaria, but the Italian doctors diagnosed pneumonia. Coppi was dead within a few days. The doctors claimed that the diagnosis didn't matter; he had been too weak to survive any serious illness.

He had been a prototype for modern celebrity. As you would expect, the vultures picked over the details of his death. Questions were asked in Parliament; there were suggestions of conspiracy. Strangest of all was the claim of a Benedictine monk in Burkina Faso that Coppi had been poisoned in revenge for the death of a local racing cyclist. The whole thing has never really been settled.

I kind of hoped that none of this was a direct result of breaking the hour record.

Of course I hadn't left obscurity behind just yet. A couple of pages further on in the magazine, and less unexpectedly, I featured in a preview of the National 25-mile championships. This was the only British title missing from my collection. Now I was heading for it in what was hopefully the form of my life. After the underwhelming National 10, I was planning to give the 25 everything. Set the stall out, so to speak, and show what I'd got. Chris Boardman had prepared for his first hour record by winning this race. Ten years on I was going to do the same.

The race was only a few miles south-west of London, at Farnham, on a Saturday afternoon. Louisa and I drove down that morning. It was a nice luxury to spend the night before the race at home. I hoped that everyone else had had a sleepless night in a cheap hotel listening to a wedding reception through the floor. (There is no song you can play that doesn't remind me of a crummy hotel somewhere. Trust me, you don't go downstairs and ask them to turn it down if the first dance is 'The Ace of Spades'.)

I signed on at the HQ in Farnham. Instead of staying there to get ready, we got back in the car and drove off to a quiet country lane a mile or two from the start. I parked on a wide verge, under some trees. I'd picked the spot a couple of weeks previously when I'd been out this way. I like to plan these things.

It's important, because the events that have gone badly for me have always been the ones where I got distracted. If you hang around the HQ, friends stop to say hello and strangers come looking for autographs. It's a sad reflection on the fans I have that all the autograph-hunters are middle-aged men who usually claim it's for their sons. Curiously, the sons in question have never been able to make it to the race. Even more interestingly, they always have the same name as their dad. Someone once asked me for an autograph for his daughter, whose name was David. I actually signed that one 'Marilyn Monroe'. It seemed appropriate, and so far as I know his daughter didn't have the nerve to complain.

No, I wanted to avoid that kind of thing. I needed to be left alone so that I could visualise how the race was going to be. The sights, the sounds. Even the smells and the metallic tang of adrenalin that would be in my throat at the start. I wanted it all to be familiar before it happened. If you rehearse it in your mind, it's easier to get it right in real life. A quiet roadside verge was the perfect place.

The usual preparations. Inflate tyres. Put the wheels in the race bike. Put the warm-up bike on the home trainer, and try to find a level spot for it. Sunlight dappled through the trees onto the grass, and the birds were singing. The gentle breeze was as warm as a sigh. We should have been having a picnic, not riding a bike race.

Then, with everything ready, Louisa and I sat in the front seats of the car watching the time. It got windier, and the sun went in. Suddenly it was quite cold. I don't think we said anything, but even if we did I don't think I would remember it. I was trying to commit as much as I could to this race, to make it part of the hour itself. If I was going to break the hour record, I had surely to win this.

Finally, the warm-up on the trainer: 20 minutes or so, gradually increasing the pace until I was at about race intensity. Still thinking about the race, what it was going to feel like. Another look at my watch. Off the trainer. Onto the race bike, and off down the lane to the start. As I emerged onto the dual carriageway that formed the course, the roar of the traffic seemed impossibly loud.

The start was in a scruffy lay-by. The ground dropped away behind it to miles of fields, so it was exposed to the wind. The sun was out again, in a gap between the clouds, and for the moment it was hot. I had to wait three or four minutes for my start, and I half-watched the preceding rider being held upright on the line and setting off. I was still trying to concentrate on my race. I rolled up to the start.

I settled well after the sharp effort of the starting acceleration. Within a couple of minutes I was at full pace, breathing well and under control. It felt pretty good, even into the headwind. Low over the bike to reduce the wind-drag, with my head tucked down into my shoulders, my eyes peering from under their brows. Sweat already trickling down the edge of my sunglasses.

First 180 degree turn, at a roundabout. Could have taken it a little faster. But okay. Another acceleration out of the turn. Tailwind now, turning a big gear and going very fast, up over 40mph.

Back past the end of the lane I'd warmed up in and, on the roadside with a watch, Louisa signals that I'm leading. But Stuart Dangerfield is behind me, and I'm not going to know about him until it's too late. Concentrate; don't think about him, think about me. Smooth, powerful pedalling. Low on the bike. Feeling balanced, relaxed – trying to make it feel like it did in the perfect mental run-through.

Another turn. Big roundabout this time, lots of traffic, and inevitably I get held up a little. I shout incoherently, in surprise and anger at a car that swerves in front of me to block me for a moment. It's being driven by the wife of another rider. Forget it, Michael. Concentrate. Headwind again. Getting tired; keep the rhythm. Sweat blows into my right eye, and there is salt on the inside of my glasses. Breathing close to the limit. The very edge of what you can do. That's good, that's strong.

The last turn, at the smaller roundabout again. Last tailwind blast to the finish, and control doesn't matter any more. Just give it all I have left. Past Louisa again, who's signalling I'm down. But that must be from the last pass, so it doesn't mean much. A last acceleration for the line, past the flag. And release, let it go. Whatever happens, it's over now. It's time to go home.

I didn't win. I was second, again behind Dangerfield. Unlike the 10, this time I was pissed off. This time I'd made myself care. When Louisa asked, 'How did it go?', I snapped, 'It was fucking terrific, how do you think it was?', which wasn't very reasonable of me; and when some well-meaning stranger at the race HQ said, 'Well done', I just glared at him. I normally manage at least to look like a good loser whatever happens – I regard it as part of the job – but now the cracks were beginning to show. I was angry that despite the capital I had invested in the race and the lack of any obvious mistakes, I'd lost. That ten years earlier Obree had been beaten in the 25, but had still broken the record, didn't make me feel any less frustrated.

Stuart Dangerfield's generosity of spirit was not much in evidence after the race either. When asked if he fancied a go at the hour record himself, he said, 'I'm no Eddy Merckx or Chris Boardman, I would have no chance.' If I was feeling sensitive I might have taken that as an insult. As it happens, I was feeling sensitive.

Most people were more supportive. But you could see what they were all thinking: how does this guy think he's going to break a world record if he can't win the National 25?

It wasn't all anger and frustration. I met Jamie Pringle, an exercise physiologist from the University of Brighton. He'd rung me the morning the attempt went public to offer any help he could. It's illustrative of the generally misanthropic mood I was in that the first thing I thought, was not 'How kind', but 'How did you get my number?' I think I may actually have said it.

Jamie had the distinction of being almost the first

member of Team Hutch who wasn't making it up as he went along or, in some notable cases, just standing about watching. I'm sorry I didn't meet him earlier. There were a lot of questions to which he knew the answers, and by now it was too late to ask most of them, let alone do anything constructive with the information.

For instance, Jamie knew the answers to the questions: 'What is glycerol, and how might it help an hour-record attempt? What ethical issues attach to its use?', and 'Discuss the issue of heat fatigue in endurance athletes, with specific reference to the cycling hour record.' In fact he'd written me essays on these and other relevant matters, and bound them into a report. So now, as well as being able to train for the hour record, worry about the hour record and argue with people about the hour record, I could read about it before going to sleep at night. And – hurrah! – that meant I could dream about it too. Saturation point.

The heat question was one that had been worrying me (as if fitness, wheels, frames, helmets and general logistics were not enough). As I've said, the hotter the air at the track, the faster you go. To a more limited extent, humidity makes it faster too. But, obviously, working out in a sauna is no one's idea of fun. I was planning to wind the Velodrome thermostat up as far as it would go, and then just hope for the best. Not wildly scientific, I know, but given that in the eight years of the Velodrome's existence it had never made it above a comfortable room temperature, it didn't seem a very great risk. (That's not quite true: the first night of track competition at the 2002 Commonwealth Games there was a capacity crowd, with the heaters on and the windows closed to try to create hot conditions for the sprinters, for whom heat fatigue is not an issue. We were all breathing straight nitrogen and the walls dripped like a subterranean nightclub. Apparently sprinters like that kind of thing.)

My only heat defence so far had been crude acclimatisation training. My kitchen has a glass ceiling, facing south-east. On sunny summer mornings it is sometimes so hot that you can't stand on the floor barefoot. That's before I shut the door, and put a fan heater in there as well. Then I got going on the home trainer. The temperature was usually up around 35°C. When you set about an interval session, that's hot. On one occasion I misjudged it and let it get to 40°C, at which point the corks started pushing out of a couple of bottles of wine I'd left there.

Actually, this hadn't been as barking mad a scheme as it appears. In fact, according to Jamie's dossier, I'd got it more or less right. All I'd forgotten was the pan of boiling water on the cooker to get the humidity up. Jamie had offered weirder suggestions than that, though. Another heat-beating tactic was to try to lower your body temperature before the event, using an ice-vest like one of those rapid coolers you slip over a wine bottle. So when you start getting hot, you're starting from a lower base.

The ice-vest was a very odd item. You soaked it in water and put it in the freezer for a few hours, whereupon it went rigid. Then you prised the front and back of the thing apart, and pulled it on over your head like a plywood pullover. And it was cold. In a fit of teenage bravado on a school trip I once jumped off the end of a jetty into a Swiss mountain lake. It was just like that. In the notes Jamie supplied with it, he described this surreal object as 'very practical'. He also suggested 'cooling the blood flow to the brain'. Mercifully this translated into 'Point a big fan at your face, fat boy' rather than anything more invasive.*

The hassles were still bubbling along. *Cycling Weekly* wanted to organise a corporate hospitality event at the hour, which meant more phone calls. Some tyres I'd got for the spare bike turned out to be the wrong size and needed to be replaced. I ended up having to order a spare set of wheels for the spare bike and trying to sell a couple of bikes from my collection to pay for them. Just stuff. All the time. It was no-brain stuff that someone else could easily have done, but there wasn't anyone else. Well, that's not quite true; it just felt that way. To my lasting gratitude, Andrea had taken on the task of organising the officials for the attempt; the UCI notifications, the time-keepers (manual and electronic), the UCI commissaires and the dope control. If I'd had to do that lot myself, I'd probably have given up.

My training diary records that on the afternoon of 12th June I spent an hour in my hammock 'watching the aeroplanes flying towards Heathrow'. The fact that I bothered to write it down suggests it was a bit of an event. In an ideal world, with a couple of weeks to go I'd have been spending hours of every afternoon in a hammock watching the aeroplanes.

* On the subject of invasive, I stopped reading at the bit about temperature probes. I had a nasty feeling about where they went, and what effect they might have on what we might delicately call the rider-saddle interface. The hour was going to be long enough already, I felt.

Every hour attempt has its logistical problems. It goes with the territory. You're effectively organising an international race and having to make sure it's all done by the book. While you do that you have to organise your team, your equipment and your training programme. As well as doing whatever other races you are committed to. The pros have people to help them deal with all this, but I suspect no one has ever had it easy.

Take Chris Boardman. He made three successful attempts. The third one was the athlete's hour mark I was trying to beat. That had proved nightmarish – mainly because the rules kept changing as the UCI vacillated over (among other things) whether it was a new record or a continuation from Merckx, and they only produced a definitive set of rules with a couple of hours to go.

Chris's first hour in 1993 had been just as difficult. He hadn't been able to persuade any sponsors to back the attempt fully, so he ended up paying for most of it himself. Then he'd had trouble getting himself and his team and equipment to Bordeaux. In the end they managed – incredibly – to borrow one of the Rolling Stones' tour trucks, only to get to customs and find they didn't have the correct documentation. You can imagine:

Bemused Customs Official: So this is your truck? (Looks at large 'tongue' logo on truck.)

Team Boardman: Well no, actually it belongs to the Rolling Stones. We borrowed it.

BCO: Of course you did. And can you give me Mick Jagger's phone number so I can check with him?

TB: Ah, you see, he's on tour in America, so you can't really get in touch with him. But we're on our way to break the world hour record, and Mick is a really big cycling fan so he lent it to us. We've got lots of bikes in the back, and this is Chris, he won an Olympic gold medal.

BCO: Please get out of the truck and come with me . . .*

Then, a few days before the attempt, Boardman woke up to find that Obree had broken Moser's nine-year-old record. Understandably, he was a bit put out. Chris said he felt Obree's timing had been unsporting, presumably because the attempt was announced only after Boardman had made his own plans public.

Not surprisingly there was continuing tension between the riders. When Obree came back the following year and took the record back from Boardman, Chris said that he felt Obree's approach had devalued the record. 'It's not a magical thing any more. When Graeme said, "Look at my bike, it's worth fifty pounds and made of washing-machine parts", it didn't help the record.'

Boardman wanted to be part of the elite of world cycling. He found that hard to reconcile with having his record broken by someone as wilfully offbeat as Obree, a man fuelled by cornflakes and marmalade sandwiches, who built his own bike and then rode it as if he was a circus act.

I could be thankful for one thing: it seemed unlikely that my target was going to move. I'll admit, though, that I did check the cycling news websites each day just in

* Mick Jagger actually *is* a cycling fan and, improbable though it seems, he and Charlie Watts were in Mexico City to see Francesco Moser's second hour ride in 1984. His personal assistant told *Cycling Weekly* that the track Moser used was just like the one in Welwyn Garden City. I'm prepared to bet that is the only similarity between Mexico City and Welwyn Garden City.

case. Maybe one of the stars was having a secret go at it – there were always rumours about Lance Armstrong. Or maybe some wild Italian version of Graeme Obree would come out of the bushes and break it, presumably on a diet of Nutella, with his mother holding the stopwatch.

I should really have been concentrating on things that might actually happen.

I had only two races left before the big one. One was a 20-mile national series event in Kent, on a hot, sunny afternoon. I won pretty comfortably, catching second-placed Gethin Butler who'd started two minutes before me, shortly before the finish. I'd expected to beat him, but not by that margin.* More to the point, I rode strongly. The data showed that my power output had been well above what I reckoned I had to manage for the hour record. After the difficulties of the two national championship events, I really needed a good, relaxed performance like this one. I know it's easy to perform well at a race that is not tremendously important, but that doesn't mean you don't go home happy.

The following weekend's race was good too, another national championship, this time over 50 miles. I won, again fairly comfortably. Even if the earlier, more fiercely contested championships had hardly gone to plan, at least I was going into the hour with a couple of wins. It meant

---

* Gethin is a top-class bike rider, most noted for his long-distance rides; he holds the Land's End to John O'Groats record with 1 day, 20 hours and 4 minutes for the 840 miles. He then doodled around northern Scotland in the lashing rain for another 7 hours 55 minutes so that he could break the 1000-mile record as well, which I think shows a certain fortitude. Though, as he pointed out himself, 'There's not much else to do up there.'

that *Cycling Weekly* could unapologetically puff the attempt a bit, with more big pictures and the leading news article. It ended with the Italian cry of encouragement: *Forza Hutch!* It was, for *Cycling Weekly*, an uncharacteristic piece of dynamism.

The level of general enthusiasm continued to surprise me. There was a genuine swell of support, from the press, and from people at the races I did. I felt I was being cast – a bit prematurely, granted – as the successor to Boardman and Obree. It was nice to be taken seriously as a contender. I'd been prepared for rather more hostility.

The Internet message-boards, for instance, I carefully ignored. I was expecting rather a lot of 'What the hell is he playing at?', 'Who does he think he is? How dare he try and break Boardman's record?', 'Wanker!' I'm thick-skinned enough not to be too worried, but there didn't seem a lot of point in spending what spare moments I had reading abuse. I only looked at the messages some months later. What most of them had really said was: 'Best of luck to him', 'It's great to see someone having a go.' I wished I'd read them earlier.

Cyclists are a hard-bitten lot – years of fighting losing battles with the modern car-centred world, I suppose – and rarely given to outbreaks of enthusiasm about anything. All the warm messages of support and good luck were a little unnerving. I guess this was how a band-wagon looked when it got going. It was nice to know that if I slipped up, it was right behind me. Ready to run me over.

Ah yes. Slip up. I *still* didn't have the famous frames, and I was going to look pretty daft trying to break the hour record without a bike. Dave and I were edging back onto speaking terms after a row – I don't remember what about, but I'm sure I remember being right. Dave's peace offering had been to ring me the morning the attempt went public and say, 'Michael, I was wondering what I should put on the company website. I wouldn't want to get it wrong; I know how much that would annoy you. So I thought I'd better clear everything with you.'

I could tell we were talking again because he rang me another three times that morning to clear each sentence of his announcement: 'We're proud to announce that Michael Hutchinson will be attacking the Hour Record on 2nd July. The attempt will be at Manchester Velodrome at 7 p.m. Contact the Velodrome for tickets.' I told him it was barely capable of being improved upon.

I always had to remind myself that Dave was helping me with this project for free; it wasn't really going to do much in the way of generating publicity for his business. In the end he was doing it out of friendship, and for the love of it. I tried, if I could, not to be too demanding. But by the Monday after the National 50 we had only ten days to go until the attempt, and there was still no sign of the frames. While I didn't want to look hysterical, it was time for a bit of prodding.

Dave told me that the frames were in Holland, at Giant's European head-office, and would be with me the following week, probably the Monday that was two days before the attempt. I was not impressed.

'No, Dave!' I took a deep breath, 'I'm not cutting it that fine. I'll end up trying to build the damn bikes in a hotel bedroom with a Swiss army knife.'

'That's the next shipment, there's nothing they can do.'

'Don't they have couriers in Holland?'

'Yes, but it has to go with the delivery. That's the way they always do it. It's not worth arguing about.'

It was time to press the nuclear button. I had acquired, somewhere along the line, the phone number for one of the Giant Europe big cheeses. This was a man who was a long way up the food chain. I'd never had the nerve to use the number, which was probably a bit anal of me, because Dave was my contact with Giant and I hadn't wanted to go over his head. I was going to use my advantage in a clever and original way, one that meant I didn't have to invest any more than the bare minimum of effort.

'Dave, I've got this number here. Why don't I just give him a ring and see if I can sort something out with him myself?'

There followed a short silence.

'Leave it with me, Mike.'

And so it was arranged. Someone from Giant would be dispatched to bring the frames personally to Heathrow. I would meet them, collect the frames, and they would fly back to Holland on the next aeroplane. Now that (albeit a month late) was more like it. That was the relationship a record-breaker had with his sponsors.

It was still going to be tight, though. The handover was scheduled for Wednesday, and I had my last track session the next morning. If anything went wrong, at the attempt I'd have to ride a bike I'd never sat on before. That didn't seem a very sensible approach. But I didn't have much choice. The bike I'd been using in testing was difficult to steer and too tiring to ride on the constant curves of the track.

★

With ten days to go, the training had slackened off for a last period of rest. Rest is as important as training. It's only while you rest that you get stronger. There is always the danger of training too hard, of doing more than your body will recover from. Then you end up trying to do more and more as you grow weaker and weaker, and your form slips catastrophically away. That's why compulsive exercisers make bad athletes: they can't rest. Most endurance athletes have a story about a period, normally following some great success, where they decided the route to the next level consisted of doing more. Normally disaster follows. I can't help but suspect that Paula Radcliffe's famous crumpling in the 2004 Olympic marathon had a lot to do with the idea that more is better.★

But it's awfully hard to be that objective about your own training. It's part of who you are; for a full-time athlete it's what you're for. Most of us are no more likely to recognise that we're doing too much than we are to wake up one morning and decide over breakfast that really we're rude, ugly and that our breath smells. Even if you do, you probably won't actually do anything about it.

Unfortunately for athletes like me, even if you're highly resistant to resting, everyone knows that the last act before a big target is big rest. It's called the taper. You reduce your training load one last time to try to reach a

★ She would not have been the first; British marathoner Ron Hill used the same logic to get himself dumped out of the back of the 1972 Olympic marathon, a race he would probably have won if he'd asked no more of himself than that he train as he had before.

fully recovered state. It is, if you like, the last push for the summit of condition. Except that when I say push, what I really mean is sleep in a hammock and read a good book. It's the bit of training that looks like it's going to be a big hit with everyone.

Except that it's not, not when you have to get into your hammock and get on with it. It makes you jumpy, irritable. I always feel as if I should be doing something. As usual, it's the loss of control that gets me. So far as hard work is concerned, you can't do any more. You just have to rest and hope you got it right. Even if you taper perfectly, you're only going to get back what you invested, so all you can think about is the handful of days when you knocked off early, when it rained and you didn't feel like it.

For the first couple of days I managed the rest thing rather well, I felt. I did the sessions I'd specified for myself, and no more. I read a good book – though not so good that I can remember what it was. I ignored ringing telephones and e-mails, and I stopped opening letters. If anyone had rung the doorbell, I'd have ignored that too. I made a device for measuring the altitude of the Heathrow-bound aeroplanes out of a ruler and a bit of wood, and spent an afternoon preparing a histogram illustrating what I'd discovered. I worked out the mean altitude and standard deviation. It was nice to think that an A-level in statistics hadn't been time wasted. Once or twice I managed to forget about the hour for a few minutes.

When Louisa flustered in from work and asked me how I'd spent the day, I would explain all this from a reclining position, and then politely ask her if she wouldn't mind cooking a meal, since I didn't want to stand up and risk tiring myself out. All the energy drains out of your feet, you know. If you keep them off the ground you're okay. Yep, Monday and Tuesday went well.

Wednesday rolled round. Frame day at last. I got the Tube to Heathrow. I figured a couple of frames wouldn't be very heavy, and it would be faster by public transport. I was to meet a very tall man called Dirk, flying in from Amsterdam at 12.05 p.m.

Terminal 4 was crowded, and I had half an hour to wait. The couple of days' taper had so far made me feel restless and fretful. I felt I hadn't trained enough, and now I felt I wasn't resting enough, either. I should have been at home, but I was trailing around an airport. I couldn't even sit down; the benches were crowded and I was worried about catching a cold. That would have ruined everything. I really hated this. I felt hot and tired and grimy and pissed off.

Of course the flight was late, by 90 minutes. More wandering about, trying to stay away from other people. I might have had a coffee, but I'd given up caffeine. Caffeine is an ergogenic – it makes you go faster, but only if you're not too habituated to it. I love coffee, but giving it up was another noble act of self-denial. All this self-flagellation. Really it's a shame I wasn't born a Catholic.

At 1.30 the flight landed, and I elbowed my way to a place against the tubular-steel fence that faced the Arrivals door. I'd made a sign with a Giant promotional sticker, and I held it up like a taxi driver. Me, the star of the hour, running his own errands.

It could have been worse. A couple of places down the

fence, in the plum spot bang opposite the door, was a middle-aged man who'd been standing there since I arrived in the building more than two hours previously. He was easy to spot because he could have fidgeted for Britain. He stood on tiptoe every few seconds. Or he clenched his buttocks. Or he twisted a finger in his ear. He didn't ever actually hop from foot to foot, but he looked like he wanted to. He smelled slightly of sweat and a cooked breakfast, and he made me look relaxed and fancy-free.

What made him really stand out, though, could only be seen from the front. Like at least half of us at the fence, he was holding a sign. Unlike the rest of us, his sign was decorated with pink-and-blue ribbons and balloons and the message was written in glitter. It said, 'Kuala – Mrs David Simmonds to be! Welcome to England my Little Lady!'

I realised with excitement that this was a man waiting for his mail-order bride. I'd never really believed there was such a thing, but here he was. I was captivated. He'd been clenching his buttocks by the fence for two hours now. Had she failed to show? It looked like it. Had she missed the flight, or had she arrived on time, taken a look at him and walked on by? Had the second possibility occurred to him yet? When it did, would he start crying? How long would he stand here? Had he stood here before, waiting for a woman he'd never met?

'Michael?' Someone touched my elbow. It was Dirk, and he was as tall as I'd been promised. I'd been so immersed in projecting a fantasy life onto the man with the glittering sign and the miserable face that I hadn't noticed him.

We went to wait by the baggage reclaim, and talked about the hour, how it was going. I thanked him for coming over; having thrown a bit of a strop about the frames' delivery, I now felt a little guilty at all the trouble I'd caused. 'No problem. Just think, when you break the record, I'll be able to say you couldn't have done it without me.' I felt even more guilty.

A vast box was pushed into the baggage hall; too big for the carousel, too big for the oversized luggage conveyor. Inevitably it was ours, and I swear it was big enough to hold twenty frames. 'I think there's another bike in there. We'll have it picked up from you sometime,' said Dirk. We shook hands, and he headed back towards the gates, presumably to get straight back onto the same aeroplane back to Amsterdam. I was left alone with the box.

The guilt about Dirk's journey evaporated. A bike frame weighs a bit more than a kilo. Forks, maybe another 300 grams. Taking a couple of bike frames on the Tube would have been no problem. But now I had a box about the size and shape of an upright piano. It weighed only marginally less. God alone knew what was in it – two frames and a bike didn't weigh this much. I had no idea how I was going to get it home. This was too much.

It was too big to get on a trolley and too heavy to carry, so I just pushed it across the floor as it was. Pushing it worked okay on the polished terminal floor, but it was harder on the concrete Tube platform. My hamstrings felt tight, and my lower back ached. I lugged the bloody thing onto a train and sat down beside it. This was so far from how you're supposed to spend the last week before trying to beat a world record.

When I got off the Tube, the bus driver wouldn't let me onto the bus with it. The first two taxi drivers at whom I waved pretended they couldn't see me, and when one finally did stop, I discovered the sodding box wouldn't fit into a taxi anyway. So I dragged it all the way home, about a mile and a quarter. It was ridiculous, but I couldn't think of anything else to do. There were polar explorers who had less trouble from their luggage than this. When I finally lumped it up three storeys to my flat, one stair at a time, and dragged it into the hall, I was exhausted. The whole trip had taken almost five hours, and to hell with the renouncement of caffeine – I needed a cup of tea.

I had the tea, and I showered off the sticky feel of the Underground in summer. I wanted to be clean for the big moment. I got a penknife and slit the parcel tape. There were the two frames in there, in an extravagance of cardboard packing, and a big black PVC bag. I fished the bag out. It was heavy, and it contained a folding bike. It was that and the packing material that had made it so heavy. Never mind. Now, finally, the yellow-and-black frames themselves emerged from the box in a shower of packaging.

They were useless. They didn't conform to the regulations. Despite our sending over a specification so extensive that you could practically hop on and ride it, someone somewhere had screwed up. You will recall the UCI's specifications: all the frame tubes have to be round. On the new frames, the seat-tube (the one that joins the saddle to the bottom bracket) was a sharp, angular diamond section. There was no commissaire on Earth stupid enough to miss it. I'd had two lumps of scrap metal flown halfway round the world.

CHAPTER 9

I HAD A WEEK TO GO TILL THE ATTEMPT, AND I DIDN'T even have a bike, or any immediate prospect of one turning up. Ferdinand Bracke might only have ridden his record bike the morning before the attempt, but I'm pretty confident he didn't just turn up to the track hoping he could borrow something.

That approach has been tried, though. In the mid-1990s one of the worst hour attempts ever took place when a guy from Cambridge called Tony Adams gave it a go. He was notorious at the time locally, because his training regime was based on belting round the pedestrianised area of the city centre on a full-blown time-trial bike. For maximum effect it was apparently necessary to do this at pub closing time on a Friday or Saturday night.

Eventually the local police blew the dust off an ancient by-law and charged him with the nineteenth-century offence of 'furious pedalling'. And a good thing too, though it didn't seem to prevent him turning up on the front page of the *Guardian*, which seemed to think he'd been rather hard done by. They might have thought differently if they'd ever seen Tony careering along a crowded street in the dark, yelling at people to get out of his way.

Tony's plan was to go to the Manchester Velodrome, hire a bike and get someone (anyone) to time an hour and count the laps. Then he would presumably write to the UCI and claim the record. It seems unlikely that the UCI would have accepted this system, even if it would make record administration rather easier.

In the end it wasn't really an issue. Tony was a very long way short of setting any records. His expectations were based on covering 30 miles in an hour on a road near Cambridge, in the slipstream of a convenient bus. Unfortunately there were no buses available to pace him in the Velodrome. In any event, a Mancunian bus driver would be unlikely to last a whole hour in close proximity to a cyclist without trying to run him over.

If we rule the likes of Mr Adams out of this, I don't think anyone had let themselves get into the position I was in. Professional pride is normally at stake. For instance, Merckx's record bike was built personally by Ernesto Colnago, the most famous of frame-builders, and I find it hard to imagine him lousing the thing up. ('No, Eddy, Thursday for sure, I promise . . .') Not with a bike for Merckx anyway. He was notoriously picky about his equipment – Claudine Merckx admitted that Eddy sometimes got up in the night to go to his workshop and tinker with his bikes.

Colnago responded by building the finest bike ever made, the 'queen of bicycles' for the king of cyclists. I saw it a few years ago, painted in a flat shade of orange and looking distinctly tired from its decades of touring bike-shows and charity dinners. I felt guilty about even noticing that, surrounded as I was by a press of moist-eyed middle-aged men, finally realising an ambition by seeing it with their own eyes. Cyclists are fond of claiming religious overtones to their hobby, and nowhere more so than in the adoration of holy relics.*

Chris Boardman bikes are the most sought-after by British fans. Bikes allegedly used by Boardman have multiplied like the splinters of the True Cross, which if assembled into a single crucifix would pose a hazard to passing aeroplanes. There are hundreds of Boardman bikes out there; he must have used a fresh one every day. I'm almost the only person I know who doesn't have one.

Most successful hour attempts, like Merckx's, avoid last-minute panics with equipment. Boardman cut it as fine as any during his first attempt, when he didn't take delivery of the bikes until a week to go. In the end he wasn't much impressed; he later claimed they were 'the least aerodynamic shape imaginable' which was probably a bit harsh. Chris even managed to get the bikes for his athlete's hour ready in time, in spite of the UCI's vacillation about the exact rules to which they had to conform.

The best precedent I could find for my predicament was Obree's first hour. We all know about his home-made 'Old Faithful', but the machine he used for his first,

---

* At the risk of accusations of heresy, I'll mention a journalist who told me he'd flown from one bike-show to another, and found that Merckx's hour bike was on display at both of them. He conceded that it was just possible they were the same bike, but maintained that his journey was sufficiently direct that the bike would have had to be whipped off one stand as he left, be flown in the same plane he was and have overtaken him at the other end.

failed hour-record attempt in Norway was actually a slick carbon-fibre version produced by Mike Burrows, the man who designed the Lotus superbike.

The first time Graeme saw it was only the night before the attempt. He did a handful of laps on it, and liked it enough to use it the next day. And of course the next day he came up short, and blamed it largely on the bike. He had to go back to Old Faithful before he got the record. Not exactly encouraging from my point of view, especially since I didn't even have an old faithful of my own to fall back on.

I could see a consistent pattern. Successful record cyclists have a bike to ride. Peering dumbly into the entrails of packaging spilling from the Giant box, I couldn't see where mine was going to come from. This was a serious crisis. I had the record scheduled, the press coverage in full swing and probably a couple of thousand people coming to watch. I was planning to break the world hour record, for Christ's sake. This was not me and a few mates going down the pub to see how many beer mats we could flip. Having to call the whole thing off because I didn't have a bike was unthinkable. But I didn't have a bike. And however unthinkable it was, I couldn't think of anything else.

I sat on the floor, and not for the first time in the hour project felt dizzy. I was angry. I'd been let down; it had never even occurred to me that anyone could possibly mess up building something this simple. That was the whole point of the athlete's record – it was simple. And they'd taken so long over messing it up that I'd now got almost no chance of sorting it out.

I was tired and frustrated from my trip to the airport to

get the box, and I nursed a particular resentment towards the small, yet spectacularly heavy folding bike that had been foisted onto me. I kicked it, which made me feel a little better but didn't ultimately solve anything. Still, it was more productive than my next move, which was ringing Dave.

'You're sure it's not legal? Have you checked the rules?'

'Dave, I know the rules. This is useless. The question is what do we do.'

'Nothing we can do. We'll call it off.'

'We definitely can't get a frame done in five days?'

'You could in theory, but no one will actually do it. Frame-builders are artists, Mike. They aren't motivated by money; they do it for the love of it.'

Most of a year's work was falling in flames around my head, and this was the best Dave could offer. I couldn't believe it.

And then there was a sudden, magical feeling of release. Why not let go? Just give up. The record project was stressful and difficult and expensive. It was giving me headaches and chest pains, and I hadn't slept peacefully for weeks and weeks. I suddenly felt that, however good being the world hour record-holder might be, it couldn't justify all this. Nothing could be that good. I could let it go, and pick up a normal life again. Best of all, I could blame it all on someone else and assure everyone that, had I not been let down, I would have stamped all over the record. It vaguely occurred to me that issuing such a press release would lose me my job, but the thought of a record-attempt-free life was so attractive that it really didn't seem important.

I listened to Dave without complaint. When he'd finished, I said thank you, and goodbye. I could feel the frown I'd worn for weeks uncrinkling. I was happy. This afternoon I would read a book; I would be able to concentrate at last. Maybe I'd have a cup of tea, or maybe I'd just sleep. I needed to sleep. I rang Louisa to tell her it was over.

'Like fuck it is,' she said.

'Sorry?' Louisa and I had been together for most of ten years, and I'd heard her swear maybe half a dozen times. She swore only when she was properly angry.

'Don't walk away from this. You've spent months on it – it's all you've talked about since January. There's a problem, so we'll sort it. I'll speak to Dave. What's his number?'

This was not really what I'd expected, and in some ways it wasn't really what I wanted. I'd had a glimpse of liberty and I liked it. I hesitated.

'It's okay, I've found it,' she said. 'Speak to you soon.' She put the phone down.

Dark clouds rolled over the sun. My face folded back into the frown. Now I had to go to Manchester again. The trip had been planned as the try-out for the new frames, and to do a final record pace trial. In the few giddy record-free minutes I'd obviously abandoned the idea. But if the attempt was back on – as Louisa, of all people, seemed determined it was – then this was something that needed to be done after all. I'd packed my bag before the trip to Heathrow. I put it in the car, along with the test bike, and reluctantly headed north.

Before I left I rang my contact at Giant Europe. He wasn't there, and I left a message. I was relieved; I wasn't sure what I was going to say to him anyway.

Meanwhile, a few miles across London, Louisa was on the phone to Dave. This probably came as something of a surprise to him. He gave her the same speech he'd given me, the bit about the artistic sensibilities of frame-builders: 'They're just not motivated by money, that's the problem.'

'Rubbish,' said Louisa. 'Everyone is motivated by money. It's just a question of how much. What will it take to solve this?'

Dave maintained that no amount of money in the world would make a frame-builder work over a weekend, which would be required.

'That's okay,' said Louisa. 'Why don't you give me a few phone numbers for frame-builders, and I'll see what I can do?'

He was happy enough to do that.

Dave then rang me. He assured me that she had no chance of succeeding. 'You might be able to build a steel frame in three or four days, but it takes ages to paint it. You need several coats, and they all need time to dry.'

'Do we need to paint it?' I asked. 'It isn't going to rust in three days.'

There was a sort of offended-sounding silence. Eventually he said, 'It would look dreadful, Mike.'

I was in a hot car, stuck in the perpetual traffic jam by Birmingham, and I didn't know if there was the slightest point in being there. I'd had enough of this. I felt as if I'd got nothing left to give. I had tried my best to make this thing happen, but it had still come down to farce. Right now, staring at the back of the white transit in front, I was no closer to being able to mount a successful attempt than

I had been six or seven months ago, despite hundreds of hours of work and thousands of pounds spent on equipment and track hire fees. *And it wasn't my fault.*

As the traffic inched forwards I rang Andrea, just to tell her what was going on. There wasn't anything she could do for me, and she sounded as dispirited as I felt. When we'd finished I turned my phone off. I knew Dave or Louisa was likely to be looking for me, but I was close to breaking point. I suspected that the next time the phone rang, I would hurl it out of the car window.

Eventually I got to Manchester as the scorching afternoon started to cool into evening. Another quiet night in the cheap hotel. I spoke to Louisa. She hadn't really made a lot of progress. She wasn't very clear about what she was looking for. (Louisa: Okay Dave, what am I looking for? Dave: It's pretty complicated. I don't think you'd understand. Louisa: I don't need to understand, I just need to be able to tell them what we need.) It was hard to get anyone to take her seriously, and she was beginning to wonder if maybe they weren't motivated by money after all. She got a fair bit of 'Well, miss, ask your boyfriend what he wants and maybe get him to give us a ring' and not much else. A couple of people had laughed at her outright.

Despite a lot of panicky effort, all that had happened since I had taken the dud frames out of their box was that I'd made it to Manchester. There still didn't seem to be much point in being there.

I slept badly – no surprise there. My heart thumped all night, and I just lay awake. Properly awake, and bored, not the sort of half-asleep state where you're only just aware of time passing. It was hot and I lay on top of the covers, staring at the thin stripes of street light that leaked round the cheap blinds onto the walls and ceiling. I got up to watch TV for a while, but it didn't help. It was like jet-lag. I was still awake at dawn, so I only fell asleep just in time for the alarm clock to wake me up.

It was a lovely summer morning. It seemed a cruel counterpoint to the frustration and confusion. At the track, Andrea had been having a rummage around to see if there was anything she could find that might do as a spare if I used the test bike – wonky steering and all – for the attempt. All the dust-encrusted machinery in the bowels of the Velodrome was in some respect or other too modern for the UCI's idea of an hour-record bike.

We started to get ready for a trial that had been planned in more confident times. If we yet managed to sticky-tape an attempt together, we needed to know just where I was physically. It felt odd to worry about me, rather than the other problems. I was the least of my worries.

I'd been tapering off my training for almost a week. What we hoped we'd find in the trial was that I was in record condition already, and that the second week of rest would just be there to add a bit of insurance. Waiting for fitness that didn't yet exist, to go with a bike that didn't yet exist, would be a step too far into optimistic fantasy.

Bike ready, tyres pumped. I struggled into my new super-tight skinsuit, the one I never managed to test. In its unworn state it was about the size of a child's T-shirt. Stretched onto me, it was like a balloon, so tight that the black printing went pale grey.

It felt fast. Well, it felt uncomfortable, which usually amounts to the same thing. I couldn't stand upright in it, there was simply not enough material from chin to groin.

An absent-minded attempt to straighten up ended painfully. I was bent over, trying to clean my glasses, when the man from Giant rang me back. Standing in the posture of a man talking down a well, I told him about the frame problem. He was suitably horrified, and I was delighted that he was horrified.

I suppose he was well aware that having to cancel very publicly an attempt on the hour record because one of the world's biggest bike-makers couldn't successfully toss a couple of frames together would be pretty embarrassing – though I'm not sure that anyone would decline to buy a Giant bike as a direct result (I know my head doesn't work that way).

At the time, of course, I was functioning on a more self-centred level. I wanted help, and I didn't care about its motivation.

'We'll fix this. What did Dave say?'

'He said to call it off, that there's no chance of getting a frame built in time.'

'Who has he tried?'

'I don't know whether he's tried anyone. He hasn't told me.'

'I will speak to him.'

And he was gone. According to my phone, the call had lasted slightly more than a minute. No promises made, but for the first time I had grounds for hope.

It meant that the trial felt like something better than a waste of time. The idea was to replicate the first 20–30 minutes of the attempt. The first 10 minutes were more or less all right. Not easy, but I was about on the pace. The bike's iffy steering bothered me more than it ever had, because there now seemed some risk that it might be the only bike I would have. Whatever happened, I wouldn't be able to do myself justice on it.

From this one negative thought, the cracks spread. Suddenly I felt tired. I hadn't slept. I'd had an agonising twenty-four hours. I started to slow down, not because I was near my limit, but because there wasn't enough life left in me. I dropped away from record pace without really putting up much of a struggle.

I stopped at 20 minutes. I'd averaged 49kph, about 166m down on where I needed to be, and I'd been getting slower. In an hour I'd have been lucky to hang on to 48km. I really didn't know what to make of it. If I'd thought it was the best I could do, I'd have told the man from Giant to forget about solving the problem: we'd let each other down, and we should just leave it where it lay. He didn't have the frame, and I didn't have the legs.

On the other hand, I knew that I was in as bad a state as I'd ever tried to perform in. If I'd averaged record pace, I'd have been jubilant; I'd have known that a week of resting and other people solving problems would gain me a nice bonus to act as insurance. But it's only a bonus when you already have what you need. Now I was depending on it.

I got out of the horribly tight skinsuit and had a shower. My testicles had been squeezed back to a place they hadn't been in many years. (I subsequently found an unauthorised photo of myself wearing this suit on a Lycra-fetishist website. And my mother wonders why I won't teach her how to use the Internet.)

Back to the track centre, and the inevitable conference. 'Let's face it,' said Andrea, 'we're guessing. We don't really know much more about how you're going to get on than we did when we started. And you don't have a bike. In fact, if having a go at the hour record next week had only occurred to you this morning, we'd be in about the same position.'

'It's been a worthwhile six months.'

Elsewhere, the man from Giant had spent a few minutes on the phone. He'd found, apparently without significant difficulty, a frame-builder, at Roberts in Croydon, who was prepared to build (and paint) a frame for the following Monday. Obviously he was happy to risk being thrown out of the frame-builders' brotherhood for his embracing of Mammon.

This can't have taken very long, because by the time I'd finished the trial ride there was a message on my phone giving me the gist of it. The message was from Louisa, and quite who spoke to her I don't know.

Things were at last beginning to swing back my way. I should have made the most of it – gone back home and tried to relax. But for some reason I didn't articulate at the time, and which I can only guess at now, I decided that it was a good idea for me to stay in Manchester for another day to ride a similar trial to the one just failed. This was patent lunacy. I can only assume that London must have seemed too close to the action, and I wanted to stay out of the way of the next disaster. If I hid in Manchester, with my phone turned off, it wouldn't be able to find me. 'Go home!' said Andrea. I should have listened.

I spent another hot, restless day in my crummy hotel room. It was as hot as it had been the previous night, and the Hyde Road roaring past below the window left fresh air in short supply. Meals consisted of cereal consumed straight out of the box, because I was too scared of catching a cold to go out.* I spent most of the afternoon and evening half-asleep, and by the time night came, it didn't even seem relevant. I'd lost my grip on the whole day/night thing entirely. I drifted in and out of consciousness until morning, like a child with a fever.

Not surprisingly, the following morning's ride was no better than the previous one. It was no worse, either. It was just a waste of time, and precious energy. At last, a day too late, I packed up to go home.

'So that's it then,' said Andrea, 'next stop the hour record.'

I carted my stuff out to the sunny car park and my baking-hot car and went home. One week to go.

On this hot, sunny Friday, Louisa was at a picnic in Whitstable in Kent. This was her employers' idea of a treat. To enhance the experience, the location of the picnic was a secret; employees were divided into teams and dispatched on a treasure hunt round the town to find it.

This was a bit of a distraction for someone who had unexpectedly become the lynchpin of Team Hutchinson.

---

* Cereal is a recurring theme of Obree's book. Before his first successful attempt, he wrote that he got up every couple of hours during the night to do some stretches and eat cornflakes. Best of all, when he arrived late at the first team meeting of the pro team he signed for in 1994 and found that there was no food left, he said, 'I'd have gone hungry if I had not had my usual emergency supply of cornflakes and skimmed milk with me.' This is a man who carries his own milk supply. Now that's preparation.

Louisa had received her first phone call from Dave before the train to Whitstable had left Victoria station. He rang twice more on the train ride, once to tell her what colour he was arranging to have the frame painted, and once to check that we already had a pair of forks for it. Clearly he'd decided that Louisa was a more reasonable person to do business with than me.

Louisa's team at the treasure hunt was somewhat handicapped by having a member of staff who had lived in Whitstable. Or so she claimed. Within two minutes of leaving the station they were lost, and while the other teams started to yomp from waymark to waymark using the cryptic clues provided, her team was lost in what looked (however improbable that might be) like Whitstable's red-light district.

Louisa's team finally got to the picnic by following another team (who turned out to be following yet another team, but no matter, they all got there in the end). Fish and chips at a hotel on the front was their reward, followed by an afternoon on Whitstable beach, which was not, Louisa tells me, nearly so bad as it sounds.

Dave rang during the meal to remind her that, with an alloy fork steering-column she would need a new star-fangled nut,* and said that he would send some over. He rang a couple more times during the afternoon to tell her about various potential minor problems he'd thought of, and then again to tell her how he'd solved them.

My experience was that Dave's initial reaction to a crisis tended to be somewhere between slightly panicky

---

* This is a real component, not the cycling equivalent of a skyhook or a bucket of blue steam.

and very panicky. But after he'd calmed down a bit he was usually pretty smart. Several of the calls he made to Louisa were to identify, and subsequently announce the solving of, problems that I certainly wouldn't have thought of until they'd developed into the next disaster.

The only thing irritating Louisa was that he kept telling her about it. Her contribution to the day's discussions was no more than 'Yes', 'Thanks', 'I don't understand', 'If you think that's a good idea', 'I'm sure that's best, Dave' as seemed appropriate.

Meanwhile she was trying to give the impression to those around her that the picnic was actively enhancing her employment experience. Or that she was being more effectively integrated into the company ethos. Or whatever it was they'd been taken to Whitstable for, when they'd all presumably rather have had an afternoon off.

Her patience was not due entirely to her placid nature. She knew that if she told Dave to leave her alone, he'd ring me instead. Then I'd ring her to moan about Dave ringing me all the time, and I'd take even longer about it than Dave, because I'd have to tell her what he'd said before I could start complaining. It was easier for everyone her way.

Louisa's role in the attempt had suddenly become awfully hands-on. I suppose she'd planned to come up and shout encouragement, and give thanks that whatever happened she wouldn't have to listen to me talking about the record any more. If you've seen the film *The Final Hour*, that's pretty much what Sally Boardman spent the first half-hour of the attempt doing. Later, though, when it was clear that Chris was on the edge, she went to the trackside to do some shouting, which Chris later admitted unnerved him so much that it probably did more harm than good.

On the other hand, Anne Obree seems to have played a crucial role in getting Graeme to his second Norwegian attempt intact, after the failure of the previous day. According to Graeme, it was Anne who took command, taking him back to the hotel and chasing everyone else away to give him the peace to prepare himself.

Overall, though, the function of wives, girlfriends and assorted others has been rather more . . . well, *decorative* really. (I've had jobs I'd have been fired from for saying that, and I've just said goodbye to any hope of picking up my career as a university lecturer.) Like when Jacques Anquetil presented his wife Janine with the bike he rode in his 1967 attempt (the one he was disqualified from, for refusing the dope test). I'm sure she was thrilled.

Janine was not otherwise entirely typical, it has to be said. She was five years older than Jacques, and when he first met her in March 1957 she was already married, to Jacques' doctor. She was initially rather unimpressed by the young, hypochondriac cyclist who took up so much of her husband's time – time that she as a nurse thought he might better spend with people who were properly sick. She quickly changed her mind, as Jacques turned the full glare of his (rarely seen) charm on her.

The affair remained secret until Jacques joined Janine and her family on a skiing trip early in 1958. He asked her to come and live with him. She refused. A few days after the holiday, unable to bear the separation, he travelled from the South of France to her home in Normandy to take her away. Putting a raincoat over her nightclothes, she went with him, in a borrowed van, to Paris. Were it not for the involvement of Anquetil – a cold and decidedly unromantic figure – and the betrayal of her apparently blameless husband, it would be a rather lovely tale of a classic elopement. She bought clothes for her new life in Paris the following morning, in the most fashionable boutiques.

Jacques' aloof personality was rooted in shyness. The older, slightly maternal Janine was an essential support to his career. She turned up at races to comfort him, in an era when riders' wives were either banned or simply stayed away. No one really seemed to think there was anything odd about it; somehow the normal rules didn't apply to her. The only problem was that she couldn't have any more children. This was a terrible disappointment to Jacques.

How terrible a disappointment soon became clear, as Anquetil's hitherto only moderately scandalous private life slithered off into exciting new territory. He had a daughter, Sophie, with Janine's daughter from her first marriage (his step-daughter). Not actually incest, admittedly, but really only on a technicality. Janine raised her grandchild as her own. Eventually, though, she left Jacques and moved from Normandy to Paris.

Having a failed marriage with the older Janine behind him, Jacques decided to sample the joys of a younger woman, and started a relationship with Dominique, who had previously been married to Janine's son Alain. (Frankly Alain should have seen this coming; Jacques had cast moral caution to the wind some time previously.) She moved in with Jacques in 1984, and they had a son in 1987. It was the last great joy of Anquetil's life: shortly after the birth he was diagnosed with stomach cancer. He died a few months later aged just fifty-three.*

Louisa was not – not yet anyway – having to put up with this kind of thing. (Nor was her brother, nor her brother's girlfriend, nor her mother, nor her step-mother.)

London was still hot when I got back, and a haze of pollution hung in the air. It was Friday night, and outside every pub people were having an after-work drink. It was four or five months since I'd had a beer, or even gone out for an evening. Everything revolved around good recovery, avoiding infection.

Driving through a sticky city on a hot evening looking at the life I'd eschewed, it felt as if I'd got it wrong, and everyone else had got it right. I'd stopped enjoying this. Looking back at the sacrifices I'd made to get this far, I felt like I'd been conned. The frame disaster, the lack of help – it had all thrown me badly off course. I'd started panicking about absolutely anything that might go wrong, however improbable. (I booked a second hotel for the night before the attempt in case the first one burned down. Now that's getting paranoid.)

I'm always nervous before big events, it's part of the deal. There's a lot of truth in the idea that to perform at your best you have to be slightly on edge. But you have

---

* For much more on Jacques Anquetil, see Richard Yates's book *Master Jacques* (2001), though I've told you most of the salacious stuff already. It's a pity, from my point of view, that Henri Pélissier, a prolific winner in a career lasting from 1911 to 1928, including the 1923 Tour de France, didn't break the hour record. He was shot – five times – by his lover, using the same gun that his wife had used to shoot herself two years previously.

to make sure it's a positive force. It's not 'nervousness', it's 'excitement'. You must never be 'anxious', but 'pumped up'. Not 'weak-kneed with terror and having to be physically restrained from running away', but 'energised'.

One of the characteristics of a natural champion is that they always see it the second way. They love the feeling of adrenalin; it's something they associate with success and achievement. Think about that next time your stomach is in a knot, waiting for a job interview or going into an exam. These people would be murmuring, 'Mmm, yes. That feels *good*. Bring it on!'

That's not really my natural inclination. I get nervous like everyone else, but usually I can turn it round and feed off it. This time that was hard. Normally I go into a race with some rough idea of what is going to happen. Not this time. I knew that a lot of people (well, a lot in a cycling context) were planning to come and watch me. That's not something I should have been dwelling on, but I couldn't help it. Quite a few people were planning 300- or 400-mile round trips. To see me. I'm too nice a guy not to feel some responsibility for that.

Worst of all, the process is reflexive. I knew I should be calm and relaxed; all my best racing performances were done when I was laid-back about it all. I was clearly far from relaxed. Now I was worrying about that in itself. And worrying about worrying about it. Like the infinitely receding reflections in two parallel mirrors, all I could see was tension. I needed to break the loop, and I'd only got a weekend to do it.

I got home not long before Louisa got back from Whitstable. As was normal for those days, my first thought was not 'Hello, dear, did you have a nice day?', but 'You'd better not have caught a cold.' I'd had enough practice to say the first one anyway.

The weekend wasn't too bad. Either the heat faded a little or I'd got used to it. I did the small amount of training I'd planned for the taper. The training schedule seemed to have been written out a very long time in the past. And the taper was wrecked anyway. Too much tension, too little sleep; too long in Manchester, too little rest. The circadian disorientation that had set in at the hotel didn't really go away, and I found I was getting to sleep later and later, and getting up later and later. In fact I never seemed to wake up properly at all. I was supposed to be getting stronger and stronger. That's not how it felt.

Over breakfast on Sunday, a meal that had slipped to about midday, Louisa said, 'Let's get out for a while. Why don't we go to the park? We could rent a rowing boat or something, so you're not on your feet for too long.'

It was a good idea, and I should just have said yes. I didn't want to do anything except rest, but the more I worried about it, the less I was able to do it. Going out for an hour might have helped. Instead, the thought of doing something just filled me with panic.

'No,' I said bluntly. It was a pretty ungracious response.

'Well, for God's sake do *something*,' she said. 'You're driving yourself mad.'

So I did. I put the test bike on the home trainer, and played with the position a bit. Last-minute tweaks are not a good idea, but at least it made me feel productive and – to some extent – in control. It wasn't exactly forgetting about the record, but I'd already proved I couldn't do that. Changing the angle of the bars to see if they could be made any more comfortable, changing the way the bar tape was applied – it was therapeutic. Peering at the details meant I could lose sight of the terrifying whole.

I must have played around for a couple of hours, by which time I was as relaxed as I'd been in days. My subconscious was astute enough to make sure I didn't make any major changes to the set-up, and I measured everything carefully so that I could replicate it exactly on the new bike for the attempt. I would have it tomorrow, and I'd booked the track for Tuesday – the day before the attempt – to ride it for the first time. I didn't dare to think of the consequences if there was a problem with it.

Louisa offered to go to Croydon on the Monday to get the frame. She probably knew I was going to ask her to do it anyway. I'm not quite so much of a bastard as I make out; I even felt a little guilty as she left.

The frame was supposed to be ready by mid-afternoon. Louisa was already on a train when she got a call to say that it would be another couple of hours. It wasn't worth coming home again, so she killed some time in a coffee shop, then got some food to take to Manchester that night. She went to a bike shop, looking for some spare chainrings I'd asked for. They didn't have them, but said they'd get some from their other shop. If she could come back at six, just before they closed? That should be fine.

She reckoned she might as well go on to the frame-builders. It was most of two miles away, on the northern side of Croydon. The shop was closed. Panicky hammering on the door brought someone from the workshop at the back, who let her in. He would be just a little longer, he said, and went back to work.

After a while he re-emerged. 'What do you want me to do about the headset? Do you want the cups put in, or do you just want to take them with you?' he asked. Louisa tossed up between ringing me or Dave. (My stress levels or hers, really.) She chose Dave. She started to convey his long, incomprehensible description of what was to be done.

When he got to, 'Now make sure he does that properly, it needs to be neat', she decided that it would be best not to start telling the nice man how to do his job. After all, he'd worked all weekend (in defiance of the union) for nothing more than money. So she handed over the phone so that Dave could take personal responsibility for the causing of offence.

She could hear Dave's voice buzzing on the phone, and see the frame-builder rolling his eyes towards the ceiling. She could also see the six o'clock deadline approaching: it was half-five already. The monologue continued for some time. It was many repetitious minutes before Dave became resigned to his powerlessness and let it go.

Twenty to six. She didn't feel she was in much of a position to ask the man to hurry. When he took the frame off the workstand and handed it over, it was a quarter to six, and she barely had time to say thank you as she dashed back out onto the pavement and hoofed it in the direction of the other shop.

It says something for Louisa's determination to keep the hour project on track that she was prepared to run a mile and three-quarters across Croydon in fifteen minutes carrying two bags of shopping and a bicycle frame.* She made it, crashing though the door on the dot of six.

By the time she got home it was seven o'clock. We'd planned to go to Manchester that night, but that had been abandoned some time ago. Now it was going to be an early start on Tuesday morning. Louisa started to cook, and I started to build the frame into a bicycle.

Normally assembling a track bike is pretty simple; all the work on a road bike is in setting up the gears and brakes, and of course a track bike has neither. I'd even got the measurements from the unsteerable test bike that was now going to be the spare, though God help me if I had to use it.

This time – and looking back on it, I can see there was a certain inevitability about it – the job turned out to be rather more difficult. Despite the absurd length of Dave's instructions, the forks didn't fit through the headset. I couldn't build the frame into a usable bike.

I wanted to go and hurl the new frame into the vast box that still stood in the hall containing the Giant duds. Then I was going to drag the box onto the street and leave it there. This being central London, it wouldn't be long before someone stole it, and I'd be rid of the hour project for ever. There was a sharp pain in my chest, and for a moment I seriously thought I was having a heart attack.

The hour project had changed into an ordeal, a trial by frustration and disappointment. I'd love to say that I was

---

* There was a woman in Louisa's running club who regularly ran the six miles home from work carrying two bags of shopping, and who was capable of making the trip in fifty minutes. But she'd had substantial practice, and she didn't usually carry a bike frame as well.

determined not to be beaten. But to be honest I didn't have the strength to give up.

There was nothing for it at nine o'clock on a Monday evening but Dave. God knows I didn't want to ring him, I'd avoided him for days, but at this time of night he was the only person I could think of who might have some suggestions about this. And, bless him, he did. He explained that some of the Giant forks had been erroneously manufactured with a slightly oversized area at the base of the steering-column, where it goes through the headset. The solution was to sandpaper off the excess. It was simple.

But then he spoiled it by telling me how the manufacturing error had occurred, which meant telling me how the forks were made in the first place. And also why with most headsets the excess didn't matter, and how sanding off the excess didn't compromise the structure of the fork at all, but filing it off would be a different matter. He kept me for nearly half an hour, which I spent saying nothing but 'Must be going . . .', 'Right, Dave, thanks . . .', 'Fuck me, is that the time?' Dinner had been hot, but by then it was cold again. Louisa and I were both on the verge of tears.

CHAPTER 10

TIME. IT'S NOT JUST ME — ALMOST EVERYONE involved in any kind of exercise or sport is obsessed with the passage of time. Either exercise is a trial to be endured for the minimum time possible, worked out and monitored to the second, or it's a predetermined distance to be completed quickly. Time is of the essence. As a psychological phenomenon, I imagine it's closely related to the one that causes otherwise sane people to drive a mile to the gym to walk two miles on a treadmill, and then drive a mile home. It's about being in control.

Successful athletes are just as obsessive; Paula Radcliffe said that, as a teenager, if she got back from a 20-minute training run after only 19 minutes, she would run round the house for a minute. (Round the outside, I would imagine.) Children might be keen on running around just for the hell of it, but they have that knocked out of them pretty early on in life, normally by school games teachers — upon which subject I really ought not to get started.*

---

* I used to run around for fun, until one day in 1980, aged six and inspired by Ovett and Coe's mile exploits, I decided I'd like to run a mile. I asked my father [cont'd]

So almost everyone who takes premeditated exercise uses a digital watch or clock. It's more precise that way, and that's the point. Particularly pessimistic users set it on a countdown, so that they can see how much longer they have to go. It's a little-known fact that the world now has more digital watches than insects.

For all this we have to thank Peter Dimitroff Petroff, a Bulgarian who worked in the US space industry – among other things, he was a member of the team led by Wernher von Braun that developed the Saturn V rocket for the *Apollo* missions. In the late 1960s Petroff invented the digital watch. The watch, with a red LED display, was put into production as the Pulsar in 1971, and retailed for $2100.

The more committed exerciser will not be content with just using a watch to measure quantity of training; they will want to measure quality as well. That gives you even more control. The heartrate monitor, a digital watch with a wireless link to an electrode belt round your chest, tells you your pulse. It's an indication of how hard you're working, and a handy alarm bell. If I'm racing, and see a pulse much over 185bpm, I know that trouble is just around the corner.

Curiously enough, the wireless heart rate monitor was also invented by Peter Dimitroff Petroff, though it wasn't until the early 1990s that it became a consumer product. Petroff had a certain style. In his younger days he'd been

how many times I'd need to run up and down the garden to make a mile. He glared at me, said it would be about 100 times and went back to sleep under his newspaper. I remember running until it got dark. Some years later I measured the garden and discovered that 100 laps would have been just under four miles. And then my father had the nerve to complain I'd worn a dirt track in his lawn.

a member of the French Foreign Legion, and spent most of the Second World War in a prisoner-of-war camp (he was captured while defending the Maginot Line in 1940). After the war he worked on the construction of Arctic bases for the US Air Force, and sailed a catamaran of his own design and construction across the Pacific. Perhaps best of all, he was declared an Enemy of the People of Bulgaria by the country's post-war Eastern Bloc government, and was sentenced to death in absentia.

It was therefore largely thanks to the work of Peter Dimitroff Petroff that I could tell, as I sat for the second time in a week in a traffic jam on the M6 by Birmingham, that I was going to be late getting to Manchester, and that my heartrate was unhealthily high.

We'd been late all along, despite getting up early. I'd badly underestimated the amount of stuff we needed to take with us; it was all odds and ends of things, but by the time we'd got three bikes in the car (warm-up bike, race bike and the spare), a bucket for pre-cooling ice, a fan (the air-blowing type, not the type who wants to be your best friend), cycling kit, food, water bottles, wheels, home trainer and about a hundred other things, we were already three-quarters of an hour late. Breakfast ended up being forgotten altogether.

Then the drive up was slow, the traffic jam by Birmingham was awful – it's a permanent fixture, and I really should have managed to get used to it – and since I was pretty edgy anyway, I ended up swearing furiously at the unfairness of it all. Then Louisa and I had the argument we always have in a traffic jam, the one that goes 'Bloody traffic' v 'There's nothing you can do about it.' (For a while we tried designating our regular arguments with code numbers, so that we didn't have to go to the trouble of thrashing them out word-for-word each time. However, the primal need to complain was not satisfied.)

The rest of the trip was conducted in a hurry and a sharp silence.

The familiar cool gloom of the track was comforting. Everything slowed down a little. Even so, I started frantically spannering away at the bike to get ready for the session. Andrea shooed me away. 'Go and get changed,' she said. 'I'll get it ready. You've got plenty of time. You really want to learn to relax, you do.'

The new bike was a hell of an improvement, and that was a huge relief. I was able to sweep sweetly round the curves, under easy control, rather than having to contend with the 20-pence-piece cornering I'd been putting up with until now. I could even get close enough to the foam 'sandbags' – placed just inside the track to prevent me taking shortcuts – that I could touch them with my inside pedal, without then continuing my downward trajectory off the track altogether. At last we'd got something right.

I came down off the track and had a drink. 'Looks good,' said Andrea. I nodded. Then for the first time in a week, I grinned. I felt much better for doing something. I was back in charge again, rather than having the capricious fates of the hour record pushing me around.

Back onto the track for the final effort. A 10-minute run at record pace. I accelerated the bike down off the banking onto the racing line at the base of the track. 'Just relax!' shouted Andrea as I passed her. It felt good, there was a buzz in the air. The 10 minutes were no problem. I know I'd never yet failed to manage a mere 10 minutes at record pace, but this time I felt as if I could just have kept swinging round the curves and straights in an effortless rhythm all day.

All the same, when I glanced at my pulse monitor on the last lap of the effort, it showed the very high reading of 190bpm. That was worrying; 190bpm wasn't a pulse I could sustain for more than about 20 minutes, if that. But it didn't quite square with how I felt, and normally how I felt was more important. The high pulse probably had more to do with the Birmingham traffic than with anything here on the track.

Back down in the track centre, I took my helmet off and rubbed a towel over my shaved head. Louisa and Andrea came over from the trackside. They both looked cheerful, though I had the nagging doubt that that was because they'd been sharing a joke at my expense. Possibly concerning my absurdly tight skinsuit.

'You know,' said Andrea, 'I think this might actually happen. Perhaps you haven't been wasting my time after all.'

It was rare to hear such unrestrained optimism from Andrea. I knew, even at the time, that she pretty much had to say something like that, but I felt that she meant it.

'I'm only sorry you're not going to be able to help tomorrow,' I said. Andrea was in charge of the following night's track meeting, of which my attempt was only the first part. She'd decided that she couldn't risk being my trackside coach in case some disaster brewed up elsewhere in the meeting. I was trying to guilt her into changing her mind. It didn't work. She shrugged apologetically. There was perhaps a trace of guilt, but not enough.

On cue, Mike Ellis and Charles McCulloch arrived. Between them they were going to do the job I wanted Andrea to do. Mike coached at the Velodrome, and he'd wandered in and out of several of the test sessions over the previous few months. He'd always taken an interest in what we were doing. Charles was one of his riders, whom I knew slightly from a few races we'd done together.

On a previous run, together they'd managed to give me the feedback I needed, with Mike giving me the signals for the overall speed, and Charles indicating each lap split-time. It just seemed a shame that Andrea wasn't there for the final act. I slightly resented Mike and Charles being there, just because they weren't Andrea. That made me feel guilty (to go along with stressed, nervous, intermittently angry, occasionally morose and constantly anxiety-prone).

To complete the party, the UCI arrived at the track in the person of the Commissaire for the attempt. He'd said he would drop by on the Tuesday, to check over the bikes and offer what he called 'general advice'. He clearly took his task seriously. His UCI blazer was immaculately pressed and his shoes were buffed to a high gloss. At least he didn't have one of the UCI armbands worn by many commissaires, in the style favoured by the Warmington-on-Sea Home Guard in *Dad's Army*.

I got the feeling that this commissaire didn't take me terribly seriously as a contender for the record. His general advice consisted of telling me that I had to complete the lap on which the hour expired, to allow the calculation of the full distance. I interrupted him several times to tell him I was fully aware of this, but to no avail. Maybe he thought I was a bit thick. He also explained at some length how much he was to be paid for the rendering of his services, and the expenses that he would be charging. I told him I was aware of this also. He clearly didn't like being interrupted.

'You're lucky to have me,' he said impatiently, 'You could have had an Italian official, you know.'

'What?' I must have looked baffled.

'Then you'd have had to pay my return flight from Italy. First-class, it would have been. And I'd have stayed at a top hotel. You'd have had to pay for that too.'

Maybe he resented never having been invited to Italy to supervise a record attempt, I don't know. Certainly it seemed a bit odd. But the UCI as an organisation is capable of considerable oddness – it once helpfully specified that a bicycle be propelled only by 'the lower muscular apparatus'. Most of us would have settled for 'legs'.

Checking over the bikes was accomplished in a matter of moments; Blazer-and-Shoes just said they looked like the kind of normal track bike required, and they'd be fine, assuming the measurements were within the regulations. I assured him they were, and that appeared to be that. I'd been expecting something a bit more rigorous, especially after the painstaking checks that had been made to Boardman's athlete's hour bike. I wasn't complaining, though.

Louisa had insisted that this trip was not an occasion for my usual taste in cheapskate hotels. She'd found an apartment hotel near Piccadilly station, which meant we could cook for ourselves, pretend we were at home. It was a good idea. Except, unlike home, you couldn't see your hand in front of your face. The apartment was in a converted warehouse, which was very trendy, but also very thin on windows. We checked in at three o'clock on a bright July afternoon and had to switch all the lights on.

It was like living in a shopping mall. All natural sense of time passing disappeared. Added to the temporal dislocation I'd been suffering for the past week, the result was a bit disturbing. Three hours passed in a few minutes. But when I boiled some pasta for dinner, it seemed to take about an hour. At eight o'clock I felt as if I wanted to go to bed for the night, but at eleven I was wide awake again, with a distinct yearning for a cup of tea and a slice of toast. I was surprised when I looked out of the only window in the apartment to find it was dark. Hour-record jet-lag again.

But the pasta was nice, the sofa was comfortable, and Louisa, in a thoughtful touch had brought a DVD of *Local Hero* to try and keep me calm. It did to some extent, but it also made me wish I was in a remote fishing village, and 200 miles away, at least, from Manchester. I think I'd have felt like that anyway.

I wouldn't normally want to be somewhere else. By the night before a race, I'll accept that I've done all I can to prepare, and be curious about how I'm going to get on. I'm ready. This time I didn't feel as though I'd engaged with what I was about to do at all. I tried to change it, by just thinking it through, step by step, like the National 25. I closed my eyes and heard the start, listening to the automated countdown like the BBC time pips: 5, 4, 3, 2, 1, go. The starting effort. Then the motion and slight vibration of the bike below me and the rhythm of my legs and breathing. The concentration to keep the bike tight to the line in the curves, and the way the centrifugal force would push me down onto the bike through the bankings. (A force of about 1.5 times my body weight every 9 seconds. Not exactly fighter-pilot stuff, but very fatiguing in the old-fashioned, unsupported position. Imagine doing press-ups with Frankie Dettori sitting on your shoulders.)

And the critical speed. The magic 49.442kph. Each lap to take 18.2 seconds. I imagined 18.2-second lap after 18.2-second lap unrolling.

I slept about as well as you'd expect. The dishwasher in the apartment had a bleeping alarm that went off when it wanted to be emptied, and I was awake enough to be annoyed by it, but not awake enough to get up and turn it off. The noise drifted in and out of weird, vivid dreams: as the starting countdown beeps, as a bleeping heart-rate monitor, as the morning's alarm clock. I must have started wide awake from these dreams half a dozen times, once or twice with a cry that woke Louisa.

At least I was better off than Fausto Coppi in 1942, who was kept awake in Milan the night before his hour record by the allies bombing the city. The rest of Coppi's build-up was disturbed by the war as well; the army was billeted in the track, so he couldn't use it for training, instead having to take his fixed-gear track bike to the long, flat road near Novi Ligure.

The Vigorelli track in Milan, where Coppi broke the record, survived the war. It's still seen more successful hour attempts than any other: nine between Giuseppe Olmo in 1935 and Rivière in 1958. It was without peer, there were no records set anywhere else during this period. Even the British tandem pair of Bill Paul and

Ernie Mills travelled to the track in 1937. The tandem hour record they set lasted for more than sixty years.

Eventually I abandoned the idea of getting back to sleep – the day was finally here, and I was going to have to face it. Muttering something to myself about condemned men and breakfast, I had two slices of toasted bread with orange marmalade, a small amount of muesli, and two cups of decaffeinated coffee. Also a small stone lying on the work surface that I mistook for a sultana.

I suspect that pre-ride food tells you more about hour record-holders than a lot of the more obvious detail. Obree, obviously, had cornflakes with milk. Ferdinand Bracke had a 'ham-based lunch'. Merckx had toast and a cheese spread he'd brought to Mexico from Belgium. And Roger Rivière had a couple of glasses of Chianti (which would have enhanced nicely the effects of the large doses of amphetamine that he had planned for later that afternoon). The scientific Moser had fruit, honey and a sachet of citrus fruit powder with additional vitamin C, with three teaspoons of wheatgerm and some hazel nuts, followed by two glasses of fruit juice, 10 grams of a fruit-based powder, 50 grams of boiled rice mixed with more honey, washed down with 500ml of an electrolyte drink developed by his sponsors. Whole lot of powder there, interestingly.

All this dietary trivia is included in the hour-record press reports for a simple reason. An hour-record attempt is a massive occasion, and demands many pages of coverage. But it's not actually that eventful. So reporters have to find whatever details they can to make the story's size match its gravity.

We find out that Obree listened to Fleetwood Mac's *Rumours* before his first hour attempt. That Boardman's training partner Paul Jennings had 'Next Directory good looks'. That Rivière went to see the Milan v Trieste match the day before his 1958 ride. And that in Mexico, Merckx got up at 5 a.m. to wake his entourage. This was cited as evidence of his enthusiasm to get on with the ride. The possibility that the mighty Merckx might have had a nervous night does not seem to have been considered.

Some of the details made sense in a way they would not have done before I experienced the hour at first hand. There was incredulity when Jacques Anquetil travelled from Milan to a nightclub in Como on the penultimate night before his first successful attempt and danced until the early hours. 'What the hell was he doing?' cried the journalists. Master Jacques justified it on the basis that it would help him sleep. As a means of relieving the tension of a record attempt, it probably worked rather well. It probably also appealed to his self-image.

Weirdest of all was the home-made psycho-idiocy of Michele Ferrari, Rominger's coach, who immediately before the attempt slowly and deliberately walked towards his protégé, carefully maintaining eye-contact. He placed his fingers to Rominger's temples for a few moments. Suddenly he exclaimed, 'Concentration, Tony! Concentration!' Maybe Ferrari possessed powers of super-strength that he could transfer to others for an hour or so. Given how nervous I was, I think I'd have hit him, which the reporters would have enjoyed greatly.

After breakfast I didn't do much to get anyone excited. I rode a bike on the home trainer for half an hour, just to loosen up a little. I did an interview on the phone with a local radio station whose researchers had (understandably) confused the absolute hour and athlete's hour records. As is the way with these things, it was I who ended up sounding like an idiot. 'So, Michael, Chris Boardman's record is 56.3km. How far do you think you can go tonight?'

'Well, I'm aiming for 49.5km.'

'That's not really going to break the record, is it?'

'Well, the UCI in 2000 changed the rules for the hour . . .'

'Well, thanks very much anyway, Michael. It's news time now, with . . .' The phone went dead without so much as a goodbye.

Apart from that I stayed in bed. (Now I think about it, I did the interview in bed as well.) The bedroom was the only room with a window. Anyway, keeping off your feet is a good idea.

I wasn't totally idle. I listened to *Time Out* by Dave Brubeck, and even wasted some energy waggling a finger in rhythm. I only had the album with me because I'd borrowed it from David Taylor, the man whose suggestion had started this whole thing off, and I wanted to return it. It occurred to me that he'd done the bits of publicity I'd asked of him without at any point feeling the need actually to get in touch. Exemplary.

Dave Thompson, on the other hand, rang me to ask how he was going to get into the track, and again to ask for directions.

We left for the track at about half-past four in the afternoon. The attempt was scheduled for seven. A couple of hours was as long as I wanted to wait about. Ideally I'd have left it later, an hour say, but I feared last-minute problems – though I was hard pressed to see what there was left to go wrong.

At the track Andrea was looking hassled. She gave me the key to her office – somewhere to wait, and to warm up – and vanished immediately. Dave was hanging around the entrance. He waved, but made no move to come and speak to me. He'd probably guessed I wanted to be left alone. I went and let myself into Andrea's office.

Just waiting now. There was nothing left between me and the attempt. No distractions, no displacement activities. Just waiting is not easy. Nothing I could do would make any difference now. I couldn't make up my mind whether I wanted the time to race or crawl. I tried to read, but I couldn't retain more than a few words in my head at a time, and even a short sentence was barely comprehensible. My mind always drifted back to the coming ride.

The office was gloomy, and the fluorescent lights flickered. But I didn't want to go outside. I wanted peace. I was trying to relax, even now. My pulse thumped, I could feel it all the time. Slow it down, calm it down. Soon I could stop worrying about relaxing; I could just let go and allow the adrenalin to wash over me.

I thought of Obree, and of his determination at his second Norwegian attempt that he would only get to the track in time to get on the bike and go. He spoke to no one, in case they punctured the fragile self-belief he'd managed to build after the previous day's failed attempt. When the starter began to ask Graeme if he was ready, he was interrupted by Graeme spitting back, 'Are *you* ready?'

It came over as arrogance. It was terror: that he was going to fail, that he would go home the same person as when he left. He was more afraid of failure than of death.

God, I wished I'd been able to make the attempt in the morning. Just to get up and get on with it. That would have been nice. It could all have been over by nine o'clock. I could have been home by late afternoon. I could by now have been so drunk I couldn't speak. Outdoor attempts were often in the morning, when the air was still. That was the biggest problem outdoors, the wind. It was 1993 that saw the first world hour set indoors. Before that, waiting for the wind to drop, or worrying it would get up, was what I'd have been doing now. Before I knew what was happening I was worrying about the wind. Then I remembered I was riding indoors.

The time ticked by. One hour to go. I was so wrapped up in myself that I hadn't said ten words to Louisa all day. But now she came back to the office from some errand, and told me that the Commissaire required my urgent presence in the track centre.

I had to push my way through a crowd of people to get there. 'You can't use that set of cranks,' he said. He meant the power-measuring system. It was on the bike because the data from the attempt would be priceless if I wanted to have another go at the record, irrespective of this evening's outcome.

'Nothing in the rules about them,' I said, possibly a little bullishly. 'Anyway, I can't see the read-out when I'm riding.'

He casually waved a couple of sheets of paper at me though not so casually that I managed to read what they said. 'Says here,' he said.

'What's that?' I pointed at the papers.

'The UCI guidelines for the athlete's hour record.'

'I've got a copy of the rules, and they say nothing about power-cranks.'

'Well, this is how the record rules are to be interpreted – and you can't have any modern performance aids at all. The UCI wants to preserve the primacy of the athlete in this record, and keep it close to the spirit of Merckx's ride.'

It seemed a bit sweeping, and I wasn't happy. But there wasn't time to argue, or to appeal to a higher authority. Andrea had been right: there was no doubt about who was in charge. Suddenly the hour project I'd worked at for all these months was under the absolute command of a complete stranger.

There was nothing I could do about it. If I wanted to make the attempt that night – and for better or worse I did – I guessed it was his way or not at all. He could have me deported at a moment's notice to the UCI's prison work camp, in a high, inaccessible Swiss mountain valley, where cyclists who have displeased the Organisation make finely tailored UCI blazers and shiny black shoes at gunpoint.

Anyway, there wasn't *time* to argue. I had to get changed, get the pre-cooling under way, get my legs warmed up, try and get focused. It was all on a timetable, pinned to the office noticeboard. I looked at my watch; whatever happened, it would be over in 100 minutes, but I had to start getting ready *now*.

Skinsuit on, and the ice-vest. It was going to be warm on the track. Hands in the bucket, filled with iced water. Your mother was right: cooling your wrists lowers perceived body temperature. It even lowers your actual body temperature a little. And I could do with having my body temperature lowered a little.

Andrea appeared, with a new edict: that I could only have one helper trackside, rather than the two we'd planned. 'I'm sure Mike can manage on his own,' she said, a little doubtfully. It didn't make much difference to me. It was a bit more difficult for Mike, but it was still hardly quantum physics. Though it seemed to me that this particular demand was out of line with almost every hour-record attempt there had ever been. Just for starters, Boardman's athlete's hour should have been disallowed when his wife Sally joined Peter Keen on the trackside. Never mind Obree, Anquetil, Merckx, Rivière, Coppi. Most attempts had dozens of people round the trackside. I've got the pictures to prove it. But there was, as I've said, no point in arguing. Presumably this interpretation of the rule was a recent innovation.

I went back to Andrea's office, took a few deep breaths and started to warm up. But within a few minutes there was more noise outside; the door opened. Andrea again – the rest of her track meeting must have been going to ruin. Louisa went outside with her. Twenty minutes to go. I could hear Louisa talking to Blazer-and-Shoes, but I couldn't hear what they were saying over the roar of the fan that sat on a table beside me. The voices went on for some time.

I stopped pedalling, got off the bike and went to find out what was happening. When I opened the door, the Commissaire was clearly just leaving. Louisa looked furious.

'I was just making it clear that you're not permitted to use a heartrate monitor during the ride,' he said.

I was stunned. Where the hell had that come from? 'What?'

'The UCI wants to preserve the primacy of the athlete in this record, and keep it close to the spirit of Merckx's ride. So obviously you can't use a heartrate monitor – Merckx didn't have one.' He paused. 'Or need one.'

I suspected this might have been an insult. 'That's not what the record is supposed to be, you can't just turn the clock back thirty years. I mean . . .' I tailed off. I'd been about to name half a dozen things that had changed since 1972, starting with the fact that this was an indoor track. I stopped because I realised he could quite possibly ban anything I mentioned.

'Well, it's what the guidelines say,' he went on, turned his back on me and walked off.

So this was how it was going to end: I was about to murder a UCI commissaire. Still, probably not a sin, though of course God might have issued some extra guidelines for interpreting the commandments that said it was.

This new ban was more of a problem than the previous ones; a monitor is a useful alarm bell, especially in stressful rides where it's easy to misread the feedback you're getting from your body. It was something that I really didn't want to be without. If the UCI had been prepared to put that rule in general circulation, then I could have prepared accordingly. But that would have been too reasonable.

I abandoned the rest of the warm-up. It wouldn't make any real difference, but it was another disruption. It wasn't how it was planned, it wasn't how I'd rehearsed the afternoon in my head all those times. Now I was just wondering what would go wrong next. I didn't have to wait long to find out.

I asked Louisa if she'd go and check that the bike for the attempt was in the track centre, and ready to go. I towelled my head and neck, to stop sweat from running onto my glasses any sooner than it had to. Louisa came back, and didn't look happy. The bike was fine, she said. But Blazer-and-Shoes had further clarification to offer: 'When he says you're not allowed to use a heartrate monitor, he means you're not allowed to use its digital watch function either.'

'Oh, for fuck's sake. Why?'

'Eddy Merckx didn't have a digital watch, I suppose.'

'Go and tell him that Eddy Merckx could have had a digital watch if he'd bloody well wanted.' Merckx had a painting by Miró hanging on the wall beside his preposterously overstuffed trophy cabinet; $2100 would have been no problem.

This really was a crisis. I'd no other means of telling the time. And if you're trying to break the hour record, knowing how the time is going is essential. I couldn't look at the big scoreboard without having to raise my head from the aerodynamic tuck, and I'd no signal for the elapsed time worked out with Mike Ellis. I knew with wind in my ears, and the noise of the crowd, I'd no chance at all of hearing shouts.

Louisa came back. 'He still says no,' she said. 'He says Merckx couldn't have any electronic aids, so you can't. He did say that if you want, you can ignore him and appeal to the UCI afterwards. Apparently he's just trying to be helpful.' She paused. 'I've never really wanted to hit someone in the face so much in my life.'

The whole thing was spiralling into farce. I'd spent months, thousands of pounds, night after night in that crappy hotel, working my way towards this attempt. The last week had been awful. And now it seemed the UCI was going to do to me what it presumably wished it had done to Obree ten years earlier. The previous day, as I stood there with the cranks on the bike and the HRM on my wrist, and the two people who were going to be trackside, I'd had the very clear impression everything was just fine. Now, with minutes to go I'd lost the lot. This was *helpful*?

I exploded into fury. I shouted and swore. I threw the bucket and its contents across the office and I kicked over the warm-up bike, still clamped in the trainer. Louisa had to stop me from going to beat the stuffing out of Blazer-and-Shoes, by locking the door and refusing to give me the key, working on the assumption – more dangerous than she probably realised – that I wouldn't attack her to get it.

I'm not violent, or given to temper. I'd never been in this kind of a fury in my life, but something broke in my head that night. There was a blast of pure anger and hate that blew away all the restraints that had been carefully programmed into me, by my parents, by my school. The damage may have been irreparable. Decades of careful brainwashing undone in a few minutes. I don't think I've ever been quite the same since.

I couldn't give up. But I couldn't help feeling I was only being treated this way because I wasn't a star. It wouldn't have been like this for Boardman, or Indurain, or Armstrong. I reckon if Lance had rung the UCI and, as I did, asked for full details of the rules for the hour, they wouldn't have assured him they were simply as already published, and then have sprung a set of guidelines on him at the attempt. I've always felt that the UCI looks after its own. It's a business after all, and it's expensive to mess with the stars who bring the money in. And there was nothing I could do.

Another bang on the door. Andrea. 'Come on,' she said. 'It's time.'

So this was it, and it wasn't supposed to be this way. Andrea pretended not to notice that a bucket of iced water had been thrown across her office, or the upended warm-up bike. I picked it up, unclamped it from the trainer, and wheeled it down the corridor after her.

Down the stairs to the short, dark concrete passage that led under the track to the track centre. Mike Ellis was waiting. 'Good luck,' said Andrea, before she disappeared. Mike nodded. There was a blast of music from the track. 'That's it, time to go,' Mike said.

I got onto the warm-up bike. Nothing is as ungainly as a cyclist trying to walk in a tight skinsuit and cycling shoes. For an elegant entrance, you must use a bike. Mike gave me a push while I clipped my feet into the pedals. Up the ramp leading to the apron round the inside of the track. And the sudden emergence into bright lights, loud music, people, applause, cheering.

I rode a slow lap round the inside of the track, to get used to the different atmosphere, the lights, the people and the noise. These people had come hoping to see history made; none of them knew anything about the trials involved in getting here. Suddenly their optimism was uplifting. The hour record had jumped out of the cycling magazines and books, and had come to life. Whatever happened now, this was the hour record, and this *was* how it was supposed to be.

Louisa told me later that while I was trying to adjust to all this, she was once again head-to-head with Blazer-and -Shoes. He had taken exception to the Lycra shoe covers I was wearing, which zipped over my shoes for a marginal aerodynamic benefit. On the basis that Eddy Merckx had possessed no such assistance, he wanted them removed. When Louisa pointed out that Chris Boardman had used an almost identical pair, she was told that was of no relevance; Chris shouldn't have been permitted to wear them either. There was, apparently, no contradiction at all between his having worn a pair to set the 49.441km I was trying to beat, and my not being allowed to use them.

'Unless,' he said suggestively, 'you can give me a good reason why he should be allowed to wear them.'

'Keep his feet warm?' said Louisa.

'Not good enough.'

'He's got really scruffy shoes, and doesn't want anyone to see them.'

'No.'

'Look,' said Louisa, 'I don't know anything about the bloody rules, I'm only his girlfriend. Just tell me what you're talking about.'

'If, say, they were an integral part of the shoe?' he hinted.

'Of course they are.'

'Well, that's all right then.'

Now that *was* more helpful. I only regret I didn't think of telling him the watch was an integral part of my wrist.

I rode round to the start line, and through the gap in the fence that separated the track apron from the main infield. An official went to put the attempt bike into the starting gate – a contraption that holds you and the bike upright, and releases only as the timing starts. I sat down on a blue plastic chair on the infield side of the fence and put on my helmet – keeping my head low so the Commissaire wouldn't see it, because I was sure he wouldn't like it. Glasses on. Dried my hands.

Ready then. So. Stand up. Hobble in the cleated shoes, hunched in the tight suit, out of the infield and onto the track apron under the bright lights. Like a stage. Applause, a few shouts of 'Go on!', 'You can do it, Mike.'

Careful Michael, there's not much grip between plastic shoes and concrete, or between plastic and sloping wooden track. I clamber onto the bike in the gate. (Never an elegant moment – there's a sort of step, but it's right by the back wheel, so you have to stretch your left leg forward like a man tiptoeing through cartoon quicksand, and then slide onto the back of the saddle.) At least I make it onto the bike without falling over. An official stands on the track outside me, holding a thing like a table-tennis bat. 'Are you ready?' he says. A hundred funny answers. But I say, 'Yes, I suppose so.' I have an urge to keep talking, to put it off. The 'so' stretches: sooo.

Here it is. He'll hold the bat in the air, and the countdown will start. Except not; we have time for a little more farce. The official with the bat holds it half up, looking hesitantly past me for something in the centre of the track. I sit up on the bike, to see what's happening. I see. Blazer-and-Shoes has gone missing, and the countdown can't start without him. I don't know exactly, but there are probably a couple of thousand people here, and there's only one man in the entire building who's not ready and we're going to have to wait for him.

Then I see him; he's talking to someone over by the ramp. He's just letting us all wait. I start to get off the bike, to go and . . . well, I don't know. Nothing good, I suspect. But man-with-bat says calmly 'It's okay, Michael, just sit there.' Someone goes to tell the Commissaire he is required. The crowd is quiet; why are we waiting?

At last, he finishes his conversation and moves to his station. Man-with-bat holds bat up. Suddenly the warning pip sounds from the automated start system. The countdown display shows 30 seconds, 29, 28. Ha! It's an electronic system! With a digital display! Concentrate. Not the moment for pointing out ironies. Take a deep breath, Michael.

CHAPTER 11

IT IS VERY QUIET. I CAN ALMOST BELIEVE I'M BACK where I started, on my own in the Velodrome playing with the idea of the hour record. Sitting on the bike in the gate, only the bright light glowing off the track gives the game away. The crowd is silently waiting. I have little more than a subliminal awareness of them. The pressure of thousands of eyes looking at me.

I'm not looking at them, because I'm watching the big digital display by the inside of the track. Soon it will count up the laps, but for now it's counting down seconds to the gun: 20, 19. Fluorescent numbers on a black background. I can hear it making a 'thunk' as it changes each second. In the oppressive silence it feels as if the 'thunk' is getting louder. Like an approaching menace. Like nails in a coffin.

Oh for the love of God, think positive! It's just the countdown. It sounds a lot more like a clock than anything else. I used to catch the train from Clapham Junction each morning to my job at Sussex University, and the platform clock made exactly the same noise as I and all the familiar strangers stood ignoring each other, waiting for trains that came irregularly and usually in the wrong order. Cold winter mornings with the wind blowing the rain under the platform canopy.

That was just five years ago, but it feels like a lifetime. It seems impossible that I'm the same person listening to this same 'thunk . . . thunk' in such a different context. A sudden feeling comes, that I should be in the stands holding my breath, watching someone else doing this. And the equally sudden, reassuring feeling that I'd rather be down here. I have to be down here, because if I wasn't here I'd always wonder what it would have been like.

Impassively the clock counts to 13 seconds, then 12; 10 arrives, with a long, loud baritone 'beep' in case my attention has been wandering. I check my grip on the bars, pull up with my feet on the pedals to make sure I'm properly attached. Wiggle my shoulders, more for something to do than anything else. It's a familiar ritual, but it's never very relaxed. I can feel the crowd shuffling forwards on their seats.

From 5 seconds the beeps come each second. I slide back on the saddle ready to rock forwards between 1 and 0 to get as much forward momentum as possible at the gun.

3, 2. Breathe out on the odd numbers and in on the even. 1 . . . here we go, breathe in . . . The starting system makes a silly-sounding bang like a toy gun. I echo it with a sharp exhalation – ha! – as I jump forward out of the saddle onto the first pedal stroke.

There is an explosive release of noise from the crowd, cheering and applause, and the familiar sound of the front row, leaning over the fence at the top of the track, banging their hands on the advertising hoardings on the other side. The racket is instantaneous; they must have been sitting there with hands poised during the countdown.

My hands grip tightly; the first few pedal strokes I'm pulling hard on the bare metal bars, fighting the big, heavy gear to get up to speed. Trying to keep my upper body still, with my arms and shoulders tensed so that the bike doesn't weave from side to side. All the power from the lower muscular apparatus.

First curve, still out of the saddle. The bigger gear means it takes longer to get up to speed than a pursuit bike, and it feels a bit precarious going this slowly on the steep banking. I keep accelerating down the back straight. Pedalling fast now, and my breathing is picking up. I sit down just before the second curve and wriggle about on the saddle for a moment; I'm going to be here for an hour, I might as well be as comfortable as I can. I ease gently into the carefully researched aero position. Somehow now I'm here, there's no hurry.

Out of the second curve and back down the home straight again, past the grey-bearded Mike. No signals yet, not on the opening lap with the standing start to slow it down. He makes this clear, standing on the line beside the track with his hands behind his back. For some reason the lap counter doesn't indicate the first completed lap. Bastard machine. It was fast enough at counting down the seconds to the start.

I have to establish the pattern for the rest of the ride now, while I'm fresh. Try to be efficient, economical. Smoothly round the long curve, relax for the 3-second length of the straight, smoothly round the next long curve. Let it all flow. Eyes on the black datum line that marks the bottom of the track, just trying to let instinct guide the bike. If I think about it too hard I can't do it. It's a funny sort of look-the-other-way concentration.

This is it then. This is what an hour-record attempt is like from the inside. It's a very pure effort. No outside influences; no wind, no hills, no big trucks coming past. It's all the same. The third lap is like the second, and the fourth is like the third. Mike is the only variable in my life now. He signals that the first laps are a bit too fast, 17.8 seconds, then 18.0. I try to relax, and let the splits slip out to 18.2. The magic number. It's surprising how finely you can feel the pace.

My breathing has settled into the familiar rapid pace of racing. Full breaths, taken quickly, but just this side of snatching at it. I wouldn't be able to talk, and drinking would be very difficult. But I'm under control. Breathing is the key. If I breathe right, at the fastest pace I know I can sustain, then everything else will fall into place.

The lap counter still shows zero. This is worrying. For a lap or two, fair enough. But I've done maybe twelve laps now. I realise, with a lurch in my stomach that throws my breathing off its beat, that it must have fallen foul of the 'no electronics' rule. Shit. So now I have no watch, and no lap counter. I have no idea where I am; maybe thirteen laps now. Maybe fifteen. I should at least have tried to count. Have I done four minutes? Five? This isn't fair. The essential sensory inputs for an hour record are simply accumulated time and distance. That's all I need. But now I don't have either.

Mike is all I have left. And I don't understand what he's doing, either. He's made no signal as to whether I'm behind or ahead of the overall pace, which means I'm on schedule. That's good. But he signalled some lap times at the start that were too fast, then later some that were on pace. So I should be ahead of schedule, and Mike should have indicated that. More laps, some slower, some on pace. Still no pace information, just the individual lap times.

Another prop falls away. I thought he was going to do both his own job and that of the prohibited Charles. But he's clearly just going to do the lap times, presumably because no one asked him to do otherwise. Andrea was organising a race meeting, and I was vandalising her office. I stood with him in the passage outside the track for at least 30 seconds before I came in, I could have checked with him then, but I was too distracted. That was stupid. I was too busy cursing the Commissaire.

Another time around, and I try to yell 'Pace!' at him. It comes out as a breathless squeak. I get no response. The crowd is still making a lot of noise. I don't suppose he heard. Yelling once took me most of a lap to recover from. It got in the way of breathing. Can't do it again. All I'm going to get are the individual lap splits. It's better than nothing, but barely. No time, no distance, no overall schedule.

I have a rough idea that I started a little fast, and I've slowed down. I suspect I'm behind schedule. All I have to go on is what I carry with me: my breathing, my legs, my head. To try to feel the rhythm, to try to take the measure of an hour in my head, and the hours have been so flexible these last few days. Time itself has been untrustworthy.

The rhythms of the hour are as insistent as they are complex. My breathing is fast, but regular. Pedalling cadence is faster, about 104rpm. But not regular; it edges up a little through each curve as I lean in towards the track centre, closer to horizontal than vertical, and the wheels slingshot round the track outside me. Like a rider on the wall of death, my wheels will travel further than I will. For the 6 seconds of the curve the cadence increases as the bike accelerates and the gear feels easier. Then as I straighten up, the bike slows, the gear gets heavier again and the cadence eases down.

This is the laid-back bass line of the ride, this long, flat lazy wave of the cadence defining the curves of the track. The riff repeats every 9 seconds. And then each lap, every 18 seconds (maybe a little more now), past Mike again and his signalling fingers.

Four laps is a kilometre. It doesn't really matter now because I don't know times or distances, but I start counting off the sets of four. Or three laps, that's almost a minute. I count threes and fours at the same time.

I'm disappearing into a hypnotic world, pulled in by these rhythms as they slip in and out of phase. No distractions about how fast I'm going or how long. It's like floating underwater. Like time out of time.

As soon as each lap passes it disappears. Even if I tried, I couldn't remember it. Each lap Mike signals a split-time, but already I've forgotten the one before except for a vaguely remembered emotional response. I have enough to deal with right now; each breath, each pedal stroke, each curve, each lap, each minute, each kilometre. Except that the four laps of a kilometre stretch so far into the future that I can't imagine it. My future is never more than the next 9 seconds, the rhythm of straight to curve to straight.

I can feel the tyres on the wood of the track, the slight vibration. The lights are harsh, they show up all the track's little imperfections, maybe where a pedal dug into the wood in a crash, or where a board has been replaced. In a couple of places there is a small piece of black tape on the track – temporary repairs. Above me, painted on the track surface round the bankings, there are giant logos left over from the previous year's Commonwealth Games. They are in shades of orange and red that deepen into the curve, and lighten again as you emerge. I can just see them strobing at the edge of my vision, five to each curve.

It may be hypnotic, but it's a long way from relaxed. There is still tension, still fierce concentration. But the rhythm allows a state of balance. I'm on an edge between what I can do and what I can't. When I get the curves right, the bike seems to fall round them on its own. Sometimes I get them wrong, and have to flick the bike back on line. When that happens, my trance wobbles at a sharp intrusion of reality, a burst of real-world noise and light. Getting back on line is an effort. The rhythms are so entwined that it can take a lap to recover from a momentary waver.

The crowd seems to cheer and shout all the time, but I know that it's actually a Mexican wave of noise following me round the track. Everyone claps every 18 or so seconds; they're being pulled into the rhythm of the hour as well. The noise is quieter now than it was at the beginning.

Mike is signalling lap times that are too slow. Most of them are 18.4 or 18.5. I'm behind the pace. But I don't know how far I've let it slide. It might be 30m. Or it might be 150.

This isn't fast enough. But just pressing the pedals harder won't help. I have to keep the rhythm. It's my best tool. I can make the rhythm do the work; it's easier to concentrate on that than on something as brutal as just riding hard. Riding hard is hurting yourself, like holding your hand in a candle flame. Rhythm is an art. It can allow me to do things I would never do if I had to face them directly. I can set up a fast pace when I'm fresh, and it's easy. Then all it ever needs to keep it going is a little more, and a little more. Like a hot-air balloon: once you have it off the ground, it only needs enough energy to keep it there, a little at a time. Riding with no rhythm is like starting from scratch with every pedal stroke. I have to preserve the momentum and pattern of all the little things I'm doing to hang on to the whole.

My shoulders are getting sore, in a line up across the top of my back. Every time around a curve, as the cadence comes up a little, and the G-forces press my weight onto the handlebars, I feel it a little more. I shift my grip on the bars, to hold them on the top, a hand each side of the stem. We tested this position, for a joke really, and it was more aerodynamic than any of the others. But we didn't have the nerve to try using it for the record – I'd have been disqualified by now for sure because Eddy-bloody-Merckx didn't do it. But I'll try to slip in a few laps like this under cover of relieving cramping muscles. A couple of laps later, I'm back onto the drops. I'll repeat that every couple of kilometres now. It doesn't do very much for the pain though.

I still don't know how I'm doing. This is beginning to worry me more. I'm down. But how much? How many tenths, two-tenths and three-tenths have added up over how many laps? Could be almost anything by now. The crowd is still making a reasonable racket – I'm not dying on my ass. But that's a pretty approximate measure.

Anyway, the crowd isn't really all that interested in me, riding round and round. I'm kind of necessary, but on my own I'm not enough. Numbers are what the crowd wants. Every kilometre is checked off on the big scoreboard and matched against Boardman's record ride. It's a race. The rider keeps belting around the bottom of the track and the crowd watches the numbers he generates on the scoreboard.

I could piss off out of the Velodrome entirely, and it would be minutes before some of the crowd noticed. (At least it would be, if everyone else would keep pretending and clapped every 18 seconds.) I'm beginning to resent that everyone in the Velodrome knows how I'm doing except me. It doesn't seem fair.

I shift my grip on the bars again. Sweat starts running down the inside of my glasses. It's lonely doing this. I didn't expect that, not tonight. I can't communicate with anyone – I can't yell, I tried that once. Anyway, what would I say? This is hard? Big news. I can't even see anyone, apart from Mike, and I'm concentrating on his hands, the fingers that give me the only information I've got.

Another straight, and then I concentrate on dropping the bike into the curve smoothly. Tight to the bottom of the track, the shortest line, where the G-forces are strongest, like a roller-coaster. As I'm pressed onto the bike, the pain in my shoulders is spreading down my arms. I can't do anything about it, I'll just have to ignore it. Straight again, this time with Mike's fingers. 18.7

seconds. This isn't good. That's half a second. A second every two laps. That will be . . . (and it takes me a lap to work it out, because with all the blood and oxygen going to my lungs and legs rather than my brain, I'm getting stupider every lap) 2 seconds a kilometre.

It's worse than just 2 seconds. I'll have to get them back sometime, because the idea here is to break the record – did I mention that? 2 seconds lost in one kilometre means that I'm going to have to ride a kilometre 4 seconds faster than that one, sometime soon to make it up. I can't remember all of Mike's signals, but I know I'm losing ground steadily. *But how much?* Shit, I hate this. This was always going to be close. Now I'm just lost.

Ride fast – in the end that's all it ever comes down to. The pressure of another curve, the relief of the simple straight. But the straight's short respite is never enough. My shoulders are awful. My arms hurt. And every few seconds I have to manage another banked curve. Each one demands a little more effort, a little more concentration. As the physical toll mounts, the balance and rhythm aren't offering the protection from reality that they did. I need some sort of reassurance. Some comfort.

The only possibility is to look at the big scoreboard over the South Curve. It's what everyone else is looking at. I've only got 2 seconds each lap, after I straighten up from the North Curve, before I have to start eyeing up the entry to the South Curve. I have to raise my head to look, and refocus the vision that's been fixed at a point a few metres in front of me since the start. The first time I don't see anything at all. Next time I see some words and numbers, but it's three or four laps before I've sorted out what number is what. Laps, target time, actual time. It doesn't help that they keep changing.

The good news is that I've done half an hour. I was scared it might be more like 10 minutes. The bad news is that I'm behind by something towards the higher end of my suspicions.

It's starting to get hard. It's never been easy; I've always been on the edge. But sustaining the magical rhythm is taking more and more effort. The single fixed gear on the constant track means you can feel everything that's happening. I don't need Mike to tell me that my speed is dropping, though he's already holding up so many fingers that he looks as if he's making a shadow-puppet octopus.

The gear is just a little heavier now, and because I'm connected to it, I feel heavier too. I'm labouring on the pedals, trying to make them spin freely. If I can make them move a little faster, it will get easier again, I'm sure. The curves are all right, when the bike speeds up and the gear moves under my feet. But on every straight it gets laboured. I know the differences are small, but that's not how they feel. They set up echoes in the beat of the ride. The 9 seconds of straight-curve-straight have become 9.5.

The trance that's made it bearable is fragile now. There are more mistakes; I mistime the entry to a curve so badly that I twitch a good couple of feet up the track, past the red sprinters' line. Then I over-correct, and kick a sponge. I shake my head – concentrate. Shaking my head makes my shoulders hurt.

I don't know if that was it, but something brought reality back. It didn't come back on its own, because it was so sudden. It was violent. A whirr of bright colours in my peripheral vision and I surfaced back into bright, bright light and loud noise.

I don't slow down, but now I can feel every pedal revolution at its full value. My breathing is harsh, and snatched. It's stripping the skin off my throat, or at least it feels that way. My ribcage is being wrenched by each breath.

After the trance, this is hyper-real. The bike is still humming over the smooth boards, but it feels like it's shaking over a rutted road. And every curve now is agony. I'd have said the pain in my shoulders, arms and hands made the straights unbearable, were it not for the fact that the curves are worse. Shooting pains, from my elbows up to my shoulders and across my back to meet at the base of my neck. I'm astonished I've managed to ignore this up till now.

Back to the scoreboard. It's still going badly: 35 minutes gone, and more than a minute off the target. I can't see exactly what it is. Probably still less than a kilometre. But if I've lost a kilometre by now, then I need to get it back. That means that I have to ride the next 25 minutes more than 2kph faster than I've averaged so far. And I haven't been losing ground to the record for the sake of creating extra suspense. I've been doing the best I can.

But there's no point in just doing my best, if my best isn't good enough. That's rather the point of the hour record. That's why it is so intimidating. I knew all that before I came here. But this is what it feels like to be at the wrong end of the record's brutal simplicity. As much as I have is not enough.

I've only got one option – well, one brave option.

That's to open the throttle again, the one that I think is flat to the floor anyway. I need more. I pick up the pace, into what feels like a sprint finish. I'm sure I can't sustain this, but it's going to have to last for 25 minutes. It might work. Maybe I can do things I think are beyond me.

The cadence is picking up. But I know the rhythm isn't coming back. There is no art to this, just simple, savage effort. I've never ridden this way before. It's going to be hell, it's going to hurt all the way now. Really hurt. Mike's signals show the lap splits are getting faster, though I almost don't care about him any more. The curves and straights, the track moving under me – I can feel the tyres on the wood. The crowd claps and shouts; I can hear individual voices now.

My hands are going numb – I can't feel the bars any more. I'm scared I'm going to lose my grip. Still I try to pound the pedals round. This is like blind panic; it's not efficient, it's not considered. It's just throwing everything I've got onto the fire.

Hands, arms, shoulders, back. They're all burning. They must be glowing. I'm losing the feeling in my legs. My vision has started to darken around the edges. The effort has pulled Mike's signals back down to 18.5, 18.4. But that's not enough. To get it back I need more.

I try to pick it up again. Push harder. I can feel my shoulders rolling, the bike snaking a little with each pedal stroke.

But now there is no more. For the first time the small, slow-witted part of me that's not just trying to wrench the pedals round whispers, 'You're not going to make it. You could stop.' And that's it. As soon as it's expressed, the thought will win out. For the first time since I started the hour project, stopping is easy. I fight against it, like I fought so hard to get here, to give myself this chance. I can't stop. But now I know that I'm hurting myself for no reason. I'm going to have to stop sometime. It's going to happen. Stopping is suddenly all I can think about. The next lap split drifts out towards 19 again. And the one after that. I ride another lap; I still feel like I'm sprinting, but now I know it's a finishing sprint. The spirit is gone.

I promise myself that if Mike is signalling 18.3 or faster, I'll make myself do another lap. As soon as I come out of the South Curve, I can see he's signalling 18.9. I've given up before I even pass him.

CHAPTER 12

I'M SORRY I COULDN'T DO THE HOLLYWOOD ENDING. For you it would have been a more satisfying book, and for me, well, just more satisfying. I thought about writing alternate closing chapters, with one where I battled manfully against the hour and won out, to add my name to the great list. But this is supposed to be a factual account, and since up till now it more or less has been, it didn't seem very respectable to lurch into fiction at the last. Anyway, it would have been a bit clichéd. There are thousands of books about success. One about failure at least has some novelty value.

I've told you about lots of other riders' successes, and in the end they are more interesting. Other people's triumphs seem to change them as people, whereas your own leave you depressingly just the same. I thought for a few hopeful months that maybe breaking the hour would be success of such magnitude that it would change my whole being, make me a better person. But I'd just have been a cyclist with a story about the hour record that had a different ending. A book about that realisation would have been even more dispiriting.

When I gave up after 40 minutes I was a minute and a half behind Chris Boardman's record pace, a little more than a kilometre. It doesn't seem like very much. It is, though, and it was pretty clear that I wasn't going to get it back.

I took some flak, from friends more than enemies, for not actually riding out the hour. 'Why did you stop?' they said. 'Why didn't you just keep going?' I didn't keep going because I couldn't. I'd given everything I had to try to stay at the kind of pace needed to break the record, because that was the dream, not just riding around the track for an hour. From where I was at 40 minutes, I don't think I could have kept going at any pace. I don't give up on things lightly. If there's a dead horse that needs flogging, I'm usually first in line.

After I eased up and let the bike swing up off the racing line, all I wanted to do was get off the track, out of the building and out of Manchester. Failure is not nice, and failure in such a public way doesn't make it any better. It was humiliating. I even had a momentary impulse to pick it up again, to try to keep going, because for as long as I kept riding I wouldn't have to look anyone in the eye. But this, finally, was it. This was the end.

I did a couple of laps round the infield, not as a warm-down, but because the only way to stop a fixed-gear bike is to kick back against the gear and I didn't have the strength. I wanted to ride down the ramp from the trackside to the passage out of the Velodrome, so that I'd just vanish. But at the last minute I realised that I'd have no chance of stopping at the bottom. It would have been a moment from *Carry on Cycling*; my disappearing from view, followed by an off-screen crash as I hit the doors at the end of the ramp. Maybe a solitary buckled wheel would have wobbled back into view as Sid James laughed at me.

So I stopped at the top of the ramp, on the opposite side of the track from Louisa and Mike Ellis and the friends who'd come up to support me. I should have ridden round to them. Stopping where I did, I was on my own, and none of the riders in the track centre preparing for the rest of the race meeting really wanted to talk to me, because no one knew what to say. But here I was nearer the exit, and just as the thought of stopping had begun to block out everything else a few moments before, now the thought of leaving followed in just the same way. Simple, overpowering impulses were ruling my life.

Eventually Andy Jones, a photographer from *Cycling Weekly*, found me a chair and took my bike off me and leaned it against the fence. The pictures he took of me sitting there show me looking a curious shade of purplish-blue that clashed with the chair. I was grateful. If he'd just left me there I'd have fallen over – which would have been a better picture, but one that I'm glad isn't on my file.

I expected some hostility from the crowd. They had come to the track to watch the hour record being broken. They wanted to be able to tell their bored grandchildren every Christmas that they-were-there-when-Hutch-broke-the-hour. (Giant of a man he was, legs like pistons.) Their grandchildren would be even less interested in this version of the story.

Yet as the world reassembled itself into some sort of order, they kept applauding. By the time I felt able to stand up and walk to the track centre, they were still applauding. When I waved back to say thanks, most of them stood up. I just assumed they were leaving – and some of them were. But eventually most of them sat back down again. For people who'd been let down, they were very generous. At the time I felt as if I didn't deserve it. I would have been happier if they had thrown things.

Looking back, though, I'm not so sure. Effort on its own never feels like it's worth very much when you're not up to the task. 'You did your best' are words of consolation, not congratulation. The crowd made me feel a bit less ashamed of myself. If you just looked at what they'd seen on the track, and ignored the chaos that I'd allowed to consume the preparation, then I couldn't have done any more. I gave it what I'd got. Although I'd have disagreed at the time, that has to count for something.

I did a couple of press interviews, of which I can't remember a word. The fragments that made it into print would suggest I wasn't making a great deal of sense. I did an interview over the Velodrome public address system, and I don't suppose that was much more coherent. I remember having to breathe about every two words. But I got another round of applause, and a bunch of flowers, which I suppose was intended as a victory bouquet and still had to be disposed of somehow. It gave me something to do with my hands, and something to give Louisa's mother to say thanks for feeding the cat.

And that was it. At least this way I didn't have to go to dope control. I went to get changed. Having a shower seemed mundane, like normal life again. It would have been the same if I'd succeeded – it would have been the moment when I realised that the record was not actually a life-changing experience.

I thought about the weeks running up to the attempt, the failed trials, the traffic jams on the M6, the crappy hotels, the frame disaster, the rows with Dave, Louisa sprinting across Croydon laden like a dromedary, the obstacles placed in the way by the UCI, and more than anything the sheer nervous torment, the draining experience of not even being able to relax when I was asleep and waking up with the pain in my chest renewed. It hadn't gone the way I wanted, none of it. The whole thing had slipped out of control and spiralled into chaos. Obree building a bike out of a washing machine looked like the most sensible, rational thing imaginable. But now it was already in the past.

I stood with my face lifted to the shower head as it drained from hot to cold, and I felt as though I'd been liberated. It really didn't matter. Not very much. Certainly not as much as I'd thought it did.

So the hour-record attempt finished with the party that it was always supposed to. And I don't suppose that, looking at me, you'd have known whether it was marking success or failure. Louisa and I, and the friends who'd come to cheer, and anyone else we found who fancied it went back to a five-star hotel where one of my sponsors was staying, and ran up a bar tab that I'm sure should have made it to four figures. Fortunately, due to a bar-staff accounting error (and just how big an error I'm guessing they're only finding out now) it only came to £120. There were at least twenty of us, and we had rather more than two beers each. When they threw us out, somewhere the far side of 4.30 a.m., it was broad daylight on a fresh, bright Thursday morning.

By the time I woke up five hours later in the rented apartment, the day had slid to a dull grey to match my new mood. The relief was still there, but now it was back in the shade of the hulking disappointment, this time with a hangover to back it up. Louisa and I had breakfast in silence; neither of us could think of anything to say. The meal consisted of dry cornflakes, because we hadn't planned this far in advance. Everything had stopped the night before. After-the-hour was not something either of us could imagine.

We went back to the track to collect bikes and other stuff, and have a cup of black coffee with Andrea. The track had the stuffy air of somewhere that had recently seen a big night, but was back to its usual gloomy self.

'Are you going to have another go?' asked Andrea.

'No chance.'

She thought about it for a moment. 'You should do,' she said. 'You *can* do it, you know. The way the last few weeks have gone, you were always up against it.'

'Maybe. But I didn't spend the last six months preparing to fail. I could have failed to break the record months ago. All that work – by you, me, everyone else – and I feel like I've taken all of us for a ride. I was so far off the pace last night that I feel like a fraud. I should have abandoned the whole idea weeks ago when I couldn't manage the trials.'

What made the disappointment bite hard, looking back on it, was that failure wasn't really a surprise. Despite what I'd said to Andrea, I hadn't been miles from breaking the record. But I'd never really been on top of it, either. Every red light I came to, I'd crossed my fingers that the next one would be green and just kept going. Sooner or later I was going to be flattened, and the later it came, the worse it was going to be.

'Don't worry about it,' said Andrea, 'you had to have a go. Would you rather be sat at home, not even having bothered? Just because you didn't manage it last night doesn't mean you can't.'

She was right. Andrea was normally right. I finished my coffee, and Louisa and I picked up the last couple of bags and headed for the car.

It was hard to know what to do next. If I'd broken the record, I'd have retired more or less on the spot, on the basis that things were pretty much certain to be downhill from then on. A little shameless cashing-in while the glow of success still clung to me, and then off to do something so different that for years afterwards people would point out in amusement that there was an hour record-holder with the same name as me. What the something different would be I had no idea, but given my forthcoming and considerable wealth, there would be no urgency. But on this grey, drizzly morning I was still a cyclist.

Retirement would have been suitably dignified. In more recent times, the hour has usually signalled either the beginning or ending of a career. At the age of twenty-nine I was a bit old to use it as a step up to the elite scene; it would have taken several seasons of being kicked round the mountain passes of Europe to adjust to a different way of doing things. (Though I'm sure my judgement on this matter would have been just as susceptible to being skewed by a large cheque as the next man's. No one objects to humiliation if it makes them a lot of money.)

Chris Boardman, having carefully used the hour to start his pro career, used it again to stop it. He got off his bike (well, he was sort of helped off) and retired. When I last spoke to him, he described himself as a 'recovering sportsman'. 'I go to events like the World Championships or the Olympics, and now I can't imagine racing like that.'

This is a man who, when his wife was having their second child, left her to the hospital and went home to bed, before going to ride over the course for the National 25-mile championships the next day. Not, you will notice, actually doing the championships, just seeing the course. Frankly, no time-trial course is that interesting. Maybe he was squeamish. Whatever, he was only the fourth person to hear of the birth of his daughter. 'I've got over that kind of thing,' he told me. Probably, all things considered, just as well.

I don't know of any other holders who retired on the spot. Cyclists, as with most professional athletes, tend to have careers that tail off. After all, you can earn vastly more on the way down than you earned on the way up. But there have been several for whom it's been the beginning of the last act. The hour in 1994 was an unexpected highlight of Tony Rominger's career. He won the Giro d'Italia the following year, but by his own standards little else. He retired in 1997.

The man who overshadowed Rominger for much of his career, Miguel Indurain, did almost exactly the same thing. He broke the record (just) in 1994, and won the following year's Tour de France. Then relations with his team started to sour. He was pushed towards another hour attempt, at altitude in Bogota just after the World

Championships in October. It ended in farce, because in the mornings when the air was still, the track was so slippery with dew as to be unrideable. They tried earlier and earlier in the morning, until he was riding in the middle of the night. Eventually he went home. (You will remember he didn't much like the first attempt, either.)

Indurain rode for another season, but he was not the rider he had been. In the 1996 Tour de France, the man who'd dominated the previous five editions of the race suddenly began to struggle on a stage through the Pyrenees and was dropped by the leaders, never to regain contact. He was not superhuman after all – he was as fragile as the rest of us. His team dragged him to the Tour of Spain to atone for failing to win in France, which worked about as well as you'd expect. He retired, distinctly disgruntled, before the 1997 season.

You might have expected the man who started the scientific revolution, Francesco Moser, to do something similar. In January 1984 when he set his records, he was already thirty-two years old. He won the following spring's Giro d'Italia – so far so familiar? – but then, when he should have had a season or two of riding increasingly obscure races for minor teams before announcing his retirement to an astonished world that had assumed he'd quit long ago, he embarked on a peculiar hour odyssey.

One might have thought that breaking Merckx's immortal record would have been enough, but Moser set about breaking more hour records. Not *the* record, but minority-interest hour records, like the sea-level record, the indoor record and (since there are no covered tracks at altitude) the sea-level, indoor record.* Like everyone else, Moser claimed the hour rides were awful, painful, torturous experiences. Unlike everyone else, he kept coming back for more.

The constant stream of Moser hour attempts and records devalued the currency. Before his final record attempt in 1988, Moser's coach Francesco Conconi, a man who successfully hid from the world any inclination he had towards modesty, complained that the lack of public interest in his and Moser's hour-record feats was 'almost unbearable'. Moser's fans had taken to turning up to his few race appearances with signs that said, 'Moser, enough already!' This was not the dignified retirement expected of an Italian sporting hero.

The charitable explanation was that he was fascinated by the limits of what he could still do in a tightly controlled environment. The less charitable was that it was a relatively easy way to make money. I suppose there's no reason that it can't have been both. Certainly going to Moscow to attack the indoor and sea-level records, failing and then claiming the indoor, professional record seemed a little desperate when the indoor record

---

* In total he set two absolute records in Mexico in January 1984, and two sea-level records at the Vigorelli track in Milan in autumn 1986. He failed at two record attempts in Moscow and Vienna in 1987, and finally set indoor and sea-level records at Stuttgart in 1988, at the age of thirty-seven. The final ride produced a distance of 50.664km, which was certainly impressive, probably a better ride than the one that set the absolute record. Moser unaccountably neglected the record for cycling backwards while sitting on the handlebars, currently 29.1km. There is also a record for cycling backwards while playing the violin, but that's plain silly, and if you ride too fast the music blows off the music stand that goes where the saddle ought to be. The UCI does not recognise either of these last two records.

he had failed to beat was held by Vjatcheslav Ekimov, a Soviet 'amateur'.

After Obree's and Boardman's records, in 1994 Moser came out of his six-year retirement to have another go. Back in Mexico City, he managed 51.840km using the Obree position; nearly 700m better than his 1984 record, and indeed 250m better than Obree. But it wasn't enough to break Boardman's record. I can't help suspecting that when it came to banning the Obree position, the UCI might have felt rather differently about it if Moser had beaten Boardman's mark. Indeed, before the 1994 attempt, Moser's team admitted they had long ago tried the Obree position, but that Moser had rejected it out of hand, saying that it was impossible to steer the bike. They only came back to it when Obree used it.*

Obree himself didn't have a terribly happy 'retirement'. In December 2001 he was found hanging by the neck, not yet quite dead, in a remote barn by a fifteen-year-old girl who'd come to visit her horse. She and her father managed to cut him down, and saved his life. It turned out that it had not been his first suicide attempt. Graeme Obree, the eccentric genius, had battled depression for his whole career. But Obree's phenomenal success was not despite his illness. His extreme motivation was tied in with a need to prove his own self-worth; success was the only way to avoid the failure that he knew

---

* They wouldn't be the only ones who claimed to have been there first. In 1990 Dr von der Oster-Sacken in Germany demonstrated the superiority of the Obree position, only for it to be rejected by the German Cycling Federation. I think that if you fail to put it into practice, it doesn't really count. Obree had in fact been using the position since 1987, but anyone who was not an avid reader of UK cycling magazines would have missed it.

would crush him. His self-doubt was what enabled him to do what he did. All the same, he would probably settle for no mental illness and no hour records.

The man who'd revolutionised track cycling not once, but twice, never really got his due reward. He spent years planning comebacks and more hour attempts that never came off. It's hard to see them as anything other than attempts to put the missing full stop at the end of his career. When I met him, he felt he'd got over that. 'After a lot of counselling, I can content myself. I can have a hobby. I can read a book because I want to read it, not because it would improve me as a person, or because the knowledge in it will be useful some day. Before, I'd only do something useful. Everything had to be an achievement, and there was terrible guilt at enjoying something that wasn't an achievement.' He paused for a moment, then said, 'I could still break that record, though.'

Few athletes have an entirely balanced view of the world. Remember the birth of Boardman's second child? Oscar Egg's tape measure? It's all about obsession hooked up to physical ability.* Obree would be a long way from the first athlete to have a difficult retirement. Remember

---

* Obree wouldn't be the first athlete to say that he was always in pursuit of the perfect; he gave me the example of making the world's finest jam sandwich. How he would cut the bread, apply the jam, just so, all the way to the edges of the bread in an even layer of *just* the right depth. He elaborated on this with such enthusiasm that the rest of the customers in the Carlisle station buffet stopped to listen, and to wonder why I was making frantic notes about it all. Muhammad Ali said something similar about how he would have been the world's best dustman, if that was what he'd ended up doing. Although it's hard to see him driving a bin lorry, with a grubby teddy bear zip-tied to the front and a meticulously rhyming taunt to other road users traced in the grime on the back.

Anquetil's fascinating family life? That wasn't the work of a laid-back man. He wanted a son, and by God he was going to get one.

Henri Desgrange failed to recover from a kidney operation in 1936, and spent his last years as a pissed-off invalid. Worst of all, his illness prevented him from following by car behind his beloved Tour de France. Desgrange, the man who started the hour off, died in August 1940 almost unnoticed as France was overrun by German troops.

The lucky ones are like Boardman, and get over it. But I suspect that to get over it you end up having all the competitive juices drained from your body to the point where you can't face the thought of competition. The athletes who have a happy retirement are the ones who got bored with being athletes and realised they wanted to do something else.

Chris himself explains it by saying that he's often more interested in solving the problems of a project than in actually finishing the project off. 'I've got things that I've made, which are pretty much done, but they're not varnished,' he said. (He trained as a cabinet-maker.) 'It was the same with my career. I realised in 1997 that we'd tried everything, we'd turned over all the stones. In the space of an end-of-year review meeting, I just lost interest. It was one of the reasons for doing the athlete's hour, it was a problem to solve, and it got me interested again for a while.' The word among Chris's friends at the Manchester track at the time was that he was more or less counting the days till he could stop.

Eddy Merckx called it a day in 1978. It had been pretty much downhill over his last couple of seasons, and the wins had started to dry up. The considerable difficulty he had in securing a sponsor for his team for the 1978 season was the last straw, and he retired after abandoning a training ride on 17th May. He believed he still had it in him to win major races, but at the same time felt he couldn't go on with riding and racing at all. His confusion was clear when he said that his retirement was one of the most painful moments of his life, but that it had been forced on him by mental exhaustion and depression.

Merckx, obligingly conforming to my pet theory, spent several unhappy years at a loss without riding and racing. In 1980 he started a bike factory, which gave him a new focus and enabled him to get on with his life. He's a regular fixture at major cycling events, including hour-record attempts – though he didn't come to mine. Maybe in all the confusion I forgot to invite him.

I'm not sure he'd want to see me again anyway; the only previous occasion on which we met was at the British Time Trial awards dinner in 2000, where he'd been invited ('paid' might be a more accurate description) to present the prizes. I think his famous attention to detail had deserted him, and he had omitted to ask how many prize-winners would be involved. He probably imagined a dozen. But there were hundreds, and each was introduced with a short speech. Since our god was among us, there were souvenir photographs to be taken of each prize being handed over. And then some more photos in case anyone had blinked. By this point Merckx had stopped blinking at all. Minutes became hours, and hours became days.

By the halfway point he was sufficiently exhausted that

he had to sit down between lucky recipients, who each attempted to grovel harder than the last. Some of them had to be dragged away from him. By the time I got there, only assuring him that I was the last prize-winner – absolutely the last – prevented him from wrapping the cup I'd come to collect around my neck. I imagine that even in many years of attending dull functions, this was an evening that must have stood out. Seeing me again might have set up some sort of unfortunate reaction.

I'm not sure what the future holds for the hour record. The UCI's vacillations in the 1990s have stripped away some of the glamour and prestige. Instead of being at the cutting edge of cycling, it's been left, at the moment, as a curious period piece. It's significant that when Boardman's record finally did fall, it attracted almost no attention at all.

Ondrej Sosenka was the rider in question. The 29-year-old Czech rode 49.7km in Moscow in July 2005. He was not the kind of global superstar the UCI was presumably praying for. Five-times Czech time-trial champion, and an experienced professional, he had a higher profile than me, but he still wasn't an Eddy Merckx or a Miguel Indurain. His ride was ignored by the press; the news leaked out unheralded via the Internet. It was a long way from the day in July 1993 when *L'Équipe* – in the middle of the Tour de France – cleared its entire front page for a picture of '*L'Incroyable Monsieur Obree*'.

Part of the problem is that cyclists are techies. They *like* bikes, unlike the UCI, which tends to see them as a problem.* Gather a group of cyclists together, and assuming none of them is a UCI commissaire, before long they'll be speaking a language that's hard for a non-cyclist to follow. It's part of the deal. Of course the riders are what make the sport what it is. The man-on-man battles in the mountains, the high-speed daredevilry of a big bunch sprint. But it's not just men, it's men on bikes. Otherwise we would be runners. (Or more likely, bearing in mind the UCI's world view, race-walkers. If there is a fast, easy way, or a slow, difficult way fenced all about with abstruse rules, which need lots of blazers to devise and enforce them . . .)

The hour record used to be a showcase for the most cutting-edge technology. When Merckx set his record – the one that was taken by the UCI in 2000 as the base mark for a record with no technological input – the magazines and newspapers devoted pages to the technical marvel that he was riding. It's been the same for almost every record, up to Boardman's athlete's hour. Despite what the UCI says, it's not possible to go back to a time when the bike was not part of the equation, because such a time has never existed.

It's anomalous that the hour record resembles nothing else in cycling; all the other records on the track are set on bikes conforming to different, and more modern, rules. It's as though the athletics authorities decreed that the mile record had to be set on a cinder track with leather running shoes, while all the other events could use composite tracks and modern footwear. And the idea of

* There is a significant minority who think bikes are more interesting than people; they can be easily identified by the chain-oil stains on their bedclothes.

stopping a rider using a digital watch when an analogue watch would be permitted is simply absurd.

Even if we allow that it might be a good idea – and I think I've made myself clear on that point – stopping technical progress is difficult. Attempts to do so down the years, by every type of agency you can think of, from the Luddites to the print unions to a former British time-trial champion who went to live in a cave in Leicestershire, have tended to be battles fought in retreat. The UCI can have a good go at it because they wield almost total power. But they can't make the fans and the riders like it, and they can't see into the future.

Even two records into the athlete's hour era, Sosenka's ride raised issues. He took advantage of his 2m height to ride in an unorthodox position, with his arms straight and almost vertical. Not quite so aerodynamic, but a great deal more comfortable than the way I tried to do it. Short riders can't do it Sosenka's way because the rules mean they can't put the bars low enough. Sosenka's bike also featured a very heavy back wheel, which supposedly created a fly-wheel effect and made it easier for him to keep an even pace. The rules have left more space for innovation than the UCI might have wished.

It may get a lot worse for the blazers than a heavy back wheel. I don't suppose anyone, when they were formulating the regulations, imagined that only a few years later Lance Armstrong would announce that he was planning to make an attempt on the record, and that to gain the maximum advantage he was going to build an indoor velodrome at altitude specially for his attempt, and that (and here's the punch line) he was going to take it away afterwards, so that no one else could use it.

Of course, that attempt never happened. But the idea flew in the face of a rule that was formulated to keep things simple. Subtlety was never Armstrong's strongest suit; he formed a team in 2004 to help him with the technological aspects of the hour record, and christened it the F-1 group, just in case anyone had missed the point.

It doesn't stop there. What happens when wealthy pros and their teams bring money to bear on the other problems? Frame materials, tyres, wheel construction, skinsuit materials, helmets: these are all areas where significant improvements on both Merckx and Boardman are possible. All that has stopped it happening is a lack of commercial advantage in working to the limits of the old-fashioned athlete's hour rules. It isn't possible to do with rules what the UCI wants, not even if their rules were more tightly formulated. Their only hope is if some sort of voluntary etiquette limits what riders use and, frankly, that is not going to happen.

Graeme Obree, when I pointed this out to him (quite possibly with little specks of spittle appearing around the corners of my mouth), suggested that the UCI should make a few antique-style steel bikes, in a variety of sizes, and hire them out to hour aspirants. To break the record, you'd have to do it on an unmodified UCI bike. This is an echo from the past; in the 1930s the Tour de France experimented with standard-issue (yellow) bikes. Then, one of the problems was that bike-makers resented the lack of publicity they were getting from the riders they sponsored. I suspect the same would hold true now. The athlete's hour has already created problems in this regard, since the record is no longer a showcase for a maker's best products.

Never mind, for a moment, the issues of advisability and practicality. Most of all, the time-warp is harsh on a generation of athletes who set records in good faith, according to the rules in place at the time. Moser's and Obree's hour records were their greatest achievements. To decide, years after the event (and at a point where neither of them could realistically do anything about it) that actually they don't really count is patently unfair.

The records set between 1984 and 1996 were shuffled off to a new category, of 'Best Hour Performance', where 'Best' has a slightly sniffy air about it, sort of translating into 'technologically assisted and hence a bit dishonest', and where 'Performance' means 'not a proper record, sunshine'. If you want to, you can still have a go at it. To discourage anyone from doing so, and thereby perpetuating a record that it now dislikes, the UCI has allowed Boardman to retain the 'Best Hour' mark set in the 'Superman' position, but has changed the rules, so that no one else can use the same position to attack it. The exact advantage offered by the stretched-out position is unclear, but it's certainly quite substantial. Thus the UCI applied a very effective tourniquet. I don't think that's an absolute riot of fair-play either.*

---

* Bear in mind that the 4000m pursuit record that Boardman set on the same bike in 1996 was 4 minutes 11.114 seconds, and that, at the time of writing nine years later, no one has beaten 4 minutes 15 seconds using the position now required for track events, including the Best Hour. I wouldn't want to give the impression I'm excessively on the UCI's case here (it may be too late for that), but while I was checking some of the rules relating to the Best Hour Performance, I found a rule I'd never heard of: that 'A record beaten on the same day shall not be confirmed' (UCI cycling regulation 3.5.019). So if I broke the hour record at noon, and someone else did it at 5.30 p.m., so far as the UCI is concerned, I didn't break it at all. And that doesn't seem very fair either. Rant, rant.

There might be a bigger problem anyway. Time-trialling in all its forms has been going out of fashion for the last thirty years. It makes poor television, basically. When newspapers were the major source of cycling news, time-trialling had a huge appeal, because, unlike a mass-start event, it was possible to describe the development of the race in great detail from simple split-times round the course. Television, on the other hand, is able to convey the excitement of a road race, whereas time-trials look pretty dull. The only time most of the big stars ride a time-trial now is during stage races.

It's the same for track racing – the other half of the hour record's DNA. Riders like Anquetil, Rivière, Coppi and Moser rode track races during the winter and contested the world pursuit championships. The big stars no longer ride much on the track. Indurain's and Rominger's hour attempts were their first experiences of track riding, something that would have been unthinkable for riders of their stature twenty years earlier. In 1956 Anquetil said he wanted to break the hour record, then win the world road championships and the world track-pursuit title. It's twenty years since any one rider could set out those targets without being laughed at.

The hour record used to be an extension of the things a professional cyclist did to make a living. Now it's becoming an increasingly specialised thing to do. The new rules, and their insistence on a now unfamiliar position on the bike, take it another step away from normal racing and riding. It's another reason not to do it, another thing that has to be learned. Maybe it's too far off the beaten track for the big stars now?

I don't think so. It's too simple and too beautiful an

idea, and most cyclists, and fans, are respectful of the sport's history. The hour record is still one of the ways the greats have left their mark. Even the eccentric rules under which it's now run probably won't kill it. It might well be that there are fewer attempts, with more intensive planning, testing and training to remove the risk to reputations. But that would only continue a trend; the hour has been getting progressively more frightening for most of its existence.

In 1936, for instance, Maurice Richard made two attempts on the same day (they both failed) and then went again – this time successfully – the following October. It took Anquetil three goes to break it. Now the stakes are so high that almost no one dares risk failure. Apart from me, obviously. But attempts will keep coming. It's the only way to leave a measure of what you can do, an objective measure that does more than reflect who you were racing against, that has any resonance through time. It's the only record there is. That's why it's so special.

Bernard Hinault, a five-times winner of the Tour de France, was a superlative time-triallist. He was happy enough to be sour (sometimes very sour) about other riders' hour rides, but he never attempted it himself. He's probably the greatest rider never to do so, the only five-times Tour winner apart from Armstrong not to attempt the record. It's a huge crater in the middle of his C.V.

It's a hole in mine as well. But at least no one will be able to snipe that I never had a go. In fact I had two goes at it, because I tried again the following May. The second attempt was rather better than the first, but it was rather less of a story. In fact, that's why it was a better attempt.

I even managed to ride at the magic 49.5kph for 45

minutes in a trial – a trial that we stopped only because we'd run out of track time in the session. Unless something catastrophic was lining itself up (and after hours of work on the track, I like to think I'd have known if it was), I would have ridden the record distance then and there.

But it didn't come together on the night. I don't really know why. The air pressure in Manchester was very high, and that probably had something to do with it, because it creates an effect that's the opposite of going to altitude: you get thick air. Or maybe the memories of the previous attempt got in the way at some deep level that I don't pretend to understand. It wasn't the cathartic experience I thought it was going to be.

I've come to terms with the failures. The hard part is knowing now that on a perfect day I could do it. That's not how it works, though. I can't count on the perfect day turning up on time any more than I can in any other area of life. To break the hour record, you need to be able to do it on the day you get.

The attempt in this book, the first one, was chaotic. There were so many points in the story where I ought to have had the sense to pull the plug, but it was always easier to go on. A lack of perspective, you might say. At the time I'd have called it determination, but I'd have been wrong.

It was pretty much, despite my best intentions, an exercise in how not to do it. In fact, with suitable allowances, it was an exercise in how not to do pretty much anything. A failure to make sure things wouldn't go wrong, followed by the inability to cope when they did, and the inability to learn from the experience. Lack of foresight, followed by panic, followed almost immediately by lack of hindsight.

But even a failed hour-record rider is part of the hour. Part of its texture. Eddy Merckx retired when I was four years old. Jacques Anquetil rode his last race before I was born. Fausto Coppi died almost ten years before that. The list of the record's holders is not long, just twenty-five men. Each represents something different. They are not just the progress of a record; they are the key to the history of cycle racing. The hour brought these men to life, back to their prime, and let me race against them. I didn't win, but then you have to look at who I was up against. I didn't take too much of a whipping either. I think, under the circumstances, that I did all right.

HOUR RECORD HOLDERS

Compiling a list of hour record holders is not as straight-forward as you might imagine. There are discrepancies between the UCI's official list and the contemporary sources, particularly in relation to the distances recorded in the records between 1936 and 1942. (The UCI list subtracts 73m from the distances given in most contemporary reports, except for Coppi in 1942, where it subtracts 23m.) The following is based on the UCI list because, well, it's their record.

Name	Date	Place	Distance (km)
Henri Desgrange	11.5.1893	Paris	35.325
Jules Dubois	31.10.1894	Paris	38.220
Oscar Van Den Eynde	30.7.1897	Paris	39.240
William Hamilton	3.7.1898	Denver	40.781
Lucien Petit-Breton	24.8.1905	Paris	41.110
Marcel Berthet	20.6.1907	Paris	41.520
Oscar Egg	22.8.1912	Paris	42.360
Marcel Berthet	7.8.1913	Paris	42.741
Oscar Egg	21.8.1913	Paris	43.525
Marcel Berthet	20.9.1913	Paris	43.775
Oscar Egg	18.6.1914	Paris	44.247
Jan Van Hout	25.8.1933	Roermond, the Netherlands	44.588
Maurice Richard	29.8.1933	St Trond, Belgium	44.777

Guiseppe Olmo	31.10.1935	Milan	45.090
Maurice Richard	14.10.1936	Milan	45.325
Frans Slaats	29.9.1937	Milan	45.485
Maurice Archambaud	3.11.1937	Milan	45.767
Fausto Coppi	7.11.1942	Milan	45.848
Jacques Anquetil	29.6.1956	Milan	46.159
Ercole Baldini	19.9.1956	Milan	46.393
Roger Rivière	18.9.1957	Milan	46.923
Roger Rivière	23.9.1958	Milan	47.346
Ferdinand Bracke	30.10.1967	Rome	48.093
Ole Ritter	10.10.1968	Mexico City	48.653
Eddy Merckx	25.10.1972	Mexico City	49.431
Francesco Moser	19.1.1984	Mexico City	50.808
Francesco Moser	23.1.1984	Mexico City	51.151
Graeme Obree	17.7.1993	Hamar, Norway	51.596
Chris Boardman	23.7.1993	Bordeaux	52.270
Graeme Obree	27.4.1994	Bordeaux	52.713
Miguel Indurain	2.9.1994	Bordeaux	53.040
Tony Rominger	22.10.1994	Bordeaux	53.832
Tony Rominger	5.11.1994	Bordeaux	55.291
Chris Boardman	6.9.1996	Manchester	56.375

In 2000 the UCI decided that records from Moser's in 1984 onwards had been overly influenced by advances in bike technology, to the extent that the athlete was being over-shadowed by his machine. Boardman's 1996 ride was therefore reclassified as a 'Best Hour Performance', and the official record (now known as 'The Athlete's Hour') reverted to Eddy Merckx's ride of 1972. Chris Boardman attacked this record in October 2000 as a finale to his career.

Athlete's Hour Record

Chris Boardman	27.10.2000	Manchester	49.441
Ondrej Sosenka	19.7.2005	Moscow	49.700

ACKNOWLEDGEMENTS

There are numerous people who helped me with the record attempt featured in this book, and I'm pleased to finally have a chance to thank them publicly.

First, Andrea Ingram, without whom the whole thing would have descended into even greater chaos than it did. And of course Dave Thompson: he was the only reason I ever had a cycling career in the first place.

Andy Sharpe and Tom Davies struggled manfully to keep the whole thing on its feet, and provided unconditional support which I felt unworthy of – thank you.

Jamie Pringle, Helen Carter, Simon Jones and Peter Keen offered encouragement and realism in about equal measure, and it was entirely my fault that I only listened to the encouragement. Mike Ellis also made several helpful suggestions during the project, and stepped in to help trackside on the night.

Ken Platts has been a consistent training partner for much of my career, and gave me much wise advice during the rides we shared in the weeks leading up to the attempt.

So far as telling the story of the hour is concerned, I am indebted to Graeme Obree and Chris Boardman, who both generously took the time to answer interminable questions about their records and careers.

Thanks to Robert Garbutt and the staff of *Cycling Weekly* magazine for giving me access to their archive; to David Taylor, who allowed me to borrow much of his considerable private archive of French-language cycling magazines and newspapers (or 'All that rubbish' as his wife Pat would have it); and to David Duffield, Chris Sidwells and Alasdair Fotheringham, who provided a wealth of recollections about record attempts and holders. And to Oliver Roberts, for a number of helpful suggestions.

At Yellow Jersey Press, thanks to Tristan Jones and Beth Coates for their patience and skill. It gives me great pleasure to pass off their jokes as my own.

Thanks to Peter Buckman, my agent, whose faith in the book gave me the confidence to actually write it, and to the Buckman Agency.

Finally, the most profound gratitude to Louisa, who had to live through the attempt, and then live through my digging the whole thing up and writing about it. I wouldn't like to guess which was more trying.